Decks

plan ∧ design ∧ build

Decks

plan ∧ design ∧ build

CREATIVE HOMEOWNER®, Upper Saddle River, New Jersey

VP/Editorial Director: Timothy O. Bakke
Production Managers: Kimberly H. Vivas, Rose Sullivan

Writers: Steve Cory, Mike McClintock

Senior Editor: Fran J. Donegan
Photo/Assistant Editors: Jennifer Ramcke,
   Lauren Manoy
Editorial Assistants: Jennifer Doolittle, Evan Lambert
Indexer: Schroeder Indexing Services

Art Direction/Design: Glee Barre
Illustrations: Ron Carboni, Craig Franklin,
   Paul M. Schumm
Cover Design: Glee Barre
Cover Photo: Brian Vanden Brink, Design: Weatherend Furniture

Manufactured in the United States of America

Current Printing (last digit)
10 9 8 7 6 5 4 3 2

Decks: Plan, Design, Build
Library of Congress Catalog Card Number:
2004113337
ISBN: 1-58011-148-3

CREATIVE HOMEOWNER®
A Division of Federal Marketing Corp.
24 Park Way, Upper Saddle River, NJ 07458
www.creativehomeowner.com

SAFETY

Although the methods in this book have been reviewed for safety, it is not possible to overstate the importance of using the safest methods you can. What follows are reminders—some do's and don'ts of work safety—to use along with your common sense.

- Always use caution, care, and good judgment when following the procedures described in this book.

- Always be sure that the electrical setup is safe, that no circuit is overloaded, and that all power tools and outlets are properly grounded. Do not use power tools in wet locations.

- Always read container labels on paints, solvents, and other products; provide ventilation; and observe all other warnings.

- Always read the manufacturer's instructions for using a tool, especially the warnings.

- Use hold-downs and push sticks whenever possible when working on a table saw. Avoid working short pieces if you can.

- Always remove the key from any drill chuck (portable or press) before starting the drill.

- Always pay deliberate attention to how a tool works so that you can avoid being injured.

- Always know the limitations of your tools. Do not try to force them to do what they were not designed to do.

- Always check that any adjustment is locked before proceeding. For example, always check the rip fence on a table saw or the bevel adjustment on a portable saw before starting work.

- Always clamp small pieces to a bench or other work surface when using a power tool.

- Always wear the appropriate rubber gloves or work gloves when handling chemicals, moving or stacking lumber, working with concrete, or doing heavy construction.

- Always wear a disposable face mask when you create dust by sawing or sanding. Use a special filtering respirator when working with toxic substances and solvents.

- Always wear eye protection, especially when using power tools or striking metal on metal or concrete; a chip can fly off, for example, when chiseling concrete.

- Never work while wearing loose clothing, open cuffs, or jewelry; tie back long hair.

- Always be aware that there is seldom enough time for your body's reflexes to save you from injury from a power tool in a dangerous situation; everything happens too fast. Be alert!

- Always keep your hands away from the business ends of blades, cutters, and bits.

- Always hold a circular saw firmly, usually with both hands.

- Always use a drill with an auxiliary handle to control the torque when using large-size bits.

- Always check your local building codes when planning new construction. The codes are intended to protect public safety and should be observed to the letter.

- Never work with power tools when you are tired or when under the influence of alcohol or drugs.

- Never cut tiny pieces of wood, vinyl, metal, or pipe using a power saw. When you need a smaller piece, saw it from a securely clamped longer piece.

- Never change a saw blade or a drill or router bit unless the power cord is unplugged. Do not depend on the switch being off. You might accidentally hit it.

- Never work in insufficient lighting.

- Never work with dull tools. Have them sharpened, or learn how to sharpen them yourself.

- Never use a power tool on a workpiece—large or small—that is not firmly supported.

- Never saw a workpiece that spans a large distance between horses without close support on each side of the cut; the piece can bend, closing on and jamming the blade, causing saw kickback.

- When sawing, never support a workpiece from underneath with your leg or any other part of your body.

- Never carry sharp or pointed tools or materials, such as utility knives, awls, or chisels, in your pocket. If you want to conveniently carry any of these tools, use a special-purpose tool belt that has leather pockets and holders.

CONTENTS

Tools and Materials

STEP-BY-STEP CONSTRUCTION

INTRODUCTION

A deck can enhance your life in several ways. It makes entertaining easy and provides a pleasant outdoor space that you and your friends can enjoy together: just give the deck a quick sweep; prepare some cool drinks; and fire up the grill as guests gather around. For more private times, it offers a retreat where you can lounge during the day or toast the sunset, savoring the outdoors without venturing far from the amenities of civilization. A deck improves the appearance and usefulness of your home and yard by providing a smooth transition between the two. If the cost worries you, keep in mind that a high-quality deck is bound to increase your home's resale value.

PROJECT GUIDE

1 HAMMER   Easy, even for most beginners.

2 HAMMERS   Challenging, but can be handled by do-it-yourselfers with basic tools and carpentry skills.

3 HAMMERS   Difficult, but still doable by experienced do-it-yourselfers who have mastered basic construction skills, and have the tools and time.

To ensure that it enhances your property both now and in the future, a deck must be thoughtfully designed and solidly constructed of pleasing and durable materials. An ill-considered choice of materials or design elements can clash with your house or yard. A poorly built deck made from inferior lumber can bounce under foot, sink over time, or rot in a few short years.

Decks: Plan, Design, Build can help you realize your dreams of a new deck in two ways. The photographs in the design galleries and those used throughout the book will generate design ideas you can use on your own deck.

The rest of the book is devoted to helping you actually build your deck. Part 1 tells how to create a design and plan the job. Part 2 details the tools and materials you'll need to build a deck, including information on the newest generation of decking materials. Part 3 covers the nuts and bolts of construction. It includes everything from pouring foundations that will last to creating deck stairs and railings. Part 4 ends the book with three deck plans you can build.

As you read each section, you will learn how to perform the task through clear step-by-step photography. You will also learn a number of professional building secrets in the many Smart Tips scattered throughout the book.

Use this information to design, build, and then enjoy your new deck.

PLANNING
AND
DESIGN

GALLERY
OF
DESIGN IDEAS

1 Here a seating area provides additional outdoor living space. The decking boards run perpendicular to the porch's decking.

2

2 The angled decking pattern and the broad steps make this deck appear larger than it really is. Note the cooking area.

3 This deck provides design continuity for the entire outdoor area. Almost all composite decking materials are splinter free.

4 Built-in seating and planters are not only extremely functional, they also improve the overall design of the deck.

5 Consider staining wood decks for added interest. You could use vinyl floor tiles as templates for this type of design.

4

3

5

1

2

1 If you build a multilevel deck, you'll find that each level will become a separate activity area, so plan accordingly.

2 Wide steps provide a graceful transition to the yard. Use the steps to display plants and statuary.

3 Curves add interest to a deck's design. This curved railing invites the viewer to take in the panoramic view.

4 Match the style of the deck to the design of the house. This narrow deck works well with the contemporary house.

GALLERY
OF
DESIGN IDEAS

5 The way you place furniture, deck structures, level changes, and areas under roof overhangs all help define deck activity areas.

6 Where you place a deck is often more important than the deck's design. People using this deck have great views of the rest of the property and the lake beyond.

DESIGNING
YOUR
DECK

Building a deck is one of the most satisfying and hassle-free home-improvement projects that a homeowner can tackle. Combining various types of wood and composite materials, different building techniques, multiple levels, and overall shapes leads to a practically infinite variety of final designs. And for most deck projects, you'll need only basic carpentry tools and techniques.

BEGINNING YOUR DESIGN

We all have different reasons for adding a new deck to our home. Most people find they want a new deck for a variety of practical and financial reasons. With a deck, you expand your living space and increase your home's value for a fraction of what it would cost to build an addition. And you enhance your living style as well, gaining a new space for entertaining and socializing. But for a deck to do all these things, you need to start out with a good plan.

A well-planned deck will harmonize with the house in both size and shape and provide a smooth transition down to the yard. It can offer more exposure or more privacy, and either take advantage of a cool breeze or protect you from a stiff ocean wind.

What to Expect. Building a deck is a straightforward job, and anyone with some basic carpentry skills and the time to work carefully can handle the task. The project won't totally disrupt your home life, either, as kitchen remodeling would. All the mess is kept outdoors, and as long as you have a good place to store materials, the job can stretch from weekend to weekend with no major problem.

During your initial planning, include the whole family and develop a wish list of features. Gradually, you will pare away the excesses and zero in on a design that works for your situation. Then you'll work through the project step-by-step, from drawing plans, getting permits, choosing a framing style, and selecting materials and patterns for your decking, railings, and stairs, to applying finishes and maintaining your deck.

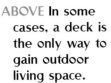

ABOVE In some cases, a deck is the only way to gain outdoor living space.

LEFT A small pond adds an unusual feature to this deck.

RIGHT TOP The proportions of a well-designed deck fit with the house.

RIGHT This deck includes a graceful transition to the yard.

CHOOSING A DESIGN

While deck materials, shapes, sizes, and costs can vary widely, there are several design decisions common to almost every deck project. Although most decks are simply wooden platforms raised above the yard, they are really an extension of the house—more like living space than yard space—even though they are outside. Because a deck connects to and expands the adjacent indoor space, deck additions are likely to be most appropriate and useful added onto living/family room areas and kitchen/dining room areas. For example, replacing a solid wall with sliding glass doors leading to an expansive deck is a quick and relatively inexpensive way to make a cramped living room seem a lot larger.

Draw a series of rough sketches as you proceed. Expect to fill a wastebasket or two with these. Don't think of them as actual designs so much as focal points for conversations—it's usually easier to point to a place on your drawing than to walk around the house.

Feel free to steal ideas from books, magazines, and other decks in your neighborhood. When you see a deck that particularly pleases you and seems appropriate for your situation, talk to the owners about how their deck works for them. Jot down some notes, and ask permission to take a few photos. Most people will be flattered that you like their deck and will be more than happy to tell you all about it.

You will probably discover lots of terrific deck ideas that you end up not using, either because you no longer like the way they look, you discover that they just won't work with your design, or the extra expense for exotic materials will blow the budget. Don't be discouraged. In fact, expect it to happen, and happen several times, before you come up with the best design for your situation.

HOW YOU WILL USE YOUR DECK

Everyone in the family probably has different visions of the ideal deck. Gather all their opinions, and figure out an overall design that will work for everybody. Consider the following items.

Entertaining and Barbecuing. Plan a convenient cooking area, probably somewhere near the kitchen. Figure out where you'll put tables for sit-down dinners as well as a good place to set up a buffet table. If you'll have a grill on the deck and plan to do a lot of barbecuing, you might want to add a small sink near the cooking area.

LEFT Begin the design process by settling on how you plan on using your new deck. Sharing meals was a prime consideration for this deck.

OPPOSITE TOP Decks are great places to entertain during pleasant weather.

OPPOSITE Built-in benches provide seating and design interest. A circular design helps promote conversation among people on the deck.

SMART TIP

START AN IDEA SCRAPBOOK

Keep your ideas and your wish list in order by starting a design scrap book. Buy a notebook that contains flaps on the covers. That way you'll have a place to keep photos you take of decks you like and pages from magazines and catalogs, as well as ample space to jot down your ideas and plans.

Lounging and Sunning. Pencil in space for a hammock or a swinging chair—a shady spot is often best. Sun worshippers will congregate on an expanse of deck that gets full sun.

Balancing Privacy and Openness. Think about whether you want the deck to feel airy and open to the world or cozy and secluded. A small deck will generally feel cozier than a large deck. Low benches and railings designed with large, open sections give a feeling of openness. A narrow deck that hugs the house will have a more sequestered feel than one that juts into the yard.

Decks are usually raised off the ground, which might mean that you and your family will be on display for all the neighborhood to see. Existing fences may be too low to shield you from view. Sometimes the problem can be solved by stepping the deck down in stages or by planting trees and shrubs.

If you feel overexposed, a well-placed trellis added to the deck can give you some nice climbing plants to look at as well as provide a pleasant enclosure and screen.

Enjoying the View. Plan your landscape along with your deck to get the best view. Orient the deck so that you will be looking at the best features of your yard and to take advantage of a nice view beyond your property line.

Planning for Children's Play. A jungle gym will probably look better in the yard, but your deck design should provide an inviting place where kids can play. Build the stairway extra wide or have a series of descending platforms, and children will spend hours playing with dolls and trucks and letting their imaginations run wild. Plan a spot for a comfortable chair where you can relax while keeping an unobstructed eye on the kids in your yard.

Lighting for Nighttime Use. Plan some appropriate lighting if you want to use the deck after dark. Whether you choose standard 120-volt wiring or a low-voltage option, plan to run the wires somewhere out of sight, maybe even underground.

Including a Pool or Whirlpool. Built with rot-resistant lumber, a deck makes an ideal surface next to a pool or spa. It's softer than tile or concrete and is slightly absorbent, making it a pleasant place to sit or lounge when you get out of the water. An inexpensive aboveground pool gains a lot of class when you surround it with a deck. If your design includes a spa or hot tub, position it for privacy as well as an unobstructed view of the stars.

Container Gardening. It is almost impossible to put too much foliage on or near a deck. Find planters that will go well with your deck and your house, or plan to build some from the same material as the decking. With enough sun, tomatoes, peppers, and all sorts of vegetables do well. An herb garden flourishes without a lot of work and still looks great after a bit of harvesting. If you're an avid gardener, consider putting cold frames or even a greenhouse on the deck.

BELOW **Plan a lighting scheme if you plan on using your deck after dark.**

OPPOSITE **Closed designs tend to make a deck feel cozier than one that is open. This design also provides a certain amount of privacy.**

LEFT Be sure to plan on connecting your deck to the indoors with passages to the most frequently used rooms in the house. Don't forget stairs that lead down to the yard.

TRAFFIC PATTERNS

Make the deck easy to reach by installing French doors or sliders—the more entrances, the better. Large windows that look onto the deck will entice people outside. If you plan to eat a lot of meals out on the deck, make sure it's close to the kitchen.

Also take the time to plan the approaches to the deck. Plan a clear, unobstructed path from indoor entertaining areas and areas where your family spends much of their time out to the deck. A door out to the deck near the kitchen and another near the living room helps avoid bottlenecks during parties. A small patio or concrete pad at the bottom of the stairs down to the yard reduces wear and tear on the grass.

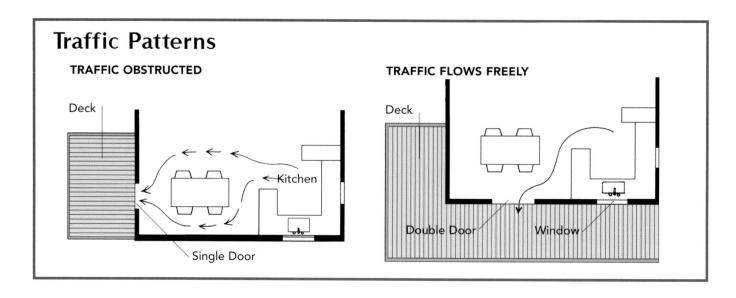

Traffic Patterns

TRAFFIC OBSTRUCTED

Deck

←Kitchen

Single Door

TRAFFIC FLOWS FREELY

Deck

Double Door   Window

Seasonal Conditions

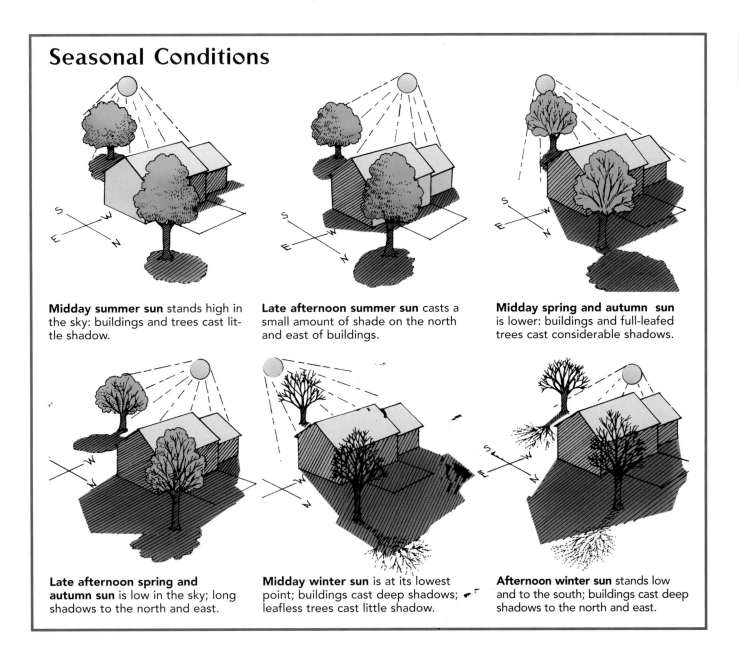

Midday summer sun stands high in the sky: buildings and trees cast little shadow.

Late afternoon summer sun casts a small amount of shade on the north and east of buildings.

Midday spring and autumn sun is lower: buildings and full-leafed trees cast considerable shadows.

Late afternoon spring and autumn sun is low in the sky; long shadows to the north and east.

Midday winter sun is at its lowest point; buildings cast deep shadows; leafless trees cast little shadow.

Afternoon winter sun stands low and to the south; buildings cast deep shadows to the north and east.

WEATHER CONSIDERATIONS

Think about how the weather and the seasons will affect the ways you use the deck, and plan accordingly. For example, a deck with a greenhouse on a southern exposure will help extend the growing season in a cold climate. The three main weather variables with which you need to concern yourself are sun, wind, and rain.

Sun. Decide how much sun and how much shade you want, and take this into account when siting the deck. A deck on the north side of a house will be in shade most of the day. This can be an advantage if you live in a very hot climate and a disadvantage for most everyone else.

An eastern exposure gives the deck morning sun and afternoon shade; this is often the best choice in warm climates. In cold climates a southwest exposure provides full late afternoon sun, making the deck warmer on cool days in the spring and fall.

Also consider the angle of the sun above the horizon. The sun is highest in the summer and lowest in the winter. This means that in the winter a south-oriented deck will receive less direct sunlight than during the summer. A fence or tree that does not block out the high summer sun may block out sunlight during other times of the year when the sun is lower.

You may want continuous shade for a hammock, afternoon shade only for an eating area, and as much sun as possible for potted plants and a sunning area. You may need to change your foliage, pruning branches or planting more trees and shrubs.

Wind. If heat is a problem and you want to maximize the breeze, plan to prune trees or remove shrubs. If you have more wind than you want, you may need to plant new foliage. A raised deck will be windier than one near the ground.

For extreme conditions, you may need to construct a windbreak of some sort. A louvered or lattice wall covered with climbing plants is much more attractive than a solid fence and does a good job of diffusing a strong wind.

Rain. Most people think of sunny, clear weather as the best time to enjoy life on the deck, but you may live in an area where it rains much of the year, or perhaps you just like to watch the rain. If your house's roof has little or no slope, consider extending it to cover part of the deck. Or install a large set of sliding glass doors between the deck and the living room, so you can open the doors and enjoy the patter of rain as it falls on your deck and potted plants.

ENVISIONING THE CONTOURS

You'll find that areas defined on sketches tend to look larger than they actually are in real life. To avoid disappointment later in the project, transfer the scale drawings to the actual building site. You can drive stakes into the ground and connect them with string to outline the deck.

SMART TIP

PREVIEW THE DECK CONTOURS

To help you visualize the actual size of a deck plan that's sketched out on a drawing, measure the rough dimensions on several of the potential building sites and stretch out an extension cord or a garden hose to mark the contours.

Arrange lawn furniture inside the deck's planned outline, and try it on for size. Imagine yourselves doing what you hope to do on your new deck, and ask some obvious questions: is there enough room for a planter here? Is this the right-size space for a buffet table if you have a party with 15 guests? Is there room for a table and chairs here, and room for people to get to their seats? Will the hammock fit over there? Where will the barbecue be? Would an L- or T-shape work better? What if you put some hanging planters or large potted plants over there, to give a sense of separate spaces? In this way, you will come up with some fairly specific ideas about the shape and size of your deck.

If it feels cramped, consider extending the deck in logical increments. Using 12-foot-long joists instead of 10-footers, for example, has little effect on labor costs and increases material costs only marginally, but may increase the deck's usefulness and sense of space dramatically.

If you have the space and the money, you may be tempted to build a very large deck. If you've got a large house and plenty of deck furniture, this can work well, but a jumbo deck can sometimes overwhelm a smaller home. Plan deck areas that feel comfortable and are scaled to the size of your house.

OPPOSITE **The surrounding area will play an important role in determining how popular the deck becomes. Create designs that enhance the views.**

IMPROVING YOUR HOUSE AND YARD

A deck usually does not stand alone; it is attached to your house and sits on top of your yard. So consider not only how the deck itself will look but also how it will fit in with its surroundings. This does not necessarily mean striving to make the deck blend in and disappear, but any contrasts should be pleasing to onlookers rather than jarring.

Although the decking boards are probably the most visible element when you look at the deck from the house, the structural elements may loom large from other perspectives. Railings, stairways, and fascia boards are often the things people will see first. If the deck is raised far above the ground, the posts, girder, joists, and

even the framing hardware may become the most prominent visual features.

BASIC ELEMENTS

There are four basic elements to consider when matching your deck design with your house and yard: shape, mass, color, and texture.

Shape. The shape you choose for the deck should harmonize with the lines of your house. The alignment of a deck should in most cases be much more horizontal than vertical. This will give it the light, breezy feeling that you want from an informal space. However, if you are building a raised deck, the posts will define strong vertical lines. If your house is tall and narrow, some of this vertical sense will be welcome, and you may want to repeat these lines. In many cases, you will want to soften the vertical aspect with a series of horizontal lines, using decking and railings.

Think about the deck's overall shape, as well. If your house has a pleasing L-shape, for example, you can repeat that shape with a deck. A house with a confusing shape can be softened with a deck that is simple, and a plain-looking house can be jazzed up with a deck that has a bold shape.

Most people choose to have a deck that is attached to the back of the house and leads to the backyard. You may want to consider other options, such as a wraparound deck, a deck that incorporates a tree, or an island or peninsula deck.

Also examine your house and your yard for existing lines: rectangles, curves, projections, even triangles. Use these as starting points, and think of your deck as

DIY OPTIONS

DECK SHAPE OPTIONS

WRAPAROUND

A wraparound deck allows you to follow the sun or the shade.

OBLIQUE

This deck is accessible from two doorways and incorporates a large tree.

ISLAND

An island deck is unattached to the house, so it can be surrounded with foliage.

PENNINSULA

With this penninsula design, you walk onto a place that feels much different from the house.

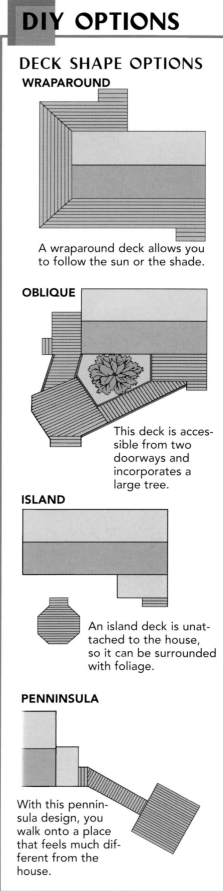

OPPOSITE Sharp angles create areas for built-in seating and planting.

ABOVE A curved deck provides the setting for a graceful railing design.

providing variations on those themes. If your existing lines are a bit boring, you will want to liven things up a bit with some new angles—octagonal and other rectilinear shapes are good choices, as are curved lines. But if you already have a good variety of lines, adding complex shapes with your deck will only make for a muddled general impression. Usually, simplicity is best: two or three lines artfully repeated are more pleasing than a jumble of shapes.

You probably can't change the shape of your house to suit your deck, but it is often possible to change your landscape in conjunction with building a deck. You can also design garden edgings or patio surfaces to complement the lines of your deck.

Mass. The size of a deck should suit the house. The most common problem is a deck that is too massive and overpowers a small house, making the house appear even smaller than it is. Decide which vantage points are the most important, and think about how your deck will appear from the yard and the house.

Many factors affect the visual mass of a deck. For example, building low to the ground or designing railings that are low or light-looking will help the deck recede and thus appear smaller. Large visible beams, railings that are densely packed with boards, and wide fascia boards all will make a deck seem more massive.

Thick 6x6 posts supporting an elevated deck might be the most obvious feature, but an interesting pattern of cross bracing draws attention to thinner wood. And the longer these posts are, the less thick they appear.

Color. When people think of a deck, they automatically think of exposed wood. The colors of wood and patterns of wood grain project a relaxed, casual mood. Redwood or cedar decking has beautiful color and looks great right away,

but some people find the green tint of some pressure-treated decking unpleasant. All of them will gradually fade to gray after a few years of weathering unless you treat the deck regularly with a clear sealer to keep moisture out of the wood fibers.

If the usual decking colors simply will not go with your house, consider staining or painting the wood. Often a combination of natural wood and stain works—one option is to stain the entire deck except for the cap piece that sits on top of the railing.

Texture. Wood has a fairly rough texture: Knots, minor cracks, and rough spots are usually considered part of the charm of a deck. Such casualness goes well with almost all landscaping, but it may be unsuitable beside your house. If you need to clean up the lines a bit, buy more expensive wood with fewer knots. Some composite decking materials—made of recycled plastic mixed with wood fibers and epoxy—have an embossed surface that imitates clear wood grain. (See Chapter 5 for more on these products.) Other options include metal railings, glass windscreens, latticework, and rough sawn lumber.

TOP **Plan the size and shape of your deck so that it works with the design of the house.**

RIGHT **Consider how the deck will form a transition from the house to the yard or garden beyond.**

OPPOSITE **This decking complements the textures of the garden.**

SMART TIP

PLAN FOR A BETTER VIEW

Avoid one of the common flaws in many deck designs: a railing that blocks your view. Because most railings rise at least 36 inches above the deck surface, it's wise to place them far away from glass doors and windows. Even on a sloping site where you want the main deck area close to the ground, you can add platform steps near the house, and install the railings around the perimeter of the main deck area. Place shade structures close to the house where they won't block the views.

BRIDGING HOUSE AND YARD

Your deck will be a destination for outdoor living, but it will also be a bridge linking your house and your yard. In fact, a well-designed deck will feel something like a bridge, not only because it is suspended over the ground but also because it balances the amenities of the indoors with those of the outdoors. In addition to the basic elements of mass, shape, color, and texture, here are some specific ways to ensure that your deck makes a graceful transition:

Stepping Down. Where possible, avoid long sections of stairway. Use a series of landings on multiple levels to step down in a way that feels more natural and graceful. Often the challenge is to make sure that each level is a usable and visually pleasing space. Solve this by making the levels cascade—falling off each other at different points or even at different angles—rather than just progressing downward in a straight line like huge steps.

Even if you build a normal stairway, consider making it wider and longer than the usual size. A standard 36-inch-wide stairway starts to look like a ladder if it is more than six steps long. An accurately scaled drawing can help you visualize the best design.

Patio Transition. The stairway from your deck might lead down to a lawn, but a patio or path at the bottom of your steps might work better. Materials that echo your house—bricks, concrete pavers, or colorful crushed stone—are good choices because they strike a nice balance. Patio materials can be rustic or formal, ranging from rough landscaping timbers to mortar-set tiles. Natural stone and brick, which are midway between formal and rustic, often work well. Plan the lines of your patio carefully—they are a con-

tinuation of the lines in your deck, which in turn should be tied to the lines of your house.

Configuring Planters. It's hard to go wrong with foliage, as long as you can keep it healthy. Any color combination looks great—nature doesn't agonize over paint chips. You can make a planter of the same material as the deck, and use plants in it that are similar to those in your yard to create a tie-in between deck and yard. And if you can build a planter that harmonizes with the house's exterior, then you can tie in all three elements.

Incorporating Trees. If you have a tree that looks great next to your house, don't cut it down. Build your deck around it, instead, to take advantage of the shade and help the deck blend into the site. Trees near the edge of the deck work well too, forming a sort of arch from yard to house, with the deck in the middle.

SAFETY

DESIGN FOR SAFETY

Don't forget these elements when designing your deck:

- A railing system that complies with building codes
- Adequate lighting for nighttime safety

OPPOSITE A series of broad deck levels guides people from the main area down to the pool.

RIGHT TOP An open deck includes a planting area. Decks give you the option of incorporating shrubs and trees in the design.

RIGHT Wide steps provide plenty of room for placing container plants and other yard and garden accents.

A great deck usually has a stunning focal point, something that immediately grabs your attention. Perhaps you already have one—a beautiful tree, a lovely view, an inviting pool. Or you can supply a new eye-catcher yourself—a hot tub, a huge potted plant, a series of flower boxes, a well-kept greenhouse, or a statue. Play to your strengths, and position the deck and furniture to accentuate your focal point.

DESIGN CHALLENGES

Every design project hits a snag now and then, whether it turns out that your railing hits the house in the middle of a window or the stairs end in the middle of the driveway, but learn to see these challenges as opportunities to create pleasing points of interesting detail. Solutions to some of these problems are given later in the book but now is the best time to start thinking about them.

Storage Space. Add storage space by providing access to the area under your deck or by building an attached shed. List the things you need to store, and make sure you have enough room, or they will clutter up your deck.

Lighting. Installing a lighting system adds a lot of charm to your deck, and if you plan now, you can hide at least some of the wires by running them through parts of your deck framing. This is much easier to do before you put the decking down.

Drainage Problems. Drainage will only be a problem in the future if it is a problem now. For minor problems, plan a gravel-filled trench in the ground to collect runoff from your deck and direct it away from the site. If you have major water problems, such as frequent standing water or significant erosion, be sure to deal with them before you build the deck.

Adding an Outbuilding. If a gazebo, shed, or play structure is in your future, include it in your plans now. There may be a simple way to tie it to the deck and the house. For example, make the roof of the same material as the deck, and paint the rest of the structure the same as your house. You can often build the play structures of the same materials as your deck.

Theme and Variation. The best decks take one or two great ideas and then work out variations on those general themes.

The theme could be a gently curved line that you use in several places, such as the edge of the decking, the railings, and a path next to the deck. Or you may experiment with a unique decking pattern: have three or four sections that break off of each other at similar angles, for instance. If you have a large octagonal-shaped projection, you may be able to add a smaller version of it elsewhere on the deck, or you can echo the shape by building an octagonal table or bench.

The most visible elements of a deck are often those that project vertically. Choose railings or benches to harmonize with the overall structure. Planters should echo the deck structure.

OPPOSITE The designer of this deck extended the railing design up to the trim on the gazebo roof.

RIGHT If you are planning on adding a shade structure, incorporate it into your plans from the beginning.

BELOW Pergolas and arbors add vertical visual interest to deck designs.

LEFT In addition to being compatible with the surroundings, this deck conforms to the site.

Sloping Sites. A sloping site makes the construction process more difficult but also presents an opportunity for an interesting, multilevel deck.

Trees. Trees on a deck site also present a chance to do something stunning, such as building the deck around the tree. Consider the age of your tree and how fast it will grow, and plan to leave ample space.

Pools and Hot Tubs. Building a deck with a pool, hot tub, or spa requires precise planning, engineering, and cutting. Think carefully about how high and wide you want the decking around pools and tubs for maximum sitting and sunning pleasure. You'll need to beef up the structure under a hot tub, adding extra joists or an additional beam.

Shade and Access. If you want some shade but don't have foliage overhead, add some louvered structures or brightly colored awnings. For areas with heavy rainfall, build a roof extension.

Plan access hatches so you can get at plumbing or electrical service junctions underneath the deck, just in case something needs repair someday. Little trap doors and hatches that would look tacky inside are charming on a deck.

Railings are usually required on any deck over 18 inches above the ground. Plan now if you want to include any custom design features or unusual patterns in your railings. A built-in bench adds visual interest to a long expanse of railing as well.

OVERLOOKED DECK LOCATIONS

Decks aren't always found hugging the ground right next to the back door. An island deck isn't attached to the house at all, so it can go virtually anywhere on your property.

And don't forget to look up when you're searching for the perfect deck location. A rooftop deck usually offers better views, more breeze, and a more private setting.

Almost any patch of flat or low-slope roof can support a roof deck. You can also run posts down to ground level, but the easiest system is to make removable platforms that lie down directly on the roof. The panels must be removable because you may have to fix a roof leak at some point. If the decking were permanent you would have to rip it out to make a roof repair.

One popular option is to build a private deck off the master bedroom and change a window into a door.

TOP A new deck need not be built tight against the house. This section of deck juts out into the garden for a better view of the surroundings.

RIGHT When planning, think of the various uses for your deck. Here having a shaded spa was an important consideration.

DEVELOPING
A
PLAN

Now that you've figured out where your deck will go, made some general choices about its size and shape, and scribbled some rough sketches, it's time to get serious about drawing your plans. Think through every detail on paper before you even drive the first nail, and you won't waste time figuring things out as you go.

MAKING THE DRAWINGS

You'll generally need to make four types of drawings. First, a site plan maps the sections of your house and yard that surround your deck site. Second, a plan drawing gives an overhead view of the deck, showing the sizes and locations of all the main components. Third, elevation drawings depict your deck as it will appear from the sides and the front, including railings and stairs. And fourth, detail drawings show how you will deal with complicated portions of the deck and how you'll build any deck enhancements, such as benches, storage boxes, and overhead structures.

The design process rarely proceeds in a smooth, orderly fashion, so don't be surprised to find yourself skipping back and forth between elevations, plans, and details, changing each one several times.

DRAWING TO SCALE

Your finished drawings must be to scale. The most common choice for overall deck plans is to draw in ¼-inch scale, where ¼ inch on the paper equals 1 foot on the finished deck. Detail drawings tend to use a larger scale—often ½ inch to the foot.

All you really need to make these drawings are some large sheets of paper, a pencil, a drafting square, a ruler, and an eraser, but a few extra tools might make the job easier. An architectural scale, for example, provides foot and inch markings for several common drawing scales, which help you quickly transfer your project's full-size dimensions onto your scale drawing. Graph paper, with ½- or ¼-inch grids, can also help you produce a correctly scaled drawing. A sheet of tracing paper taped over a drawing lets you experiment with different designs without marking up your clean copy.

CREATE SITE ELEVATIONS

To plan a deck over a sloped site, take several measurements to create a side view of the grade. Pay particular attention to the areas where you will need foundation piers. To estimate the maximum height on a small deck, simply prop up a board, and check it with a carpenter's level. Over larger areas, enlist a helper to rig a long string from a fixed point where the deck will be near the ground to a pole where it will be most elevated. Use a line level on the string, and measure down to the ground. Even with an accurate layout, it's wise to cut your posts on the long side and trim them as you add the girders and joists.

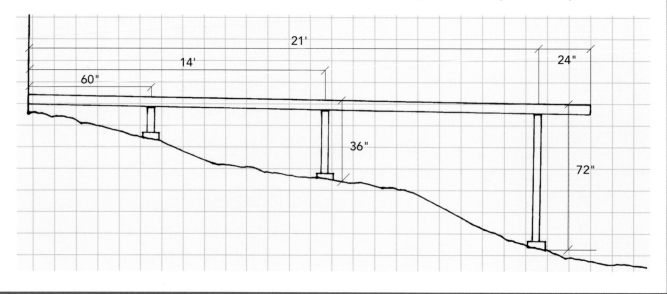

SMART TIP

BEFORE YOU BEGIN

Check with the local building department to see what drawings are required and how detailed they need to be. It's usually a good idea to do more than the required amount of drawing.

RIGHT A rooftop deck is a good solution when space is tight. The design of this shade area matches the house's roof.

BELOW When planning your deck, keep activity areas in mind. Remember to set aside space for lounging.

BELOW RIGHT When building on a slope, take several measurements when setting the posts to get a level deck.

It is to your advantage to try and make your plans as professional looking as possible. If your deck plan includes curved edges, circular cutouts for trees, or round hot tubs or gazebos, a compass or template with various curves and circles will give your drawing a professional look.

Drawing a Site Plan. Your site plan will simply show where your new deck will sit on your property. Inspectors will use it to check setbacks and other requirements. In most cases, you will be able to find some sort of scaled drawing or survey of your site as reference. It may be with your home's title in that file folder marked "House Papers," or maybe your local building department has some original construction drawings. You'll probably need to rescale it and update it with past improvements.

If you have a site on a steep slope, draw a site elevation, or side view, of the terrain as well. This will give you a more-accurate idea of how far you might have to step down with stairs or with different levels.

To get the measurements for your site elevation, you'll need a helper or two, string, a line level, and a measuring tape. Hook one end of the string to a reference point on the house. One person holds the other end of the string in the air—on a stepladder if necessary. Another person checks the line level, and a third person makes measurements from the house to a point on the string and from that point down to the ground.

Now that you have a site plan and a definite notion of the location and general shape of your deck, it's time to start planning the structure and designing the deck itself.

DIY OPTIONS

SHADE STRUCTURES

When including a shade structure or a sloping arbor on your deck, try to mimic the slope of the roof of the house. If adding roofing materials, use the same materials as those on the house for a seamless design.

SMART TIP

ADD SUPPORT
If a deck extends far enough down a slope, one edge may be more than 8 feet above the ground and require 6x6 posts plus some cross bracing.

OPPOSITE Elevated decks often require more support than is necessary for decks built close to the ground. Check with the local building inspector for details.

DRAWING AN ELEVATION

Overview: Add as many details to your plan as possible. But all the local building department really needs is something they can read. In addition to labeling the components of the deck, add a section for notes listing the lumber dimensions for posts, girders, joists, decking, and rail parts. Also remember to list the size and type of fasteners and anchors you'll use to make the connections. In some cases, as here, you may want to omit backgrounds for clarity. (See page 61 for a plan view of deck and house.)

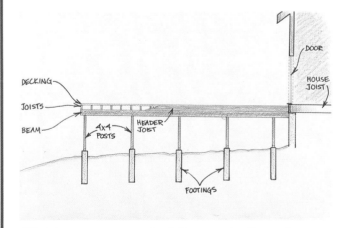

3 Joists come next, building up the frame in stages that can hold the surface boards. Ideally, they will be just below the floor level of the house.

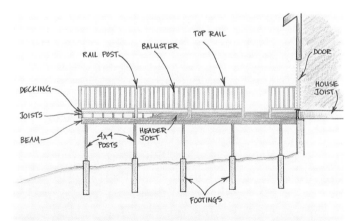

1 *Build your deck on paper, starting with concrete piers and support posts for the main beam. Cover the plan with tracing paper to try different layouts.*

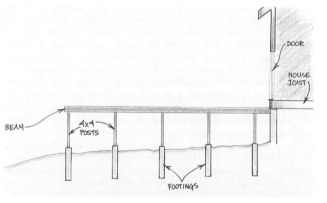

2 *Two 2x10s bolted to the posts form the beam or girder. Typically, the combination of a ledger on the house and a girder on posts holds joists.*

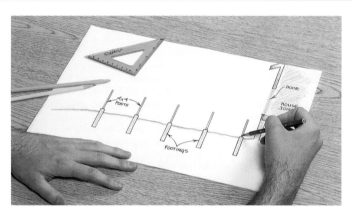

4 *Posts support the combination of railings and balusters. Remember that the spacing on railing systems is controlled by local building codes.*

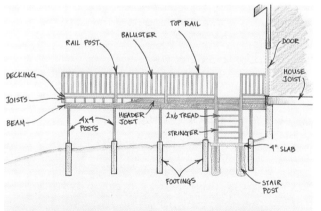

5 *Leave room for stairs that run from the deck to a landing pad in the yard. Make copies of your completed plan, and continue to refine the design.*

LEFT To hide the understructure of a deck built close to the ground, use low-profile shrubs and potted plants. A lattice screen is another option.

way the post and footing look when viewed from the side.

If you cantilever the joists out 24 inches or more beyond the girder, people probably won't be able to see the imperfect footings.

Hiding the footings well under the deck also hides the girder, so if the deck and the girder aren't perfectly aligned, it will not show. And the large members used for girders—usually a pair of pressure-treated two-by boards or a single four-by girder—are often ugly, so hiding the girder under the deck will make your deck look better. This is especially important if you include high-end materials in your deck design, such as cedar or redwood for the decking.

And with a low deck, cantilevering joists past the girder can be attractive because it makes the deck seem to float above the yard.

Let the Lumber Run Wild. Though all the parts of your deck will end up trimmed neatly to exact lengths eventually, try to wait until the last minute to make the final cuts. Leave the posts, joists, and decking too long when you first install them, and cut them to size later. This is called letting the lumber run wild, and it's an important technique for building good-looking decks. Professional deck builders have used this trick for years.

If the wall of your house bows out, for example, and you cut all your joists to exactly the same length before you install them, you'll

FORGIVING DESIGNS

Whenever possible, choose design options that either de-emphasize imperfections or make it easy to correct mistakes. There are a number of examples that you can try on your deck.

Hide the Footings and Posts. Posts sometimes end up a little bit off-center on top of the footings. An inch or so won't affect the strength of your foundation, but you might not like the

simply duplicate the bowed-out wall on the header joist. Let the joists run wild, snap a chalk line across the tops, and cut them all off in perfect alignment.

Attach Built-up Girders to the Post. If you choose to place a girder on top of several posts, you'll have to trim all the posts to exactly the same height before you install the girder. This is difficult—especially for a long girder spanning four or five posts.

An easier method is to let the posts run wild upward and build a girder composed of two or more pieces of two-by lumber attached to the side of the post with lag screws. With this design, you can check and recheck the girder for level before tightening the screws, and correct any mistakes as you work. Cut the posts flush to the top of the beam only after the girder is in place and fastened securely.

To avoid confusion during construction, your drawings should make it clear which method you'll use when framing the deck.

Use Overhangs and Underhangs. Where one piece of lumber supports another, it's tempting to trim the upper piece flush with the bottom one to create a smooth, crisp corner. But a gap may open up over time, especially when dealing with deck lumber prone to expansion and contraction.

In many cases, a planned overhang or underhang looks better than a flush cut anyway. It is usually best to let decking overhang the joists by an inch or two; railing pieces often look best overhung as well. Letting a rail overhang a post is also a good way to prevent water from collecting in the end grain of the post.

Though less commonly done, it is best to underhang framing pieces—such as letting the girder extend well beyond the end joists if the girder is especially attractive. To put their personal stamp on a project, some deck builders even carve the ends of the beam or cut them on an angle as an artistic detail.

Install Added-on Railings. You can design a deck so that the posts supporting the beam come up through the decking and continue onward to become part of the railing. This sounds convenient, but a longer post is more difficult to install perfectly plumb, and if the railing posts are not plumb or not exactly aligned, then your railing will probably look awful.

DIY OPTIONS

PLAN TO HIDE FOOTINGS

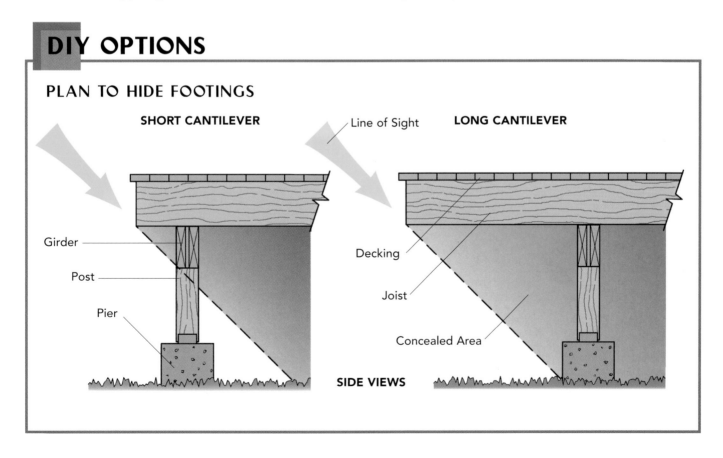

A much more forgiving technique is to build the deck first; bolt railing posts to the outer joists or fascia; and then add the rails and balusters. Properly engineered, these added-on posts are just as strong as a design that uses a continuous post.

Build the Stairway after the Deck. Stairway design is complicated; it takes some figuring to find out just where the stairway will end, for

instance. So wait until the basic deck is finished before you figure the position of the stairway posts and the landing slab.

Posts supporting the stair railings often need extra lateral support. Rather than the typical post-on-footing arrangement, you can extend stair posts down inside the footing forms and pour the concrete around them for extra strength.

Use screws rather than nails. If you ever need to reposition a baluster or pull up a deck board temporarily, you'll find it a whole lot easier if you used screws rather than nails to attach it in the first place. And the piece will probably be re-usable, too. If you have to dig nails out of the wood using a cat's paw, you'll probably ruin the board for future use on the deck.

PLANNING REMINDERS

Because you'll build your deck in unencumbered out-door space, you'll avoid a lot of the aggravations associated with indoor projects: dust in your home, fitting new work to out-of-level floors and crooked walls, navigating narrow doorways with building materials, and rerouting utilities. And you've got a pretty free hand in terms of design. Just be sure to consider a few minor limitations:

Planning for Drainage and Stable Footings. If you have a soggy site, don't expect a deck to solve the problem. In fact, it might

OPPOSITE Build the deck's stairs after the main section of the deck is completed. For tall stairs, use a switchback to make the design more appealing.

RIGHT For wraparound decks, follow the contours of the house. Jogs like this add visual interest and help create areas where people will gather.

BELOW Master suites become much more attractive with the addition of a deck, even a small one as shown here.

Planning for Electrical and Plumbing Lines. Mark the exact locations of any buried pipes or wires on your site, so you can avoid hitting them when you dig the footings. Contact your utility companies if you're not sure where things are. In most cases, the customer service department will come out and mark pipe and wire locations for free. Many local building departments require this step be taken before building.

In addition to checking on buried pipes and electrical lines, consider moving any overhead power lines that may interfere with your deck. If you want to install new plumbing service or electrical wires, plan to bury

make things even worse. Unless you plan some drainage, you can end up with the same amount of water on the ground but less evaporation, because the site is now in the shade.

Don't place footings in unstable or mushy soil. If erosion is a potential problem—usually the case only if you have a very hilly site—take care of it by improving the drainage on the site before it undermines the footings.

as many lines as possible under the deck. Check into low-voltage lighting systems before you go to all this trouble—they're relatively inexpensive and easy to install, and you don't have to bury the wire.

If the deck will cover up any utility access points, such as septic covers or electrical boxes, plan to provide an access hatch so you can get at these things without tearing up the deck.

Check Building and Zoning Codes. The local building department will probably want to get involved with your deck; a large outdoor structure is difficult to miss. Take a trip to the inspector's office before you start planning the deck to ask for a list of basic requirements (often called a handout), and to establish a reputation for yourself as a person who wants to do things right.

BASIC TERMS

The illustration below shows the essential parts of a typical deck. Starting from the ground and working upward, here are some terms you should know.

A *footing* is a solid piece of concrete, usually set in the ground, which supports the deck. Footings often incorporate metal rods or wire mesh for reinforcement. On top of the footing is a *post anchor*, a metal framing connector designed to keep the post from moving and to hold the post a bit above the concrete so it stays dry. *Posts*, usually cut from 4x4 or 6x6 lumber, are vertical members supporting either the deck or the railing. A *girder* is a massive horizontal piece of lumber—either four-by material or doubled-up two-by boards—that supports the joists. Beams sit either on top of the posts or on the sides of the posts secured with lag screws.

Joists, made of two-by lumber and spaced evenly to support the decking, usually rest on the girder on one end. The other end sits on a *ledger*, a piece of lumber bolted directly to the framing of the house. Sometimes pieces of *bridging*, made of the same material as the joists, are attached between the joists to keep them stable. *Outside joists* and the *header joist* form the outside frame of the joist structure. *Fascia* boards sometimes cover the outside joists and header

Building Terms

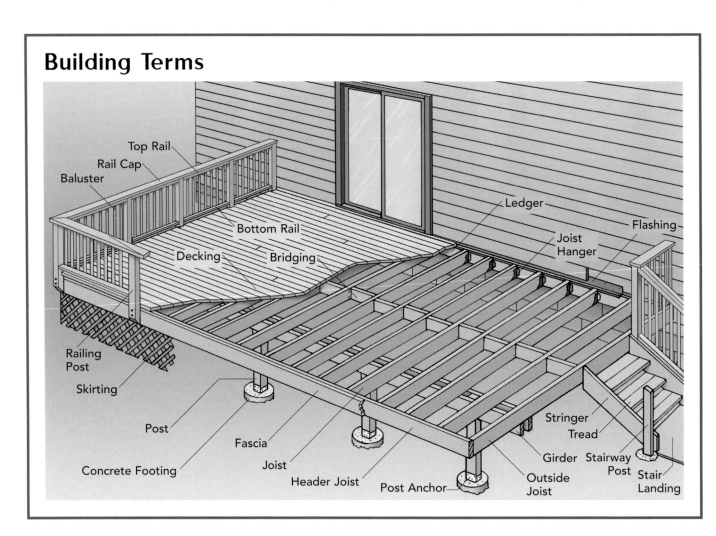

for the sake of appearance. *Decking* boards sit on top of the joists, with nails, screws, or special decking clips holding them in place. Decking is commonly made of 2x4, 2x6, or ⁵⁄₄x6 material.

A typical *railing* setup includes posts for support and *balusters* (sometimes referred to as pickets), usually 2x2 or 1x4 vertical pieces evenly spaced between the posts. Balusters typically run from the top rail down to a bottom rail, though they sometimes continue down and attach to the fascia. A *rail cap* tops the whole thing off.

Stairs have *stringers*, the downward-angled 2x12s on the sides, which are the main support. *Treads* are the steps you walk on. A pair of 2x6 boards typically serve as a tread. *Risers*, usually pieces of 1x8, may cover the vertical spaces between the treads. Stairway posts support handrails and balusters.

ABOVE Most building codes do not require railings for decks that are less than 18 inches high.

BELOW Building codes specify both the railing height and the spacing of balusters.

SMART TIP

COMPUTER DECK SOFTWARE
Programs that run on your home computer or laptop can help you organize your design ideas. Produced by a number of companies, software packages make simple work of drawing decks, railings, planters, and other deck amenities. Some versions show your designs in three-dimensional rotating images that allow you to make a virtual tour of the deck and the surrounding area. The programs can also provide materials lists and building instructions.

ABOVE Although a number of new products are available, treated wood is still the most popular.

BELOW Solid railings are uncommon, but they make a definitive statement and provide privacy.

DECK MATERIAL OPTIONS

There are a number of deck materials available, including hardwoods such as mahogany, meranti, and ipé, which are usually special-order products. The more common deck materials include the following.

- **Redwood,** bottom, is a premier outdoor wood and available in many varieties from knotty utilitarian grades to very expensive clear heartwood.
- **Cedar** is another deluxe wood with many of redwood's weather-resistant features. But it's not as strong and is used on the surface more than the structure.
- **Pressure-treated** wood, top, is ideal for structural timbers because it is infused with preservatives. But there are variations, so you need to check the labels.
- **Vinyl decking** sounds bad but looks pretty good. It won't rot or warp and needs no finishing, and you can clean off the surface with a garden hose.
- **Composite decking,** far right, is becoming more available. Each company has a different formulation, but many consist of recycled wood and PVC. Composites offer low maintenance and durability.

PLAN TO AVOID WASTE

If you plan carefully, you'll avoid paying for lumber that you don't need when you build your deck. For example, because lumber is sold in 2-foot increments starting at 8 feet, if you need a joist that is 14 feet 1 inch, you'll have to pay for a 16-footer, and you'll have a possibly worthless 23-inch piece left over.

Scrutinize your plans to see whether you can make any adjustments to your design now to avoid this kind of waste. You may be able to plan your joist cutoffs so they are the right length for bridging, for example. A change of just an inch or two in one dimension will sometimes solve a problem.

Getting as detailed as this may seem wearisome, but an hour or two of careful thought now could save you lots of work later and plenty of money as well.

Plan a way to use the decking boards efficiently, too. If your deck is too long for single decking boards to span across it, plan where the butt joints will go and whether the cutoffs will fit somewhere else on the deck. Angled decking patterns often call for several small corner pieces—a perfect place to use up those cutoffs.

Don't plan on using full-length boards, however. Sometimes you will need to trim off an inch or so from a board's end to eliminate a split or square up an end. And though some dimensional lumber may come with an extra ½ inch of

length, don't count on this. If, for example, you plan for decking boards that are 11 feet 10 inches long (rather than 12 feet), you will be able to use 12-foot decking pieces with confidence.

It's easy to get confused and miss by an inch or more when figuring this, so here are some common errors to look out for:

■ Include the overhang for decking boards.

■ For decking boards cut at an angle, always figure the length of the longer edge when planning.

■ In some designs, the outside joists will be either 1½ or 3 inches longer than the interior joists, because the outside joists overlap the header and ledger, while the interior joists butt against them.

PLAN THE FRAMING

You'll build your deck from the ground up, of course, but to begin the design process, you should think about the job from the top down.

With a typical deck design, start by locating the top surface of your deck boards a comfortable step down from the door to the house. This step works okay at anything up to about 6 inches, but 2 or 3 inches usually feels best.

On the wall, measure down from the top surface of the decking by the thickness of the decking to find the top edge of the ledger and the joists, and make a mark. Then drop down the width of the joists to find the top of the girder; mark again; and measure down by the width of the girder to locate the top of the posts.

Posts and Footings. The posts that transfer the weight of the deck down to the footings might vary in height to compensate for a sloping site, but a rough idea of their size will help you plan the rest of the structure. On a very low deck, you might skip the posts and place the girder directly on the footings. A deck attached to the second story of a house might call for 6x6 posts.

The type of lumber you choose will also affect your plans. For instance, if you use ⁵⁄₄x6 cedar decking, you'll have to make your joists closer together than if you use 2x6 pressure-treated decking. It's usually best to choose the lumber first, based on your budget and taste, then plan accordingly.

Although many different types of wood are available, chances are that the best lumber choices for you will be treated lumber for the ledger, deck posts, girder, and joists, and either cedar, redwood, treated lumber, or composite materials for the decking, fascia, and rails.

TWO BASIC FRAMING CONFIGURATIONS

Most decks use the joist-on-girder framing technique to support the joists. A large horizontal girder (or more than one, if the deck is large enough) supports one end of the joists, while the other ends of the joists sit on or are attached to a ledger board bolted to the house framing. This arrangement works well for building large plat-

forms and gives you the option of hiding the beam and footings under the deck by extending the decking beyond the girder.

Joists Attached to Posts. Another arrangement uses a doubled or tripled header joist instead of a girder. Lag screws or through-bolts secure any joists that fall next to a post. This technique works best for short joist spans.

There are three advantages to this configuration. First, it is simpler; you avoid building and installing a heavy girder. Second, the posts here can continue upward to become part of the railing system, if you wish. Third, with this system you can build decks closer to the ground because there is no girder.

On the down side, the footings will be visible, and this design is not very forgiving, because all the posts have to be exactly correct for it to work. This arrangement works best when you need to build a deck close to the ground or when the deck is fairly narrow.

LEFT As with porches, deck framing usually consists of joists supported by girders and a ledger that is attached to the house.

ABOVE Easy access from inside the house will make your deck more inviting.

BELOW Existing trees can provide natural shade for parts of your new deck.

SMART TIP

AVAILABILITY OF MATERIALS

Some manufacturers of engineered decking sell their products nationally, but many companies have only regional distribution. Before you become set on using one type of product, make sure it is available in your area.

POSTS AND FOOTINGS

If the finished walking surface of your deck is 6 feet or less above the ground, you can build with 4x4 posts. Anything higher than 8 feet requires 6x6s, which are a great deal more difficult to handle and are often unsightly. Between 6 and 8 feet is a gray area—check with your local building-code officials.

The most common post-and-footing arrangement calls for a post that is set in a post anchor on top of a concrete footing. Posts are sometimes set into postholes, which are then backfilled with concrete, giving the posts more lateral strength. But a post set into the concrete is more likely to rot over time, so use this sort of footing only for posts without a lot of other lateral support, such as stairway posts.

DIY OPTIONS

POST AND FOOTING CONNECTIONS

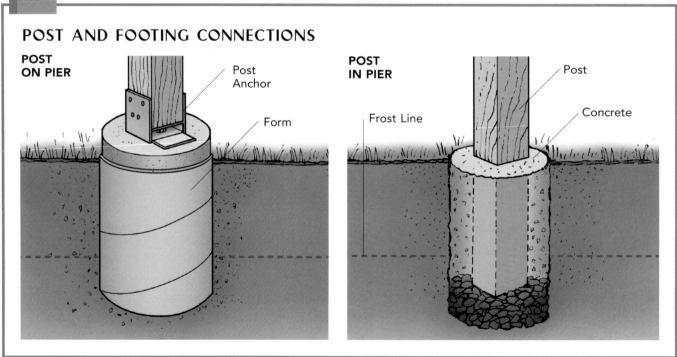

POST ON PIER

Post Anchor

Form

POST IN PIER

Frost Line

Post

Concrete

You will probably need to dig and pour footings for each post. Your drawings should include notes about the depth of the holes, the type of concrete forms you will be using, and the anchoring system.

GIRDERS

A girder made of a single piece of four-by lumber (4x8, 4x10, etc.) can save you a lot of time because you won't have to build your own girder. Unfortunately, lumber that is 4x6 and larger tends to be full of seasoning checks, difficult to find, and very heavy.

There are times you may want to use a solid girder anyway, but usually it's easier to construct built-up girders with two-by lumber. One way is to sandwich strips of pressure-treated ½-inch plywood between two two-by boards, making a total thickness of 3½ inches—the same as a 4x4. This girder will fit all framing hardware designed for use with 4x4 beams.

You can also bolt two-by lumber to the sides of posts, either on opposite sides or both on the same side.

BRACING FOR ELEVATED DECKS

If your deck is raised 72 inches or more, you will probably need some sort of angled bracing to stabilize the deck—check to see what your local building department recommends. You can always add some bracing later if the finished deck feels unstable. And bracing does not have to be an eyesore. Symmetrically placed pieces of bracing lumber add visual interest to an otherwise boxy shape.

BRIDGING BETWEEN JOISTS

In some circumstances—especially when your joists span more than 10 feet—you'll want to install bridging, also referred to as bracing. These are usually solid pieces of lumber, the same dimension as your joists, that span the distance between joists to maintain joist spacing and prevent excessive warping. Installed tightly around the middle of the span, bridging adds rigidity to the substructure of the deck.

Cross-brace bridging also works well, either 2x2s mitered to fit between the joists in an X-

OPPOSITE **This beachfront deck provides a transition between the dunes and the house. Note the angled braces that provide added support.**

ABOVE **This elevated deck provides a sheltered areas at ground level. Note the sliders which may indicate that these areas are used often.**

shape or preformed metal cross bracing, sold to fit a variety of joist sizes.

CHOOSING A FRAMING CONFIGURATION

Sometimes defining one aspect of your deck will dictate other design choices. For instance, if you use 2x6 decking, you can space the joists 24 inches apart (also called 24 inches on center), but if you use thinner ⅝x6 decking boards, the supporting joists should be closer together—with just 16 inches between joists.

You'll also factor in the length and size of the joists, and how much weight they can carry, when determining the size of the girder and where to place the posts and footings. Different species and grades of wood vary in strength.

As you delve into your project, you'll find that it's not as confusing as it sounds. Once you have chosen the materials you'll be using, use a joist span chart to figure the sizes and lengths of the girders and joists as well as the positions of the footings and posts. There is a joist span chart in Chapter 9.

DIY OPTIONS

NAILING DETAILS
ANGLED CORNERS

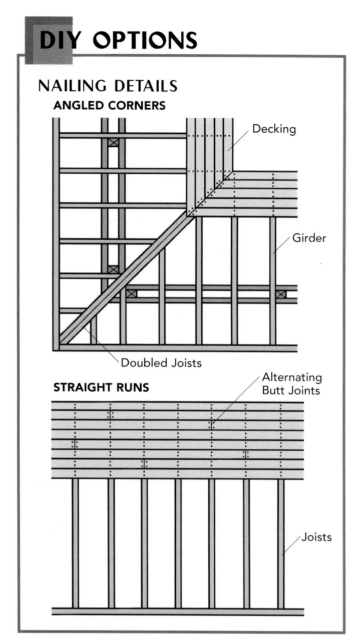

Decking

Girder

Doubled Joists

STRAIGHT RUNS

Alternating Butt Joints

Joists

DECKING SIZE AND PATTERN

When someone walks onto your deck for the first time, they'll probably check out one of two things first: the view or the decking material and pattern you have selected. While you can't do a whole lot to adjust the view, you can plan an attractive decking design.

Don't hesitate to pick a complex pattern, such as a herringbone or parquet design. Installing the decking is actually one of the simpler aspects of deck construction, and with patience you can construct some interesting and intricate deck surfaces.

Bear in mind, however, that an unusual decking pattern usually wastes more lumber, which increases the materials cost. The extra cuts and fitting take more time as well. Installing decking for an angled design will take you about twice as long as installing boards that cross the joists at right angles.

Vary Decking Widths. One way to increase your decking's visual interest without adding any materials expense and without much extra work is to use different widths of decking boards in a repeating pattern. You can alternate between 2x6 and 2x4 decking boards, for instance.

Whichever decking options you decide to use, include notes about the size, pattern, and the spacing between boards on your drawings.

Sometimes an unusual decking choice will require extra joist work. Think through the deck

Simple Stair Design

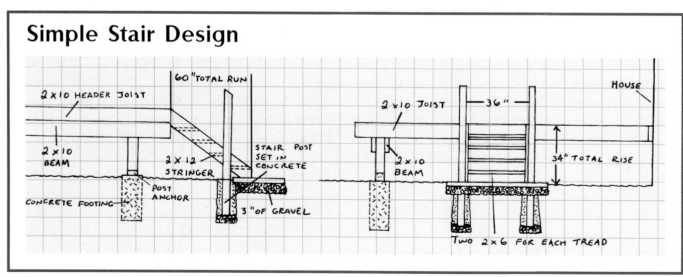

60" TOTAL RUN

HOUSE

2 X 10 HEADER JOIST

2 X 10 JOIST

36"

2 X 10 BEAM

34" TOTAL RISE

STAIR POST SET IN CONCRETE

2 X 12 STRINGER

2 X 10 BEAM

CONCRETE FOOTING

POST ANCHOR

3" OF GRAVEL

TWO 2 X 6 FOR EACH TREAD

design, and be sure that every decking board has solid support at each end. Butt joints in a run of decking are usually fine on a single joist, but plan for a double joist where the decking makes a turn and you have miter-cut ends meeting at the corner.

PLANNING STAIRWAYS

Laying out a stairway requires some fairly complicated figuring to be sure all the steps will be the same height and so that you end up where you want to.

You probably don't need to make a detailed drawing of the stairs, but for your own purposes, you will want to find out what length 2x12s you should buy for the stringers, how many treads you need, and approximately where the concrete, masonry, or gravel pad at the bottom will fall.

If you find this difficult to figure at this point, you may want to wait until you have built your deck; then figure your stairs—as long as there is no danger that the stairs will end up where you don't want them.

RAILINGS AND BENCHES

There are dozens of ways to make a safe, attractive railing, and even more possibilities if you include the countless finishing options. You can use horizontal boards between posts, vertical balusters, diagonal lattice, and other patterns. However, ladder-type railings that are easy to climb are usually prohibited by the building code. But you must make sure to meet local codes, which are much tougher than they used to be. Generally, you can leave no more than a 4-inch space between posts and balusters, and locate the railing no lower than 36 inches above the deck. Be sure to check the limits with your building department.

One approach is to attach railing posts to the outside joists. This is the easiest system because you can build the railings after the decking is completed. Another approach is to use extended posts that continue up through the deck to sup-

port the rail system. This provides great strength but requires straight lumber, and some notching work. Yet another approach is to build your railing into built-in benches. Generally, you need to do some of this work before the perimeter decking goes down—for example, attaching seat supports to the joists.

Add Finishing Touches. To help your benches blend in, use finishing details such as recessed, round-headed carriage bolts instead of machine bolts. You'll also want to spend some extra time on finishing and sanding; for example, making smooth, rounded-over edges instead of square edges that can catch you uncomfortably under the knees.

Your elevation drawing should show how you will attach the railing posts, top and bottom rails, and balusters. Make a detail drawing for any built-in benches.

BELOW **Many people prefer wide treads for stairs that lead up to a deck. Check with your local building department for specific requirements.**

FINAL DRAWINGS

Once you have made all your decisions regarding site, substructure, decking, stairs, and railings, you are ready to finalize your plans. The finished drawings should be clear: do not rely on scribbled-over and often-erased sheets—take the extra time to draw a clean set of plans because they will be easier to follow.

The set of deck plans at the end of this chapter is a good example of what you'll need to produce in order to get your building permit. After reviewing these drawings and your site plan, your building department will either issue you a permit or ask for some changes.

PLAN DRAWINGS

Plan drawings show the deck framing from above. For these drawings, it is common to leave out the railings and decking. Be sure to include

- Correct dimensional drawing of the perimeter.
- All joists, girders, posts, and footings.
- Dimensions for all lumber.
- The distance spanned by girders and joists.
- Indication of size and direction of decking. (It's not usually necessary to draw this.)
- Hardware, such as joist hangers, angle brackets, and bolts.
- Exact locations of doors and windows.
- Any electrical and plumbing fixtures and lines.

ELEVATION DRAWING

An elevation drawing shows the deck in cross-section from the side. Draw at least one elevation, including these elements:

- A detailed drawing of the railing system, including all dimensions that pertain to local codes
- Views of the concrete footings, with dimensions showing how deep and wide they will be
- Hardware list including sizes of post anchors, tread cleats, and bolts
- Height of the tallest post
- A rough approximation of the site's slope

DETAIL DRAWINGS

Draw close-up views of complicated spots on your deck. Sometimes you will need to make a detail drawing to satisfy the building department. At other times, you may need it yourself in order to figure things out. Draw details for situations like these:

- Where the stair railing meets the rest of the deck railing
- Hatchways for access to electrical and plumbing
- Framing around trees or hot tubs
- Changes in level
- Any area of the deck with special framing, such as extra joists under a section of deck that will support a portable hot tub
- Flashing around ledger

Sample Detail Drawing

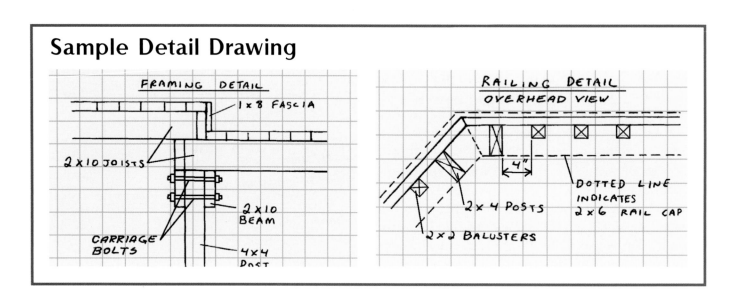

Sample Plan Drawing

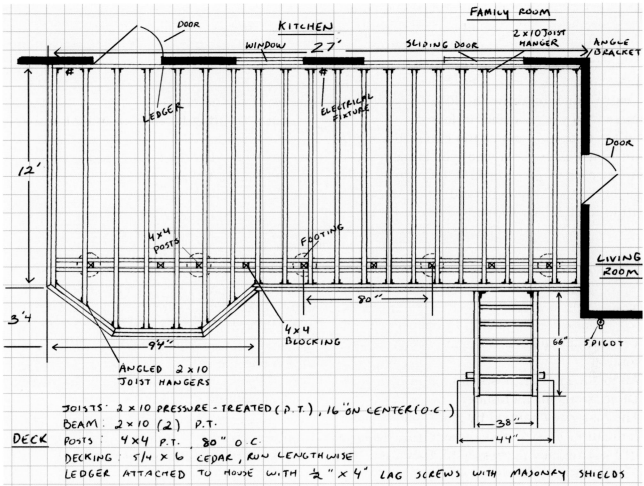

Sample Elevation Drawing

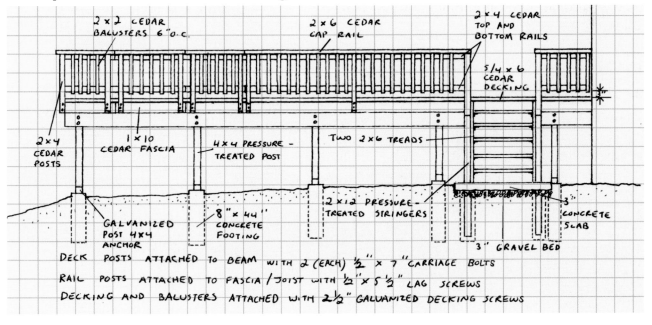

DECK POSTS ATTACHED TO BEAM WITH 2 (EACH) ½" x 7" CARRIAGE BOLTS
RAIL POSTS ATTACHED TO FASCIA/JOIST WITH ½" x 5½" LAG SCREWS
DECKING AND BALUSTERS ATTACHED WITH 2½" GALVANIZED DECKING SCREWS

PLANNING
FOR
CONSTRUCTION

3

Whether you build a deck completely by yourself or enlist pros to handle some of the work, the job will run more smoothly if you start with a good plan. You need blueprints, of course, but it also pays to plan for deliveries, materials storage, access to the site, and details that many DIYers overlook, such as finding a place to put all the dirt from your foundation.

PLANNING THE JOB

Building a deck is probably the most straight-forward type of home construction, which makes it a project that many homeowners can tackle. But even if you have an architect and a general contractor handle the job for you, it pays to do some preliminary DIY planning on site. This chapter covers some of the most important elements of planning a deck project.

Let's assume at this point that you have developed a basic plan on paper. You still have time to make alterations, of course. (It's always better to make a change on paper than to rip out joists.) But whatever plan you've settled on and wherever you envision your new deck (typically off the back or side of the house), it's also wise to take the time to plan the job itself.

Create the Outlines of Your Deck. First, make some full-scale measurements on the actual site. Drive a few stakes to see how much space you'll have and how much yard you'll give up. If the ultimate deck will overrun some protective bushes or a beautiful shade tree, the best plan may be a practical compromise.

To get a realistic sense of the space, mark the deck outline with a garden hose or long extension cord. Arrange a table and some chairs (or paper templates) inside the perimeter to see how the space works. And climb a few steps up a ladder to see how the view changes at different elevations. Height often presents several compromises—between light and shade, breezes, different views, and an increase or decrease in privacy.

ESTABLISHING A DECK HEIGHT

To reach the deck from the house you can step down, even several steps. But most decks work best as outdoor extensions of indoor space, which means the deck surface should be nearly as high as the finished floor inside.

On many houses, a step down of only an inch or two works well. First, it allows a little clearance for the decking boards to tuck under weather-shedding doorsills. Second, and even more important, it allows you to tie the deck structure directly into the house floor framing. On decks that are a foot or more below floor level, you will likely miss the framing and have to anchor the deck to the foundation. That's possible, but more difficult (and for DIYers more risky) than fastening the deck to a wood frame. This is the kind of detail you might miss by designing your deck on paper but catch when you take some on-site measurements, pry off a piece of siding, and find out where you can make the safest and most practical connections between the deck and the house.

Sloping Sites. On a sloping site, a floor-level deck may look good and work well from the house but project high above the backyard, creating a dark cavern underneath. In that case, consider building the main section at floor level and breaking the stairs into sec-

SMART TIP

SETTING POSTS

Don't cut your posts to the desired height until they are attached to the concrete piers. Then strike a level mark near the tops of the posts to create a line of level supports for the main girder or girders.

OPPOSITE This deck's railing is an unusual combination of metal and wood.

RIGHT Plan deck height so that it is a small step down from an exterior door.

tions with their own landing platforms. A more gradual step-down effect will help to anchor the main deck to the site.

Once the main level is established, you need to plan the structure from the surface down to the foundation, allowing for decking, joists, girders, and foundation.

LOCATING SUPPORTS

On almost any site, flat or sloped, the most versatile approach is to use a combination of concrete piers and wooden posts. You can dig a few piers (without calling in a contractor with a backhoe), mix concrete by the bag in a wheelbarrow, and pour it into round, prefab, fiberboard forms. Mount post-holding hardware in the piers before the mix hardens, and you're ready for posts.

PICKING A STORAGE SITE

No matter what type of lumber you decide on, select a storage site that is easy to get to from the street and close to the job site. Most suppliers bring a large order of lumber banded together on a truck and simply slide off the load.

You should be there when the lumber arrives, of course, and lay out a grid of lumber (a few treated 4x4s work well) to support the lumber above the ground.

Once the load is dropped, you may discover that some of the wood isn't exactly dry. (That's a nice way of saying the lumber quality has deteriorated.) In that case, reshuffle the pile and insert lattice strips between layers. This allows air to flow around the lumber and can make the wood easier to handle even after a few days of air-drying.

WORKING WITH PROFESSIONALS

You may be able to handle a difficult deck project. But for a typical DIYer, there are some circumstances where professional help is likely to pay off.

For example, a deck raised 10 feet or more can be dangerous to build without the right equipment and experience. A deck supported by angled braces attached to the house (rather than to posts set on the ground) requires special engineering.

A deck set in swampy or otherwise unstable soil is likely to need the sort of foundations or pilings that are difficult for a do-it-yourselfer to build. Similarly, a deck set on a site that is hilly can be a problem. If your yard is severely sloped, think through the work involved: are you going to be able to set up and support every post and raise a heavy girder on top of them as well? A deck that must support heavy loads, such as a spa or a hot tub, calls for professional assistance at least in the design phase.

WHO WILL DO THE WORK?

Though a deck may look like an imposing project, it is well within the reach of a moderately skilled homeowner. In fact, it's probably the most popular large-scale do-it-yourself project there is.

If you are reasonably handy with tools, have been successful with other carpentry projects, have a reliable helper or two at your disposal, and have the time and patience for a large project, you can succeed in building a deck on any fairly level site.

But before you get started, be honest about yourself: do you tend to finish jobs, or are there lots of half-done projects around your house? Are you in a position to devote plenty of time to deck building, or are you short on free time already? If you have any doubts, consider hiring a professional, at least for part of the work.

OPPOSITE If adding a pool or spa to the deck, be sure the deck can support the weight.

BELOW Wide steps add a graceful design touch.

RIGHT Ground- or low-level decks are the easiest for the do-it-yourselfer to tackle.

A large tub doesn't weigh very much by itself but can overwhelm standard construction lumber when it's filled with water and a person or two.

SAVING WITH SWEAT EQUITY

If you don't do all of the work yourself, you might find a contractor who will split the project with you and give you a lower price. You might do the grunt work, such as digging holes for piers and cleaning up after the contractor builds the deck. But be careful when setting up this kind of arrangement. It's easy for misunderstandings to arise, and more often than not, both contractor and customer end up thinking they are doing more work than they bargained for. Be sure your duties are clearly spelled out and that you will be available to do your part of the work when the contractor needs you.

If you decide to tackle the job yourself, you will probably still need at least one helper. Building by yourself can be quite laborious and time-wasting. Preferably, your helper will be someone with carpentry skills, but you can make do with someone who is just there to help carry things and hold things while you do the cutting and nailing.

PERMIT PITFALLS

$ome homeowners try to build a deck without a permit to keep the local tax assessor from raising their real estate taxes. This is a bad idea.

- **It's illegal.** Improvements and additions involving concrete piers, girders, and joists always require a building permit.
- **It leaves loopholes.** Without a building inspector to check the plans and the job site, a disreputable contractor might cut corners.
- **You could be fined.** If a disgruntled neighbor reports you, you could be liable for fines on top of the costs of rebuilding the deck to code.
- **It creates resale problems.** If you beat the system initially, an illegal project may complicate negotiations when it comes time to sell your home.

HIRING A CONTRACTOR

If you decide to hire a professional to build your deck, it pays to spend some time to be sure that you weed out the bad apples and hire a reliable pro. Check first with friends and neighbors, who will not be reluctant to tell you their opinions of contractors they have employed. If possible, inspect a contractor's work. Ask his customers whether he gave them the finished product they were hoping for, finished on time, and responded quickly to any complaints. If you can't find a contractor by word of mouth, try contacting local trade associations. You might also check with a local mortgage banker, home insurance agent, and other people who regularly come in contact with contractors on a professional basis. Get several references, and check the final candidates with your local consumer protection agency. In many areas, builders and remodelers must have a license. The contractor also should be insured for liability, property damage, and worker's compensation.

The Bidding Process. If possible, get bids from two or three contractors before hiring one. Don't just go for the cheapest deal. Compare the estimates point by point to see whether one contractor is providing a service or using a particular material another contractor has left out. Make sure the contractor understands what you want. It's also wise to have a lawyer look at your contract if you're not sure that everything has been covered. The contract should include the exact specifications of the work to be performed, with the plans and elevations appended. All the materials to be used should be fully identified, including lumber grades and hardware types. There are many standard clauses that help to protect your interests. To find out about them, you can check with your local consumer protection agency, and inquire at professional

LEFT On low-level decks, benches not only add convenience, they also function as a barrier or railing.

OPPOSITE Plan on deck lighting to increase the hours you can spend outside.

SMART TIP

DAILY TOOL INSPECTIONS

When putting your tools away at the end of the day, take a few minutes to give them a quick checkup. Look for dull saw blades, dead batteries, and damaged and missing parts. This daily inspection will alert you to problems that need solving before you resume work on your deck the next day.

groups such as the American Institute of Architects, which sells generic-language agreements (for remodeling work and whole houses) that are industry standards.

ORGANIZING THE WORK AREA

If you plan your work space with care, the project will proceed more quickly, you will be less likely to strain your muscles, and everyone—onlookers as well as workers—will be safer.

Here are a few hints that can help:
- Use power tools carefully and according to manufacturer's instructions.
- Centralize power tools and cords, so you always know where the tools are and you're not always tripping over cords.
- Have a cord for every tool, so you don't have to constantly stop working to unplug one tool and plug in another.
- Use a workbench or a set of sawhorses, so you can do most of your cutting from a comfortable standing position.
- Store your lumber near the cutting station to cut down on toting time.
- Stack lumber neatly, and keep clear walking paths to all areas of the job.

CORRALLING TOOLS

Tools have an annoying habit of "walking away" from a work site, even when you're working by yourself. One way to prevent your tools from "sprouting legs" is to mark off an area where each item should be returned whenever it is not in use. An old blanket or scrap sheet of plywood works well.

At the end of the day, make it a point to put away your tools on your own. That way, you'll know exactly where something is because you're the person who put it there.

PERMITS AND INSPECTIONS

Even though your home is your castle, you can't go ahead and build whatever deck you like. First, you need to get a building permit. And when that paperwork (and fee) is taken care of, you have to have periodic inspections on-site to make sure that the approved plans are being followed. And yes, you will almost certainly need a permit. Different regions have different rules, but a permit is required everywhere when a project requires a foundation (and piers count as a foundation) and when structural alterations are made, such as adding a ledger board to your house and cutting an opening for glass doors.

Dealing with Inspectors. Some building departments are receptive to homeowner jobs. (Some even offer generic building plans.) Good inspectors tend to feel a lot of responsibility because they are the last line of defense against shoddy work. They will get tough if necessary. In extreme cases, they can impose fines and make you dismantle illegal work and rebuild to code.

On the other hand, some inspectors have a natural distrust of do-it-yourselfers based on jobs where they have seen shoddy work done by nonprofessionals. So show your inspector that you mean to do a good job. Check ahead of time about zoning requirements and property line setbacks. If you will be doing any plumbing or electrical work along with your deck, let your inspector know about it. Get a list of require-

ments ahead of time, and find out what things are most important to the inspector. Present clean-looking plans that clearly address his concerns. Even if the inspector is an annoying person, respect the fact that he is there to make your neighborhood a safer place to live. If you do things well, you will probably find that even a hard-boiled inspector will deal fairly with you.

You may think all this is not worth the hassle and the money and be tempted to skip the permit. But look on your building inspector as an asset. If he or she spots a design problem in your plans, it could save you a lot more money than the cost of the permit. And if you ever sell your home, it will be an advantage to have a document showing that your deck was inspected and certified to be safe and sound.

JOB-SITE VISITS

Your inspector will probably want to make two or even three on-site inspections: for the footings, the framing, and the finished deck with rails and stairs. Never cover up anything important that hasn't been inspected, and never force your inspector to crawl around to look at something. For example, if your deck will be raised, so the substructure will be easily visible from below, it's probably all right to fasten the decking before the framing inspection. But if your deck will be low to the ground, have the framing inspected before you start decking.

NEIGHBORHOOD REGULATIONS

You may also want to check at your building department or planning board about more-specialized regulations. Some communities set their own architectural standards, either to preserve local traditions or to beautify the area. Not only will compliance with these standards help maintain good neighborly relations, but some communities actually codify these standards into local laws.

CODE COMPLIANCE

Your deck plans create more strength than you need. But codes add a safety margin that translates to deck durability.

- **Professional plans.** A licensed architect or engineer should be familiar with local building practices and provide plans that meet local codes.
- **Stock plans.** Deck designs in plan books promise code compliance. But be prepared to make alterations.
- **Preapproved plans.** Some building departments provide generic plans that include lumber and span options so you can alter the basic layout to suit your site.
- **DIY plans.** In many areas you can draw your own plans for a deck. But you need to specify sizes, dimensions, and construction details.

LEFT Check all local codes regarding railing heights and designs before building.

RIGHT If your deck is built low to the ground, don't add the decking boards until the framing is inspected.

PLANNING FOR CONSTRUCTION

TAX IMPLICATIONS

Like it or not, there's a good chance that your deck will affect your real estate tax bill. As soon as you apply for a building permit, your tax assessor will know that your house's value is about to increase. Once the deck is completed, there's a good chance that your property will be reassessed.

QUESTION YOUR INSPECTOR

Inspectors come in a wide variety of dispositions: some are friendly; some are surly; some like to be asked for advice; some don't want to be bothered. But any inspector will treat you more like a professional remodeler if you appear organized and deal with problems quickly. Along this line, ask the building department office secretary for literature that can answer common questions. Here is a list of common issues that may arise.

- How close can your deck be to your property line?
- What are the lumber requirements for posts, girders, and joists?
- How deep must your footings be?
- Are there special requirements for the concrete footings, such as rebar?
- Which method of ledger installation is preferred, and how should it be flashed?
- If your deck will be raised above the ground, will bracing be required?
- What are the requirements for the pad at the bottom of the stairway?
- What are the codes for railing height and baluster spacing?

DECK CONSTRUCTION SEQUENCE

1

Remove sod; install concrete piers.

2

Attach ledger to house; attach posts to piers.

5

Install decking following manufacturer's directions.

6

Frame stair landing; add stringers.

REALISTIC SCHEDULING

After all of your careful planning and designing, actually building the deck may seem to move quickly. Try not to lock yourself into a rush schedule, however, and leave enough time to work carefully and safely.

How much you can get done in a day depends on many factors, such as your skill level, site conditions, and lumber quality. So there's really no way to predict just how long it will take you.

But you can use these general guidelines to help plan the amount of time you'll need for the project. Any one of the four jobs listed below may be accomplished by a skilled nonprofessional working with a helper for an eight-hour day.

■ Lay out and pour up to seven footings, 8 inches in diameter and 42 inches deep.

■ Build the substructure, which includes installing a ledger board, setting posts on footings and a girder on the posts, and installing joists for a deck of 200 square feet or less, not raised very high, and straightforward in design.

■ Deck approximately 400 square feet if laid straight; 200 square feet if laid at an angle.

■ Install standard railings and stairs for a deck up to 400 square feet.

These estimates assume that you are familiar with basic carpentry. Be conservative in your planning because some trouble spots are bound to arise. It's better to be surprised by how much you've done than disappointed because you did not meet your expectations.

3 Attach the girder to the tops of the posts.

4 Attach joists to ledger and girder; add end joist.

7 Install stair treads. Some stairs also have risers.

8 Install deck railing system.

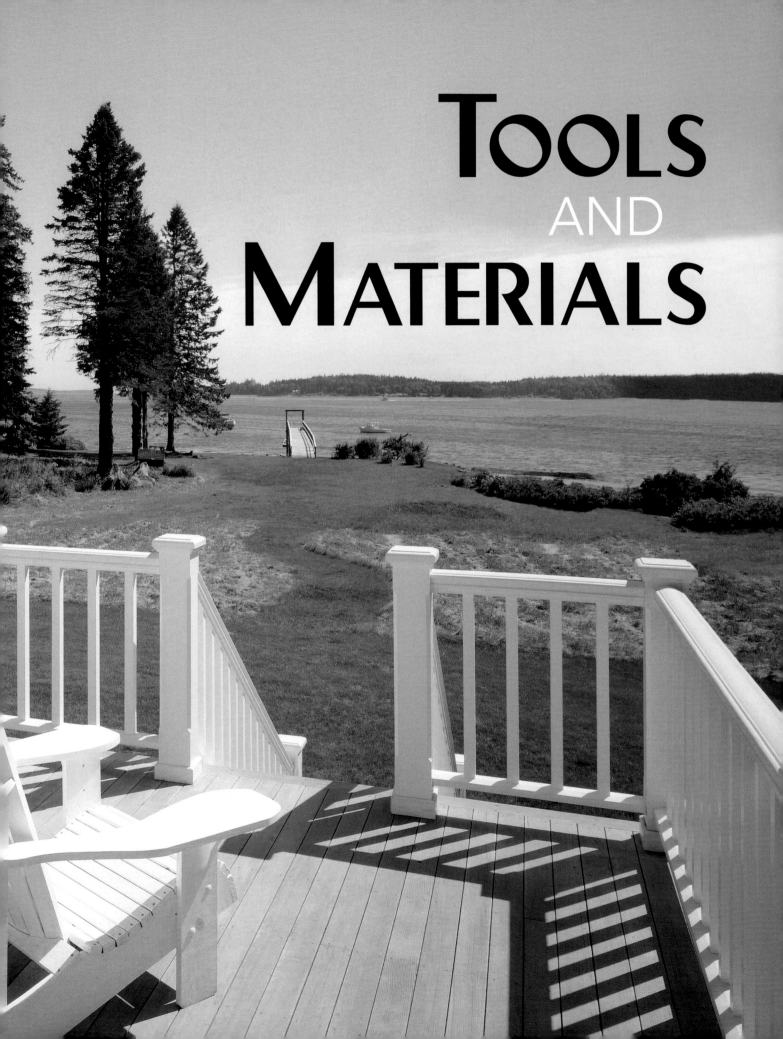

TOOLS
AND
MATERIALS

1 Although most decking is either protected with a clear waterproof sealer or stained, railing systems are often painted to contrast with the color of the deck.

2 Designers recommend selecting a deck material and color that complements the material and color scheme of the house.

3 Redwood decks resist insects and decay naturally. Choose either "clear" or "clear all heart" grades for visible areas.

4 Cedar and redwood decks will weather to a natural gray finish if untreated. You can also apply a finish to achieve that weathered look.

GALLERY OF DECK MATERIALS

GALLERY OF DECK MATERIALS

1 Top-grade lumber works the best when designing a deck for a contemporary house.

2 The retained level of preservative determines whether treated lumber is suitable for ground or above-ground contact.

3 Stained decks look distinctive and resist the ultraviolet rays of the sun better than unstained decks.

4 Composite decking materials offer the look of wood without the maintenance.

5 Natural wood decking provides a look that goes well with most style homes and surroundings.

6 An innovative railing design calls for using clear plastic panels rather than traditional balusters.

2

3

4

5

6

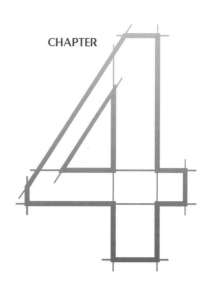

DECK BUILDING TOOLS

A fairly modest set of tools is all you need to build most decks. More-specialized tools will sometimes make the work go faster, but think before you buy: if you will rarely use the tool after the deck project is completed, is it really worth the price? And if there's a tool you've just got to try, consider renting it for a day instead of buying it for a lifetime.

TOOLS FOR BUILDING DECKS

The people on TV home-improvement shows always seem to have an endless supply of specialized tools for their projects. If you can find a tool manufacturer to sponsor your deck, you'll probably have a big pile of tools too, but chances are that you'll need to build your deck with the tools you own now, plus a few additions.

Once you decide which tools you actually need to buy, the next decision is how much to spend.

Should you buy the $279 cordless drill, or will the $39.99 model work just as well for the kind of work you'll be doing?

Typically, the answer lies somewhere between these two extremes. The high-end, professional model will probably build dozens of decks before breaking down. But you probably don't need that kind of durability if you're working on only a few projects every year. Conversely, a bargain-basement tool might quit before you finish one project. For most DIYers, a midpriced model is

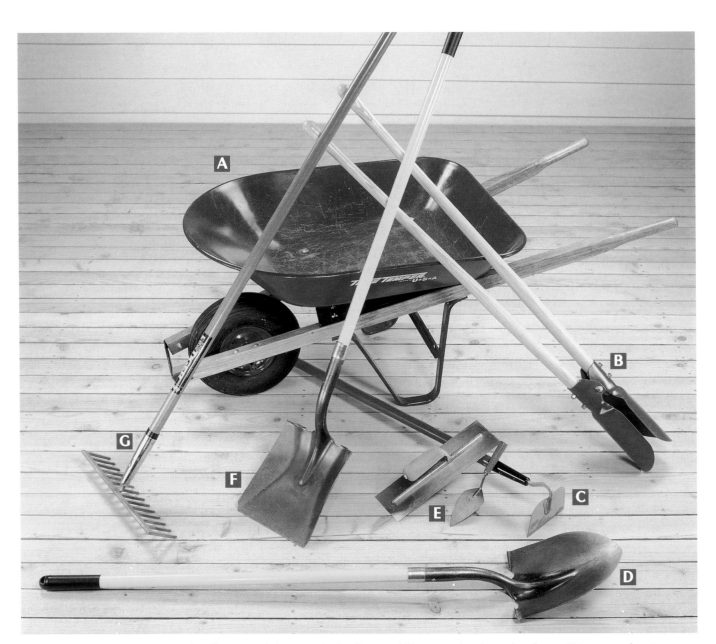

EXCAVATION TOOLS   (A) a wheelbarrow, (B) a posthole digger, (C) a standard garden hoe, (D) a round-point shovel, (E) a selection of trowels including a finishing trowel and a pointing trowel, (F) a square-nosed shovel with a sharp front edge, and (G) a metal garden rake.

a practical compromise. It will serve on a heavy-duty project, such as building a deck, and still be around for ongoing repair and improvement projects around the house.

You'll need the standard supply of basic hand and power tools, of course, including a circular saw with a sharp blade and a drill-driver (cordless or not). You probably have most of them already. But you may want to check into some of the more specialized tools and gadgets (included throughout the book) that are available today.

EXCAVATION AND CONCRETE

Posthole Digger. Whether you use tubular concrete forms or pour your concrete directly into the ground, you will need to dig deep, narrow holes for your footings. Essentially two mini-shovels hinged together, a posthole digger picks up dirt in "bites" as you spread the handles. This tool allows you to work directly above the hole without creating sloping sides.

Round-Point Shovel. The most basic digging tool there is, the round-point shovel gets plenty of use on a deck site, from excavating to spreading gravel. Use a file to keep the edge of the shovel sharp—it'll cut through small roots like a hot knife through butter.

Hoe. A standard garden hoe is handy for mixing concrete; a special mason's hoe, which has two holes in the blade, works even better.

Wheelbarrow. This is a handy place to mix and transport small amounts of concrete—one 80-pound, premixed bag fits nicely in most wheelbarrows. You'll also use your wheelbarrow to transport gravel, soil, sod, and sand.

Square-Nosed Shovel. The front edge of this shovel is perfect for cutting sod when you need to remove grass from your building site. You'll also find that this is the best shovel for scooping up dirt or gravel from a driveway.

Metal Rake. For spreading soil or gravel, and for sloping a site for drainage, a metal rake, or garden rake, is the best tool.

Trowels. For finishing and shaping concrete, a selection of trowels will be useful.

MEASURE AND LAYOUT

Measuring Tape. Purchase a high-quality measuring tape. A 25- or 30-foot tape is preferred, and a 1-inch-wide blade is far superior to one that is ¾ inch wide, since it is more rigid and will not quickly fold when you extend it.

Reel Measuring Tape. For large decks, where you are laying out long distances, it's helpful to have a 50-foot or 100-foot reel measuring tape. This tool doesn't automatically retract, like your 25-foot measuring tape—you wind in the plastic or metal tape the way you turn a fishing reel.

Carpenter's Pencils. Have plenty of pencils on hand—they have a tendency to disappear. Flat carpenter's pencils are better than regular pencils because they need sharpening less frequently.

Chalk-Line Box. The tool that aligned the ancient pyramids, a chalk line will enable you to mark long, perfectly straight lines in just a few seconds. Use blue chalk because the other colors are so permanent that they often can't be washed away.

Mason's String Line. You'll pull your string line very tight and it needs to last, so it's a good idea to get the professional stuff—nylon is a good choice.

Carpenter's Level. An accurate carpenter's level is crucial when building a deck. A 4-foot level is a good choice; a 2-foot level will probably do, but an 8-footer is often awkward to use. A level made of wood and brass is more durable than the cheaper aluminum levels but not necessarily more accurate. An aluminum model is an excellent choice for the occasional carpenter.

Take care of your level; all it takes is one good drop or a hard hit to make it inaccurate. Test the level regularly, especially before you buy it. To test, set the level on a smooth surface, and note where the bubble is. Then flip the tool end-for-end and put it in exactly the same spot. The bubble should read the same.

Torpedo Level. You will find a 9-inch torpedo level handy for leveling small objects. It fits easily into your toolbox or your pouch.

Line Level. A line level consists of a single bubble vial that clips onto a tightly stretched

SMART TIP

SAFETY EQUIPMENT

Common sense should tell you not to do carpentry without first having some basic safety equipment, such as eye and ear protection. Wear safety goggles or plastic glasses whenever you are working with power tools or chemicals. Both earplugs and earmuffs will protect your hearing. Whichever you choose, be sure that it has a noise reduction rating (NRR) of at least 20 decibels. Protect your lungs, especially if you are working with pressure-treated wood.

A simple dust mask is good for short-term use, but a respirator with a replaceable filter is best for toxic dust and fumes from finishing products. Work gloves are nice for avoiding hand injuries—catching a splinter off a board or developing a blister digging post holes is not a good way to start a workday. Steel-toe work boots will protect your feet and prevent injuries from dropped boards or tools. Flexible steel soles will protect you from puncture by a rogue nail.

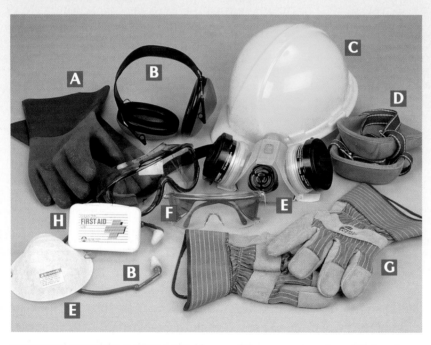

PROTECT YOURSELF WITH *(A) gloves, (B) ear protection, (C) hard hat, (D) knee pads, (E) respirator/dust mask, (F) safety glasses, (G) work gloves, (H) first-aid kit.*

Water Level. For some decks you will need to check for level over long spans. For this task, a water level is ideal. The water level is more accurate and more expensive than a line level. It is basically a water-filled hose with clear tubes attached to each end. Because water always seeks its own level, the water in the two tubes always settles out at the same height. This is especially useful when you need to level two spots around a corner from each other.

Post Level. If your design calls for any long posts, consider getting a post level. This very specialized but inexpensive tool straps onto the post, so you don't have to keep holding up a level while you are moving heavy material. A post level usually has two bubble vials set at 90 degrees from each other so you can check for plumb in both directions at once. Some post levels use a single, round bull's-eye vial to show perfect plumb instead.

Plumb Bob. To pinpoint the location of posts, you will need to drop a perfectly straight vertical line from a given spot. A plumb bob hangs from a string and tapers to a sharp point.

string line. When reading the bubble, make sure the string is stretched taut, and place the level near the center of the string line. Check the level by taking it off the string and reversing it. If the reading is the same both ways, then your line level is accurate.

Once the bob stops swinging, gravity ensures that the top of the string and the tip of the point are in perfect plumb alignment. The tapered shape of many chalk-line boxes allows them to double as suitable plumb bobs.

Framing Square. This L-shaped piece of flat

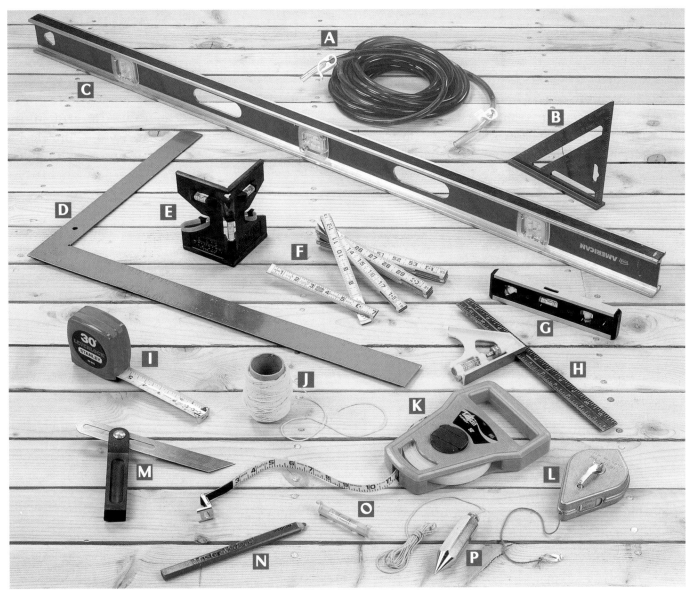

LAYOUT TOOLS *(A) water level, (B) angle square, (C) 4-ft. level, (D) framing square, (E) post level, (F) ruler, (G) torpedo level, (H) combination square, (I) measuring tape, (J) string, (K) reel tape, (L) chalk-line box, (M) T-bevel, (N) pencil, (O) line level, and (P) plumb bob.*

metal measures 16 inches along one edge and 24 inches along the other. Use it for laying out stair stringers and also for checking the squareness of your layouts and string lines.

Combination Square. This square has an adjustable blade that slides up and down. It shows both 90- and 45-degree angles, and the adjustable blade is handy for transferring depth measurements and as a pencil guide for running a line along the length of a board.

Angle Square. Often called by the brand name Speed Square, this triangular piece of aluminum is extremely versatile, yet it is tough enough to

get banged around on the job and not lose its accuracy. Its triangular shape enables you to lay out a 45-degree angle as quickly as a 90-degree angle; it also enables you to find other angles quickly, though not with great precision. Held firmly in place, your angle square makes a good cutting guide for a circular saw. You will probably find it the most useful of all the squares you may own.

T-Bevel. If you need to duplicate angles other than 45 or 90 degrees, use a T-bevel (or sliding bevel square). This has a flat metal blade that can be locked into place at any angle.

Folding Rule. If you get a folding rule, find one that has a sliding extension on one of the end sections. This is a great tool for getting interior measurements—such as the length of a handrail between two existing posts. Many carpenters prefer a folding rule for short measurements.

CUTTING AND SANDING

Circular Saw. Most carpenters and do-it-yourselfers prefer circular saws that use 7¼-inch diameter blades. This size will allow you to cut to a maximum depth of about 2⅜ inches at 90 degrees and to cut through a piece of two-by

lumber even with the blade beveled at 45 degrees.

You can get a rough idea of a saw's power and overall quality from the amperage the motor draws and the type of bearings it uses. A low-cost saw will pull only 9 or 10 amps and will run its drive shaft on sleeve bearings. This will mean less power, a shorter life, a tendency to heat up during continual use, and sometimes less precise cuts because the blade might wobble a bit.

Better saws carry a 12- or 13-amp rating and use ball bearings or roller bearings on the motor's shaft. This combination of extra power and smoother operation makes for long life and more precise cutting. As is often the case, a mid-priced model may well be your best choice.

Worm-drive saws have the most powerful motors and the longest-lasting bearings. They're built like tanks and weigh almost as much. These are primarily professional contractor's tools, and they take some getting used to. They last quite a long time, but do-it-yourselfers should probably avoid them.

A plastic housing is no longer the sign of an inferior tool, because many new plastic composites are actually tougher than metal and highly impact resistant.

Check out the saw's base carefully: if it is made of thin, stamped metal, one drop from sawhorse height could bend it out of shape for good. Look for a thicker base that is either extruded or cast aluminum.

Use carbide-tipped blades in your circular saw. These cost a few dollars more but last up to five times longer than comparable blades made from high-speed steel (HSS). A 24-tooth blade is usually the best choice for deck construction and general use. There is a trade-off between the number of teeth and cut rates and quality: a blade with fewer teeth will cut faster, but the cuts will tend to be ragged. More teeth will pro-duce a finer cut, but your saw will have to work harder to move more teeth through the wood, and it will cut more slowly. Have an extra blade on hand; wet wood and dense treated lumber can dull your saw's blade quickly.

Though you can use a file to touch up a damaged tooth on an HSS blade, send it to a sharpening shop when it needs a major tune-up. Take your carbide-tipped blades to a professional sharpening shop as well.

Power Miter Saw. If you need to make a lot of angle cuts or if you don't feel able to make consistent, precise cuts at all angles, it may be a good idea to buy or rent a power miter saw. These tools (also called chop saws) are simply circular saws mounted on a pivot assembly that allows you to make precise, repeatable cuts. Make sure you get a chop saw that will do the job: a saw with a 10-inch blade will not be able to completely cut a 2x6 at a 45-degree angle.

Another version of the miter saw, called the compound miter saw, makes both miter and bevel cuts in one pass. You probably won't need this ability on a deck, but if you are buying a miter saw and plan to install interior molding, it may make more sense to get a compound miter saw.

You can put together a jig that will help guide 45-degree cuts with a handheld circular saw. But it won't work as well as an adjustable chop saw, and will pay off only if you're using an angled decking pattern where the end of each board needs the same angled cut.

Saber Saw. This is a good choice if you need to make cutouts or if you want to make some curved cuts. If you need to do a lot of this kind of cutting, get a heavy-duty saber saw. With a standard do-it-yourself model, you'll cut through two-by lumber very slowly, and the saw will have a tendency to wobble, which produces a ragged-looking cut.

Reciprocating Saw. For demolition and for cutting off posts, a reciprocating saw works well, but don't buy one just for building a deck—a handsaw will work fine for the few cuts of this kind on your deck.

Router. Though by no means essential for deck-building, a router equipped with a cham-

CUTTING AND SANDING TOOLS (A) power miter saw, (B) circular saw, (C) router, (D) belt sander, (E) reciprocating saw, (F) saber saw, (G) pad sander, (H) block plane, (I) sanding block, (J) handsaw, (K) hacksaw, (L) chisel, (M) aviation snips.

fering or roundover bit can be quite handy for adding detail to your deck.

Handsaw. Though not used much anymore, the handsaw can come in handy for finishing cuts that a circular cannot finish—such as when you are cutting out stringers or cutting off posts in awkward places.

Block Plane. You may occasionally need a plane for trimming or smoothing wood and straightening irregular edges or bevels. Properly set, a block plane will trim one thin shaving at a time, allowing you to achieve tight-fitting joints.

Chisel. This is useful for cleaning out dado cuts, finishing notch cuts, and other trimming and wood-shaving tasks.

A 1-inch-wide chisel works well for this kind of work.

Aviation Snips. For trimming metal flashing at the ledger, metal snips are the most accurate tool.

Belt Sander. Use a belt sander to clean up your decking and to round off the edge of the deck and railings as a finishing touch. Use this tool with care; it's easy to oversand, especially if you are working with soft wood such as cedar or redwood. With practice, you can round off the whole deck quickly.

Sanding Block. A more common tool for rounding off sharp edges and smoothing splinters is the sanding block. There are several types, and they are all far superior to simply using a sheet of handheld sandpaper. In most cases, a power vibrating sander will not do any better than a sanding block. Use a belt sander only if you are doing heavy-duty rounding off.

Pad Sander. A vibrating or oscillating pad sander is great for smoothing decking and railings, but a sanding block will often suffice for a deck project.

FASTENING TOOLS

Cordless Drill. If it's in the budget, a cordless drill is very useful. You can safely steer clear of the high-end systems with batteries rated at 18- or 24-volts or more. Some of these drills weigh more than 6 pounds and are very tiring to use

all day long. Several models in the 12- to 14.4-volt range are easy to use and will do everything you need them to. A good cordless drill will come with a charger and an extra battery so that you'll always have a fresh battery available.

Read the owner's manual carefully, especially the part about charging batteries. Don't wait until a battery is completely dead before you charge it—pop it in the charger as soon as it starts to show signs of weakening.

Hammer. Your hammer is always at your side and constantly in use, so get a comfortable one. A 16-ounce hammer is a comfortable weight that will do the job, but the extra weight of a 20-ounce hammer will drive large nails more quickly. A straight-claw hammer is better for demolition work, while a curved-claw is better for pulling nails.

Nail Set. For places where the nails will show, you want to avoid the smiles and frowns caused by the hammer hitting the wood when you strike the nail with that last blow. Use a nail set, a small shaft of metal with one square end and one end tapered to a blunt point. With this, you can either drive nails perfectly flush with the wood or countersink them into the wood.

Pipe Clamps. Pipe clamps are sometimes helpful for holding pieces of lumber in place temporarily—so you can check the level one last time before fastening, for example.

Bar Clamps. Bar clamps do some of the same jobs that pipe clamps do, but are usually a little easier to set up. You can adjust some models with just one hand so you have the other hand free to hold things in place.

C-Clamps. A pair of large C-clamps is useful when you need to reach past obstructions to apply pressure to the center of a board. Squeezing a pair of 2x12s on the outside of a 4x4 post prior to fastening is a good example.

Ratchet Wrenches. If you will be installing lag screws or carriage bolts, a ratchet wrench with

FASTENING TOOLS *(A) nail gun and compressor, (B) drill, (C) pipe, bar, and C-clamps, (D) pry bar, (E) hammer, (F) caulking gun, (G) cat's paw, (H) nail set, (I) zip tool, (J) ratchet.*

SOME USEFUL ACCESSORIES (A) nail aprons, (B) hammer holster and belt, (C) extension cords with GFCI protection, (D) stepladder, (E) leather tool belt, (F) and sawhorses, either plastic, steel, or made with 2x4s and metal brackets.

the right socket is much faster than a crescent wrench.

Caulking Gun. Though it is used sparingly on a deck, there are places that benefit from a good bead of caulking.

Compressor. If you plan to frame or fasten your deck with a nail gun, you'll need a compressor to supply the air. Choose carefully—if the compressor is too small, you'll waste lots of time waiting for it to supply enough pressure for the next shot.

Nail Gun. A typical framing nailer shoots nails from 2 to 3½ inches long. Choose one with a restrictive or two-step trigger—this makes it much harder to fire a nail accidentally. Though safe when used properly, a nail gun can cause serious injury in a fraction of a second, so read and follow all safety precautions, especially the part about wearing safety glasses.

Flat Bar and Wrecking Bar. The flat bar is more versatile, but the wrecking bar (sometimes called a crowbar) gives you more leverage. These are handy for demolition such as removing siding before installing a ledger board, for prying deck boards into position, and for moving or breaking rocks you run into when digging holes.

Cat's Paw. This tool is for pulling framing nails back out of wood. By striking the back of its claw with a hammer, you can drive it under a nailhead, even if the head is below the surface. Then you push or strike the top of the tool to pull the nail out. A cat's paw always gets its nail but often seriously mars the face of the board in the process.

ACCESSORIES

Tool Belt. A tool belt or apron is a definite must; without it, you will spend untold hours looking for that tool you used just a few minutes ago. You can get an elaborate leather belt or a less-expensive canvas one. The belt should comfortably hold those objects you use most during a working day: your square, measuring tape, hammer, chalk-line box, nail set, chisel, pencils, and utility knife; and it should have a pocket for a good-size handful of nails. Be sure you can holster and unholster your hammer, pencil, and measuring tape with ease.

Utility Knife. No carpenter's apron should be without a utility knife. You'll use this inexpensive tool for all sorts of things: sharpening pencils, slicing away splinters from boards, shaving pieces of lumber, and opening bundles and packages. Get a better-quality, heavy-duty knife. Blades of cheap knives can slip out when you bear down hard. Replace a blade as soon as it gets dull. Be sure to get a retractable knife.

Extension Cord. Always check the wire-gauge number on an extension cord—the phrase heavy-duty on the package doesn't guarantee that it will supply enough current to your tools. The owner's manuals that come with your tools have specific guidelines on acceptable gauges and cord lengths.

Sawhorses. Usually used to set up a temporary cutting station, sawhorses should be strong and stable.

Hammer Holster. When you know you're going to do nothing but drive nails for a while, you might want to drop the full tool belt and put on a simpler tool holder with just one pocket and a hammer loop.

Small Sledgehammer. For driving stakes, a standard 16- or 20-ounce hammer will usually do the job, but a small sledgehammer is faster.

Putty Knife. This is for filling holes in damaged wood or holes left by countersunk screws.

Tool Bag. A tool bag is a great way to transport and organize all those tools that don't earn a permanent place in your tool belt.

SMART TIP

RENTING TOOLS
When you need a specialized tool for just a few hours, check with your local rental yard. Chances are they've got what you need and will rent it to you for a day or two. Some yards even rent by the half day, so if you're fast, you can save a little money. Think carefully before renting any tool for longer than a week: after a point, it makes more sense to go out and buy the tool yourself.

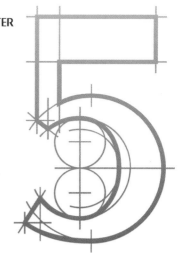

MATERIALS
FOR
DECKS

Many types of construction-grade lumber will do for a deck. One basic option is treated lumber, which many people use for the posts, girders, and joists that are somewhat hidden by the deck surface on most designs. But you can use redwood, cedar, one of many other wood species, or one of the newer composite decking materials.

ABOVE Decking products must be able to withstand the extremes of weather.

LUMBER

Because your deck is out in the weather all the time, you want to use wood that will resist decay and insects.

There are several choices, but the most popular are treated lumber, redwood, and cedar. Other options include cypress, recycled plastic decking, untreated lumber, and tropical ironwood.

To get the wood that's right for your project, it's not enough to choose a certain species. Other factors that influence a wood's performance include moisture content, method of drying the wood, what part of the tree the lumber comes from, and the quality, or grade, of each individual piece.

You also want to choose wood that won't warp or check after it's installed. All wood swells when it gets wet and shrinks while drying, so you should expect a certain amount of twisting, cupping, and splitting, but choosing the right type of lumber for the different locations on your deck should keep this problem under control.

LUMBER BASICS

Most of the lumber you buy is surfaced—smoothed, with rounded edges—on all four sides. This is called S4S, meaning surfaced on four sides. If you want a rough-sawn look (for the fascia or for posts, perhaps), you should be able to find cedar or redwood that is either rough all over or is smooth on only one side. This lumber may be a bit thicker and wider than S4S.

Lumber Sizes. The nominal size of a piece of lumber—for example, 2x4—refers to its size prior to drying and surfacing. So the 2x4 you buy will actually be 1½ inches by 3½ inches; a 2x6 is actually 1½ by 5½; a 1x8 is ¾ x 7¼, and so on. In most cases, lumberyards carry pieces in 24-inch increments beginning at 8 feet: so you can buy 8-footers, 10-footers, and so on.

Many people use either cedar or pressure-treated ⁵⁄₄x6 ("five quarter by six") boards, for the decking and sometimes for the top cap on the railing. This material is actually 1 inch thick and 5½ inches wide. Rounded edges minimize splintering. Often only one face will be usable, so choose your boards carefully. To satisfy most codes and to build a strong deck, you will have to space joists no more than 16 inches on center to use this material.

In addition to the ⁵⁄₄ decking with rounded edges, there's another type that has two parallel grooves cut down the length of one side and extra sanding on the other side to produce a slight crown across the width of the board. The grooves on the bottom provide some stability to the lumber, and the crown encourages water to run off the boards easily. With this material you can build a deck that is perfectly level without worrying about puddles forming. However, because it's not a big problem to build a deck with a tiny slope for drainage, these boards may not be worth the extra expense unless you happen to like the appearance.

Most people choose deck boards that are 5½ inches wide, such as 2x6 or ⁵⁄₄x6, either because they like the wider appearance or because it is less work to install. But the price for wider boards is rising fast because more lumber now comes from smaller trees, so 2x4 decking is becoming a more economical choice. However, lumber prices tend to fluctuate, so it makes sense to price out both types.

Lumber Density. As a general rule, lumber of greater density will be stronger but also more prone to splitting and warping. Likewise, lower-density wood is weaker and may splinter and twist less. This is because lower-density wood can act like a sponge, absorbing moisture when the weather is wet and drying when the sun comes out. Dense wood does not have the ability to transfer moisture quickly, and the internal stresses cause warping and splinters. Treating lumber does not affect density but only adds temporary weight in the form of moisture.

So higher-density wood—Douglas fir or southern yellow pine, for instance—works well for the substructure, where strength is important and splinters and warping do not matter as much. And because you want to avoid splinters on the decking and rails, lower-density wood may be a better choice.

LUMBER GRAIN

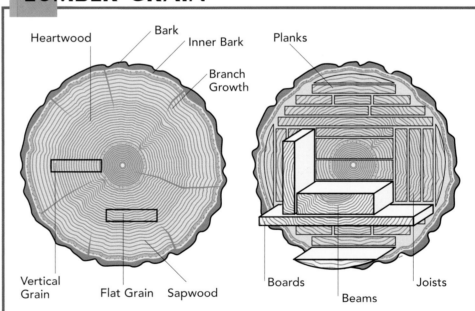

Heartwood · Bark · Inner Bark · Planks · Branch Growth · Vertical Grain · Flat Grain · Sapwood · Boards · Beams · Joists

All trees have two types of wood inside: sapwood and heartwood. Sapwood is located toward the perimeter of the tree and carries sap to the branches. Heartwood comes from the center of the tree and is denser than sapwood because it is older. It is also more stable than sapwood. All parts of the tree can be used, and lumber taken from either the sapwood or heartwood region is graded accordingly. Because a lot of lumber today is cut from younger faster-growing trees, you may find fewer distinctions between the heartwood and sapwood areas.

DIY OPTIONS: LUMBER GRADES

Number 1 grade of most common lumber has few, if any, knots.

Number 2 grade has more knots and defects than Number 1. It's the type specified as a minimum requirement in most building codes.

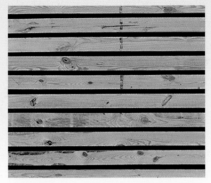

Number 3 of most common lumber has many knots and defects. It may not be approved by your local building code.

Heartwood and Sapwood. The wood near the center of the tree, which is inactive because it has not been growing for some time, is called heartwood. Lumber milled from this portion of the tree is more resistant to rot and insects and less porous than sapwood, which is taken from the area of the tree near the bark. This is a significant difference: decking made of redwood or cedar heartwood will last far longer than will sapwood decking of the same species.

Vertical and Flat Grain. Different sawing techniques at the mill yield different grain patterns on the boards. Lumber generally either has vertical grain, with narrow grain lines running along the face of the board, or flat grain (also called plainsawn), with wider lines that often form rippling V-shapes. Most boards are a combination of

the two, and in any given load of lumber, you will find boards that are both primarily flat grained and primarily vertically grained.

Vertical grain is less likely to shrink and warp, and most people think it looks better. But you don't have to go to the extra expense of specifying vertical grain when you order; when you

DIY OPTIONS: TYPES OF DECKING

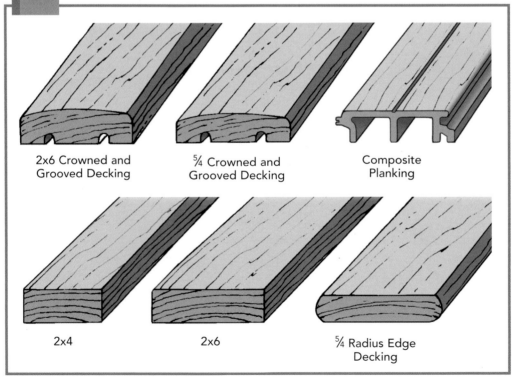

2x6 Crowned and Grooved Decking

⁵⁄₄ Crowned and Grooved Decking

Composite Planking

2x4

2x6

⁵⁄₄ Radius Edge Decking

choose boards at the lumberyard, just pick as many of the ones with narrow lines as possible.

Moisture. Freshly cut trees delivered to a sawmill have a lot of moisture in them. And after sawing and surfacing, pressure-treated lumber gets saturated with liquid chemicals, making it even wetter. It dries out some before it gets to the lumberyard, but some lumber you buy may have a moisture content of 30 or 40 percent.

Wood that is wet—whether from natural moisture or from chemicals—will shrink as it dries out. Wood shrinks most across its width. The lengthwise shrinkage is minimal unless the board is especially long. Butt joints in a long run of decking may open up over time if the boards are installed wet. If your lumber has a moisture content (MC) of less than 20 percent, shrinkage and warping should be minimal.

The grade stamp on lumber indicates the moisture content, but don't trust this number completely; wood can pick up moisture from rain or humidity while sitting in the lumberyard. Your local yard may be willing to check some boards with a moisture meter. If not, try driving a nail into a board and see if any water squeezes out around the shank. If it does, it's too wet.

Lumber Grades. Lumber is sorted and graded on the basis of number, spacing, and size of knots, milling defects, and drying technique.

The highest-quality—and most expensive—lumber is called select structural. This lumber has the fewest knots and other imperfections.

Most often, you will be dealing with common lumber, which is graded No. 1, No. 2, or No. 3. No. 1 is the strongest, and usually the best-looking wood as well. No. 2 is the grade most commonly used in deck framing. No. 3 lumber is less structurally sound.

Another grading system uses the words Const (for construction), Stand (standard), or Util (utility). These three classifications are generally used to grade 2x4 and 4x4 lumber and No.1, 2, and 3 grade 2x6 and wider stock.

No. 2 is the most common grade and will be fine for most applications. Chances are, your building codes will require "No. 2 or better."

For the railings and other areas that are highly visible, you may want to spend the extra money to get No.1 or even select structural lumber—if you can find it. Good lumber is getting much harder to find these days. Lots of lumber is now cut from corporate forests, where fast-growing trees mature quickly but have widely spaced growth rings and yield less lumber.

ABOVE **Lumber is graded on the size and number of knots. Clear wood provides the most finished appearance.**

LUMBER SPECIES

REDWOOD

The redwood trees of northern California are legendary for their size and the quality of lumber. Redwood's beautiful straight grain, natural glowing color, and weather resistance have traditionally marked it as the Cadillac of outdoor building materials. It is a pleasure to work with, easy to cut and sweet-smelling. Unfortunately, overlumbering has made redwood expensive and hard to get.

Because of its high price, you might want to use redwood only for the highly visible portions of your deck, such as the decking and railings. Redwood works for structural support as well, though you may have to use slightly larger joists and beams than if you were using regular pressure-treated lumber.

You can usually tell sapwood from heartwood by color: the sapwood is much lighter and hardly looks like it comes from the same tree. Redwood heartwood has the deep, rich color and is extremely weather- and insect-resistant. Sapwood may start to rot in two or three years if it has contact with the ground or if it will remain wet for long periods of time. Treat sapwood before installing it, and use it only where there will be good drainage most of the year.

If you let redwood "go gray" by not treating it with anything, it will reach a light gray color after a few years and develop a slight sheen that many people find attractive. Or you can treat it with stains and a UV blocker to keep it close to its original color.

In some parts of the country, you can find redwood that has been both treated and stained, which makes the sapwood more decay resistant and similar in color to the heartwood. This is an expensive item, but if it comes with a lifetime warranty, it's worth checking out. Inspect several pieces to make sure you like the color. The reddish-brown will fade after a few years, and the deck will turn a uniform gray unless you restain it.

The Redwood Inspection Service of the California Redwood Association establishes redwood grades. The service has two grading categories: Architectural and Garden. Architectural grades are the best-looking, most expensive grades of redwood. Garden grades are more economical and have more knots. Both categories of redwood are available kiln-dried or unseasoned and are usually surfaced on four sides.

Architectural grades include:

Clear All-Heart. All heartwood and free from knots, this wood is recommended for highly visible applications.

Clear. Similar in quality to Clear All-Heart, except that Clear contains sapwood. Clear is ideal for highly visible applications where the wood won't be subject to decay.

B-Heart. Containing limited knots, but no sapwood, B-Heart is a less costly alternative to Clear All-Heart.

B-Grade. Similar characteristics to B-Heart but contains sapwood; same uses as Clear.

Garden grades of redwood are suitable for most deck-building applications. They include:

Construction Heart/Deck Heart. These are all-heartwood grades containing knots. Both are recommended for work on or near the ground such as posts, girders, joists, and decking. Deck Heart is similar in appearance to Construction Heart but also carries a grade stamp for strength. Deck Heart is available in 2x4 and 2x6 only.

LEFT Many people use more than one type of wood on their deck. Visible areas receive the highest quality lumber.

Construction Common/Deck Common. Containing knots and a combination of heartwood and sapwood, these grades are best for aboveground applications such as railings, benches, and decking. Deck Common is similar in appearance to Construction Common and has the same uses but is also graded for strength. Deck Common is available in 2x4 and 2x6 only.

Merchantable Heart. This is the most economical all-heartwood grade. The rules allow larger knots and some knotholes. It's used for garden walls or utility structures on or near the ground.

Merchantable. Having the same characteristics as Merchantable Heart but containing sapwood, this grade is suitable only for fence boards, trellises, and aboveground garden and utility applications.

CEDAR

Cedar has many of the benefits of redwood and usually costs less. Like redwood, it is stable, easy to work with, and rarely splinters or checks. And like redwood, it is the heartwood of the cedar tree that is resistant to decay. Sapwood will decay relatively quickly. You can recognize cedar heartwood by its dark color and the hamster-cage smell you get when you cut it.

Cedar is fragrant and beautiful, though it tends to have a more informal feel than redwood, with its light brown color. Left untreated, cedar will turn gray.

Cedar is not quite as strong as redwood and isn't often used for structural posts, beams, or joists. You may want to use it in places where the structure will be visible—for example, for fascia. In other places, such as the outside and header joists, it is common to use pressure-treated lumber for the structure and then cover it with cedar fascia boards for looks.

However, unlike redwood and pressure-treated lumber, cedar is available in most any size, even up to 12x12 monster posts. So you might use it for unusually sized post-and-beam constructions.

Cedar is widely available and comes in a number of varieties. The most commonly used variety is Western red cedar. You can purchase Clear All-Heart, but this is quite expensive. Chances are, you will want to use No. 1 varieties: Select Tight Knot, taken from new growth and containing some sapwood, works well for decking that will not remain wet for long periods. Architect Clear and Custom Clear comes from old growth and should be used in places susceptible to rot. Stepping down from these grades you will find Architect Knotty, Custom Knotty, and No. 2. These will contain more knots, but probably have the same amount of rot-resistance. And you may like the look of the knots.

One of the most common decking materials used is ¾ cedar decking. This has rounded edges so you will end up with virtually no splinters. But inspect this lumber for the qualities discussed earlier. Just because some company has labeled it "decking" does not mean it will suit your needs.

Use cedar with one smooth face and one rough

SMART TIP

STACKING WOOD

When wood is delivered from the lumberyard, some of it may be a little wet, which means it can shrink and twist on your deck. You should return any waterlogged lumber that is significantly heavier than other pieces. The rest you can store off the ground on 4x4s with strips of wood laid between layers to increase air circulation and drying.

face (called S1SE, meaning surfaced on one side and two edges) for fascia. With the rough side turned outward, it has a pleasing rustic appearance. However, water trapped between a fascia board and the lumber it is covering up can promote decay, so treat these pieces well.

Sometimes cedar will develop black, slimy spots. While this could be mold, chances are that it's just natural resin leaching out of the wood. It can be washed away with soap and water.

CYPRESS

Bald cypress is the South's answer to redwood. Native to the swamps and lowland areas throughout the Southeast, bald cypress is similar to redwood in hardiness and strength, although it is not as stable. In the southern United States, local sawmills can be a very economical source for decking lumber. It's hard to get cypress outside of its native region, but your lumberyard might be willing to order it for you.

TREATED WOOD PRODUCTS

Pressure-treated (PT) lumber has been used to build wood decks for years. In the past, most lumber was treated with chromated copper arsenate (CCA), which gives the wood a greenish tint that fades over time. The treatment process provided a durable product that went into the construction of millions of decks. However, CCA contains arsenic, a known carcinogen, and safe use of the product required some special handling procedures.

The wood treatment industry has elected to

LUMBER GRADING STAMPS

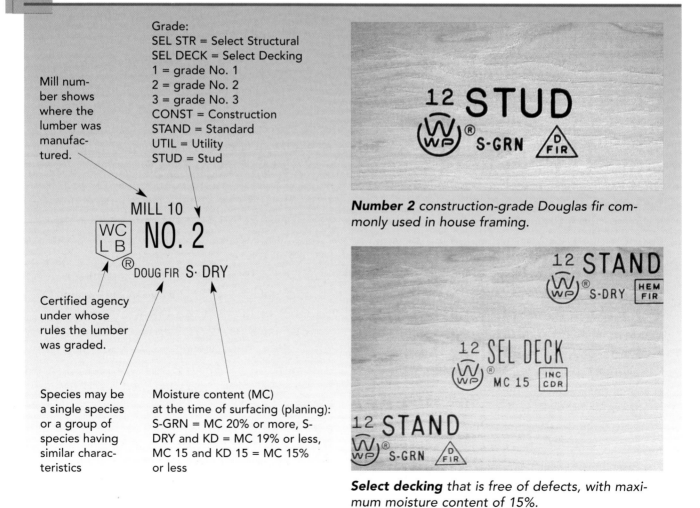

Grade:
SEL STR = Select Structural
SEL DECK = Select Decking
1 = grade No. 1
2 = grade No. 2
3 = grade No. 3
CONST = Construction
STAND = Standard
UTIL = Utility
STUD = Stud

Mill number shows where the lumber was manufactured.

MILL 10

Certified agency under whose rules the lumber was graded.

Species may be a single species or a group of species having similar characteristics

Moisture content (MC) at the time of surfacing (planing): S-GRN = MC 20% or more, S-DRY and KD = MC 19% or less, MC 15 and KD 15 = MC 15% or less

Number 2 construction-grade Douglas fir commonly used in house framing.

Select decking that is free of defects, with maximum moisture content of 15%.

stop producing CCA treated lumber for use in residential applications. Other types of preservatives are now used, including copper azole and alkaline copper quaternary. These and other types of preservatives can affect the look and structural character-istics of the lumber. Be sure to follow the manufacturer's di-rections for installation, safe handling, and proper uses.

There is nothing wrong with the millions of decks con-structed with CCA treated wood. Properly maintained, they will last for years and do not present a risk to those who use them if they follow stan-dard safety practices, including wearing a dust mask, gloves, and eye protection when cut-ting CCA treated lumber, and washing your hands after han-dling the wood. Do not sand or burn the wood.

Lumber Defects

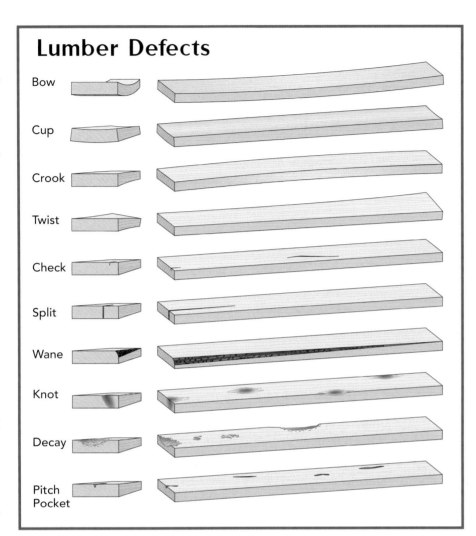

Bow
Cup
Crook
Twist
Check
Split
Wane
Knot
Decay
Pitch Pocket

IRONWOOD

If you have a big budget and a taste for the exotic, you may want to look into South Ameri-can hardwoods (sometimes called ironwoods), such as ipé and pau lopé. This lumber is extremely strong and durable. In fact, some ironwoods have roughly twice the strength and load rating as similarly sized pressure-treated Doug fir. And the resistance to rot and insects is often five times better than treated lumber found in this country.

As you may expect, these woods are quite expensive; using ironwood for only the decking and railings could well triple the materials cost for your entire deck. As they become more pop-ular, the price will probably come down. Iron-woods are also slow to install—cutting is arduous, and you may have to predrill for every screw or nail.

LUMBER DEFECTS

You probably can't afford to buy clear, select lum-ber for every part of your deck, so most pieces are going to have some small defects. Some defects are cosmetic and won't affect the strength of the board; others will cause trouble. Here is a list of lumber defects, with descriptions that will tell you whether or not you can live with them.

Bow is a bend in the wood along the wide face, from end to end. It has no effect on strength, and you can use the board on your deck as long as you can straighten it as you fas-ten it in place.

Cup is a bend across the width of a board. If it's not severe, you can try to flatten it out with nails or screws (for decking) or blocking (for joists). A cupped decking board will hold water if installed cupped-side up, and this will promote

SMART TIP

CROWNING

Most structural lumber you use for joists and girders has a natural bend, or crown. When you select these beams, sight down the edge  to find the bend, and mark an X on the up side. Setting joists and girders with the crowns up builds extra strength into the deck frame.

rot, so be sure to turn the cupped side down before you flatten it.

Crook is a bend in the wood that makes a hump on the narrow face when you sight from one end to the other. The high portion is called the crown, and joists are always installed crown side up. Most long boards have a small crook, but excessive crooking makes wood unsuitable for framing. When a deck board has a moderate crook, you can usually push or pull it into position before fastening.

Twist is a slight corkscrew-shaped distortion of the wood, and if it's severe enough to be noticeable at first glance, the lumber is unsuitable for decking or framing.

Check is a rift in the surface caused when the surface dries more rapidly than the interior. It produces patches that look like small tears in the surface. These are usually only cosmetic and do not affect the strength. Kiln-dried wood checks less than green wood.

Split is a crack that passes completely through the board at the ends. This is a serious structural weakness. Don't use split lumber on any part of your deck.

Wane is the lack of wood along one edge of a board, usually in a tapered pattern along the length of the board. This occurs on boards cut from the outer edge of the tree—where the bark once was. Wane has little effect on strength. Remove any bark that remains on the lumber because it will promote rot if it stays there.

Knots are the high-density bases of limbs. The knots themselves are strong, but they have no real connection to the surrounding wood. Avoid large knots in decking, which may come loose over time. Large knots (anything over 1 inch) in the bottom third of a joist could weaken it significantly.

Decay is the destruction of the wood structure by fungi or insects. Don't use decayed wood on any portion of your deck.

Pitch Pockets are accumulations of natural resins on the surface of a board. They have little

SMART TIP

SELECTING LUMBER

Many lumberyards store structural lumber outside. When it's delivered, you will probably find some high-quality pieces, while others have open knot holes and other defects. Most lumber today is sold in mixed-grade shipments, and unless you're paying for a select grade, you have to deal with it by selecting the best boards for the most visible area of the deck. On the deck surface, don't worry about grain direction, and simply turn the bad side face down.

effect on strength, but will cause discoloration if you paint or stain the board.

SYNTHETIC DECKING

This may be the fastest growing category as it includes composite materials, which are a combination of wood fibers and plastics, and vinyl products. Unlike natural wood, these products vary greatly from producer to producer. Some are designed to look like real wood, while others make no pretext about looking like wood and supply a different type of look. Some products are available nationally, but most of these products have only regional distribution. It is important to study manufacturer's literature for product uses and installation techniques.

On the plus side, many manufacturers say their products are easer to install and install faster than real wood. Many products feature a hidden fastener technology that provides a sleek, smooth appearance to the deck. All of these products are low maintenance.

CONCRETE

In building your deck, you'll most likely use concrete for footings to support the posts.

Concrete is composed of three elements: portland cement, aggregate, and water. The aggregate is a mixture of sand and gravel that acts to bind the cement paste together, adding strength.

It is important to get the mixture right. Too much water will weaken the concrete; too little will make it difficult to work. So the general rule when mixing your own is to add just enough water to make it workable for your needs. If you use premixed bags, read the label to find out how much water to add, and add it slowly. The mix should be liquid enough to fill all the spaces in a tube form or hole, but if it gets soupy, it's too wet.

The compressive strength of concrete—the amount of weight you can place on it before it crumbles—is determined by the amount of cement in the mix. Occasionally you will get an inspector who requires some sort of proof that you are using concrete that is strong enough.

FASTENERS

The nails, screws, bolts, and hardware you choose hold your deck together, transforming a pile of lumber into a useful, well-built outdoor structure. Some of these choices, such as what size lag screws hold your girder to your post, are dictated by building codes; others, such as whether to use screws or nails to hold down your decking, depend more on personal preference than local codes.

Whatever type of fastener you choose, remember this rule of thumb for determining the length you need: the fastener's penetration into the bottom piece should be equal to or greater than the thickness of the top piece. So unless you plan to countersink the fasteners into the top board, they should be at least twice as long as the thickness of the top board. For example, when installing 1½-inch boards, you should use 3- or 3½-inch fasteners.

SMART TIP

HIDDEN FASTENERS
Driving nails down through the surface is the standard way (and probably the easiest), to nail decking. But you have several alternatives that hold deck boards just as well without leaving any nail heads. They take longer to install but prevent nail pops and improve appearance. The most common is an L-shaped strip of galvanized hardware. One edge screws to the deck joists and the other screws up into the deck boards. Other systems use individual pieces of hardware everywhere a board crosses a joist.

SMART TIP

QUICK DRIVE
Screws have a lot more holding power than nails and can reduce cupping and twisting as your deck boards weather. The drawback is that screws take longer to drive than nails. Some pros use expensive power screwdrivers to speed up the process. You can use a screwdriving attachment (most models cost under $24), that fits onto a standard drill. The attachment locks into the drill chuck and

feeds plastic strips loaded with deck screws into position. You don't have to reload for each screw, only when the strip runs out.

NAILS
The most common, and usually quickest, way of fastening wood together is to use nails. If you choose the right nails and install them properly, the joint will stay tight for many decades.

The thicker a nail is, the more wood surface it touches, and the more wood the nail's shank displaces, the better it holds.

Nail sizes are described by the term penny, which is abbreviated to the letter "d" (which stands for denarius, an ancient Roman coin—we're talking some very old terminology here). The number originally referred to the cost of 100 nails of that size, but today it indicates the nail's length. For fastening two-by lumber together, use 16d nails, which are 3½ inches long. For ¾ decking, 3-inch-long, 10d nails work best.

Unless you are working in a place where the nails will not be exposed to weather (something that rarely happens when you're building a deck), it is usually best to use hot-dipped galvanized nails. These have a dull silvery coating that helps them resist corrosion. The coating also has a rough texture, which makes it difficult for the nail to work loose.

Stainless-steel and aluminum nails resist rust more effectively but have slightly less grabbing power than galvanized. Stainless steel is very expensive but may be worth the price in very wet situations. Aluminum nails are soft and bend easily.

A number of "deformed" nails are designed to have greater holding power. Drive-screw nails, also called screw-shank nails, have a slight thread on the shank and actually rotate as you drive them. They hold much like a screw.

Some specialized deck nails have blunted tips to minimize splitting and a knurled or ringed shank for extra holding power. A ring-shanked nail holds very well if it stays completely in place, but loses much of its holding power if it gets pried outward even the slightest bit.

Galvanized casing nails are basically big finishing nails. Originally designed for fastening window and door casings, casing nails do not have the holding power of nails with heads, though they grab a bit better than finishing nails because they are thicker.

Because they lack the holding power your deck needs, casing nails are not usually appropriate for structural connections or decking, even though they look nicer. You might, however, use them for attaching fascia or other finishing touches where less holding power is needed.

SCREWS

You have a number of good reasons for choosing screws over nails. Screws offer more holding power than nails and can pull a bowed board down flat more easily than nails.

Using screws also eliminates the "smiles" and "frowns" that hammering often produces in the wood. You can also remove them without marring the wood, so that you may not have to throw away a board after making a mistake. If using screws saves even one board, this could make up for the slight extra expense. And once you get the technique down, screwing down decking boards with a good screw gun can be just as fast as nailing.

DIY OPTIONS: FASTENERS

Regardless of the type of fastener, use only corrosion-resistant fasteners (hot-dipped galvanized, stainless steel, or aluminum).

Nails and screws. *Left to right: 10d common nail, coated rust-proof deck screw, galvanized screw, stainless-steel square drive screw, joist-hanger nail.*

Bolts. *Left to right: galvanized lag screw, stainless-steel lag screw, J-bolt, stainless-steel carriage bolt, galvanized carriage bolt, masonry shields.*

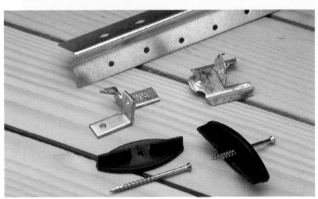

Hidden deck fasteners. *Clockwise from top: deck strip, deck board tie, slot ties, deck clip. With these and other products you don't need any surface nails.*

MATERIALS FOR DECKS

5

Deck Screws. These screws have aggressive threads and a bugle-shaped head. Two kinds of drive systems are available, Phillips and square-drive. Phillips-head screws are easier to load onto your driver bit, but the bit has a tendency to slip backward, or "cam out" of the recess in the screw head. It may take a half-second more to load a screw on a square-drive bit, but it will stay on and not cam out, even if you're screwing into hardwood.

The bits are cheap, so you may want to experiment to find which system works best for you.

Lag Screws. Also called lag bolts, these are thick screws with coarse threads and heads that will accept a socket wrench. Always use a washer or the head will sink into the lumber and will not hold as well. Use them for attaching the ledger board to the house and for other places where you need extra strength but can only reach one side of the connection.

BOLTS

Use bolts where connections must be extremely strong. The most common uses on a deck are tying together built-up beams and fastening a post to a beam.

Bolts pass through the pieces of wood they are joining and are secured with washers and nuts. Hexagonal-head bolts are easy to install because you can use a socket wrench on the bolt head. Make sure you use washers under both the head and the nut, or they will sink into the lumber. Carriage bolts have a rounded head and a square shoulder that requires no washer; use them in places where you want a finished look.

DECK HARDWARE

Besides screws, nails, and bolts, many other metal fasteners are used in the construction of a deck.

DECK FASTENERS

Specialized deck hardware allows you to securely install decking boards with no visible fasteners. You have several options here, including deck clips and continuous deck fasteners. All of these systems are more expensive than traditional fasteners, and they take more time to install, but it may well be worth the extra time and expense to have a clean, nail-free surface, especially if your decking boards are beautiful cedar or redwood.

Deck clips typically screw to the top of the joists and hold the decking boards with screws or spikes driven into the edges. They may lose holding power as the wood shrinks.

Continuous deck fasteners are long strips of metal that attach along each joist. Screws driven up through holes in the strip secure the decking boards from below. This system tends to hold better than deck clips. Continuous fasteners work well for keeping butt joints tight and generally avoid splitting problems as well.

FLASHING

Flashing installation is usually quick and easy—as long as you get the correct material. When possible, buy preformed pieces that are in the exact shape you need. You may have to buy a roll of flat sheet metal and form it yourself.

Aluminum flashing will last practically forever, but it has a tendency to expand and contract with changes in weather, causing nails to come loose and leading to leaks.

Make sure you use aluminum nails with aluminum flashing, or you'll have corrosion. Galvanized flashing might develop rust spots after some years, but it is thicker and stronger and does not react to temperature changes as readily as aluminum.

SMART TIP

TREATED WOOD FASTENERS

There is evidence that some of the newer wood treatment chemicals are more corrosive than the traditional treatments for pressure-treated wood. (See "Treated Wood Products," page 100.) Check product information sheets for specific fastener recommendations. Some manufacturers of fasteners are recommending stainless-steel nails or screws when using the newer types of treated lumber.

DIY OPTIONS: DECK FASTENERS

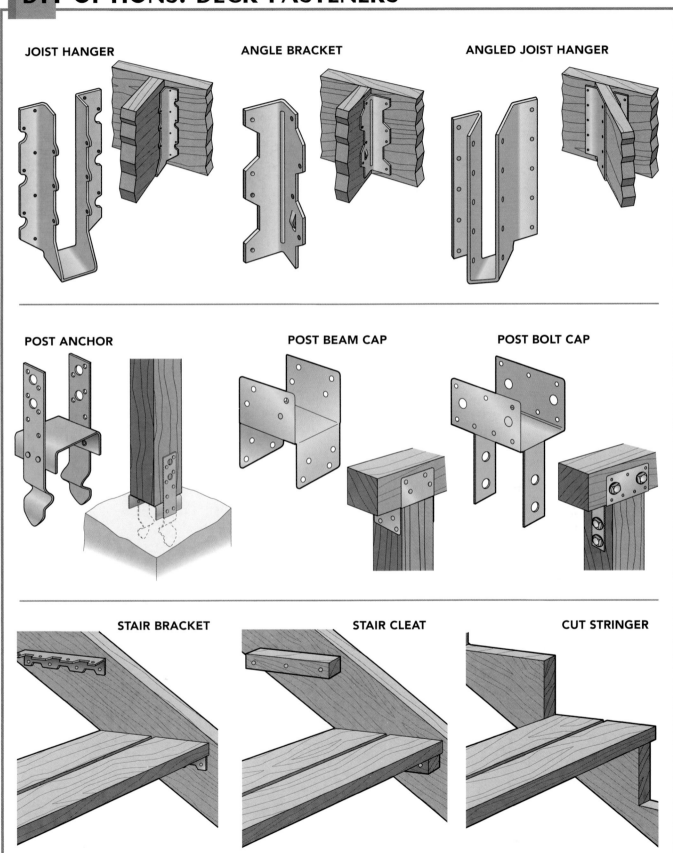

JOIST HANGER

ANGLE BRACKET

ANGLED JOIST HANGER

POST ANCHOR

POST BEAM CAP

POST BOLT CAP

STAIR BRACKET

STAIR CLEAT

CUT STRINGER

MATERIALS FOR DECKS

CONSTRUCTION

GALLERY OF DESIGN IDEAS

1 Decks need not stand alone. Here a screened-in porch provides relief from insects when this outdoor living area is in use.

1

2 Even the design of small decks in limited spaces benefits from the use of levels.

3 When it's summer in the city, this rooftop deck provides an oasis of relief from the heat.

4 Built-in seating and a multilevel design create discrete activity areas on this deck. Consider combining a deck with a patio area.

5 Don't forget about accessorizing your deck. Here a bench and candles make an interesting and dramatic nighttime display.

1

2

3

GALLERY OF DESIGN IDEAS

1 Large French doors or sliders will help ensure that your deck is considered another room of your house.

2 Ceiling fans add a cooling breeze to covered decks and porches.

3 Adding a shade structure not only provides relief from the summer sun but also creates a separate seating area, apart from other activities that take place on the deck.

4 A deck located off of a kitchen often becomes an informal eating area.

5 When planning your deck, imagine the activities that will take place there and provide the appropriate space for them.

BUILDING TECHNIQUES

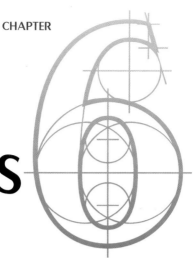

There is no one way to build decks—except the way the building inspector prefers. While inspection methods vary, all inspectors zero in on two areas: the piers, to make sure they reach below the frost line, and the ledger, to make sure the deck is securely attached to the house.

MEASURING AND MARKING

Good carpentry begins with accurate measuring and marking. Get in the habit of using the same techniques every time, and your work will be much more precise.

USING A MEASURING TAPE

You'll use your measuring tape for taking most of the measurements on your project. You will notice that the metal hook at the end of the tape is a bit loose. It is made that way on purpose: it moves back and forth ⅛ inch, which is also exactly how thick it is. This means that you will get the correct measurement both when you hook the end of your measuring tape over the end of a piece of wood, or when you butt it up against something to take an inside measurement.

Make sure you pull the tape straight before you measure. If it curves in any way, you'll get a bad reading. If a helper is calling out measurements for you to cut, make sure that their measuring tape agrees with yours—sometimes the hook gets bent, which can throw your cut off by ⅛ inch or so.

MEASURING IN PLACE

When possible, the easiest and most accurate way to measure is not to measure at all, but rather to hold the lumber in place and mark it for cutting. This usually involves butting one end of the board exactly to the spot where it will rest and marking a cut line on the other end.

If you must cut a number of boards to the same length, cut one and use it as a template for making cuts on the others.

Sometimes it's best not to precut the boards at all, but instead let each piece run wild. It's common to let the decking boards run wild initially, then snap a chalk line and cut them all off in place.

MARKING FOR CUTS

When you make that little pencil mark on the wood indicating the exact length to cut, be sure you know which part of the mark indicates the cut line. Most carpenters make a V, with the bottom point indicating the precise spot. Using your square, draw a line through the V, and make a large X on the side of the board that will be waste. (See "Smart Tip," opposite.)

To mark long lines, snap a chalk line. Have a helper hold one end, or tack a nail and hook the clip onto it. Pull the line very taut, be sure it's in position on both ends, pick the line straight up several inches, and then let go. For long lines or a wavy surface, you may need to first snap your end and then have your helper snap theirs.

For very long lines, tack the far end and have your helper put a finger on the center point, then snap both sides.

DIY OPTIONS: ACCURATE LEVELING

Here are some popular leveling tools.

1. A water level is a basic tool that's great for leveling over long distances. (See page 122.)

2. A carpenter's level normally has bubbles. This one displays a digital readout.

3. Laser levels used to be only for contractors, but some new models are in the $250 range. The red beam projects a level line against any surface on your site.

SMART TIP

STEP-AHEAD LAYOUT

To inexperienced DIYers, the carpentry technique of marking a step-ahead layout may seem a little simpleminded—after all, you just measure for a modular framing layout (usually 16 inches on center), draw a guideline with a pencil and a square, and then take the extra step of marking a large X beside the line, working in the direction of your layout. However, this way there will be no confusion when it comes time to place joists. If you always cover the X and align the joist to the line, you'll never stray from the on-center layout.

ABOVE There are usually a variety of ways to complete a building task, just be sure the way you pick will meet the local building code.

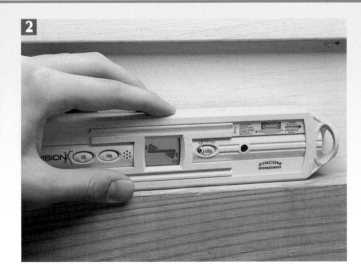

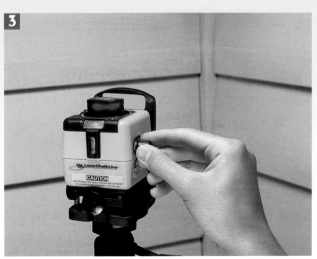

CUTTING WITH A CIRCULAR SAW

You'll use your circular saw so much in the course of building a deck that you'll soon become comfortable with the tool. But don't let that make you overconfident. When it comes to power tools, complacency can be very dangerous. A circular saw can injure you in a fraction of a second if you are careless.

So take basic safety precautions: know where your power cord is at all times; be sure your blade guard works properly. Avoid kickbacks by correctly positioning the board you are cutting. Don't stand directly behind the saw when cutting—position your body to one side. And keep your blade sharp so that it's less likely to bind.

TEST FOR SQUARENESS

You can't always trust the degree markings on your saw's bevel gauge, so take the time to verify them before you make many cuts.

Set your saw for zero-degree bevel, and crosscut a scrap piece of 2x4. Roll one of the cut pieces over, and butt them together on a flat surface. If your blade is not square to the base, you'll see a gap at the bottom or the top of the cut equal to twice the amount your blade is out of square. (See "Test for Squareness," page 121.)

If you see a gap, unplug the saw; turn it upside down; and loosen the bevel adjustment. Set a square on the base, and hold it against the blade. (See "Smart Tip," opposite.) Hold the square against the body of the blade, not the teeth; the teeth are offset and will throw off your

SAFE CUTTING TECHNIQUES

1. Adjust your depth-of-cut so that the blade extends about ¼ in. below the wood. This uses more cutting edges and increases efficiency.

2. Position the stock so that the waste end falls away from the saw. If you are cutting on a stack of lumber, hold the waste to stop it from falling before you finish.

3. Maintain maximum control of the saw by setting up a cutting station with the stock resting on a spacer. You can cut with two hands, and the waste will fall away.

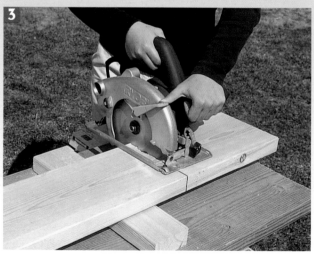

adjustment. Tighten the bevel adjustment when the blade and base bear evenly on the square.

MAKING ACCURATE SQUARE CUTS

Work on a stable surface that won't move during the cut. To avoid kickback, make sure that the cutoff can fall away without binding.

Position the Workpiece. If the cutoff will be long, don't just let it fall to the ground. If you do, the weight of the unsupported cutoff might cause the board to break off before you finish the cut, leaving a jagged piece sticking out at the end of the board. If the cutoff isn't too long, you can support it with your other hand. Or provide something for the cutoff to fall onto that is only an inch or two below it.

Align the Blade to the Line. A spinning saw blade carves a groove through the wood—that groove is called a kerf. One edge of the kerf lines up on your cut line, the rest of the blade's width should be on the waste side of the line. Standard saw blades cut a ⅛-inch-wide kerf, though you might find thin-kerf blades at the store, too. These blades cut kerfs around ¹⁄₁₆ inch wide. Because they are removing less wood, they require less force to make the cut.

Whatever size kerf you cut, be sure you cut to the waste side of the line so that your board will not end up shorter than you marked it.

Remember that the teeth on a circular saw blade are offset. One tooth veers to the left, the next to the right, and so on in an alternating pattern. Take this into account when you line up the blade to the cut line: first, select a tooth that's offset toward the cut line, and align the saw so that the tooth just touches the line. Then look at the front edge of your saw's base to find the alignment notch. Pivot the saw body until the zero-degree mark in the notch lines up with your cut line.

Make the Cut. Squeeze the trigger and saw with a light, steady pressure, allowing the blade to set the feed rate. You might want to use a cutting guide when making your first few crosscuts until you have a feel for the saw, but if you want to make a lot of cuts quickly, you should also learn to cut freehand.

This actually takes only a bit of practice. Get in

SMART TIP

SAW SETUP

To use a circular saw safely, avoid blade binding and kickback by supporting lumber so that the cut opens and the pieces fall away as you saw. Install a new carbide-tipped blade for best results (or touch up a steel blade), and check the saw shoe for square.

An arbor lock *freezes the blade.*

A file *sharpens steel blades.*

A square *checks the blade angle.*

the habit of keeping your eye on the leading edge of the blade, and become acquainted with the best way to align your saw. When you cut, push through smoothly, without micromanaging the cut by making little turns back and forth. Soon you will easily be making accurate cuts.

For precise cuts, use a guide. An angle square works well (photo 2, opposite). Make sure your saw's base butts up well against the guide and won't easily slide over on top of it. Hold the square in place against the edge of the board, and set the base of your saw so that its edge bears firmly against the edge of the square. Slide the square and saw until the saw blade lines up with the cut line. Make sure the square doesn't slip during the cut.

CUTTING MITER ANGLES

A mitered cut doesn't go straight across the board—it angles across the face to leave one edge of the board longer than the other. The most common miter angle used in deck construction is 45 degrees, and it's typically used where the decking or handrails meet at a right-angle corner.

Miter cuts can be hard to get exactly right. Sometimes the blade guard hangs up on the edge of the board at the beginning of the cut, making it difficult to start straight. And you're working in an unusual position, which takes some getting used to. If your decking or railing design calls for a lot of miter cutting, you may want to consider renting a power miter saw.

ABOVE **Built-in seating makes the deck more functional and provides a distinct design touch.**

SQUARE CUTTING

Whenever possible, keep two hands on the saw during a cut.

1. Use a square to mark the cut line. Then set the saw with the shoe parallel with the line; align the front guide notch; and start cutting.

2. You can use a square guide to help with precise cuts, but this method leaves only one hand on the saw.

3. Use a rip guide to control long cuts in line with the wood grain. The T-shaped guide comes with most circular saws.

Test for Squareness

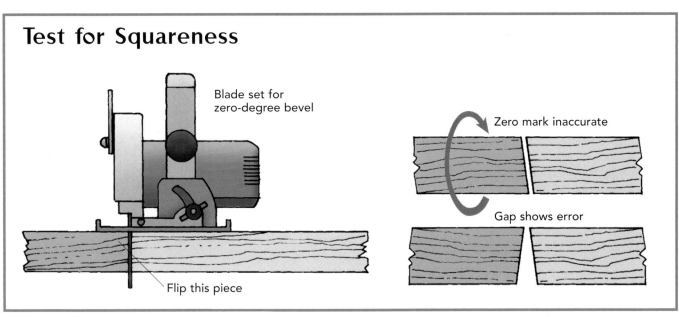

Blade set for zero-degree bevel

Flip this piece

Zero mark inaccurate

Gap shows error

RIPPING

When ripping lumber with a circular saw—that is, cutting it the long way to make a board narrower—a ripping guide comes in handy. (See photo 3, page 121.) The guide has a shoe that runs along the side of the board as you cut it along its length. This is a steel guide designed to fit your particular saw and usually attaches to the base with a thumbscrew.

CUTTING DADOES AND RABBETS

Technically, a dado is a groove cut across the grain of a piece of lumber. A rabbet is similar to a dado, except that a rabbet is on the end of the member. In deck building, you might cut dadoes into railing posts if you want rails to be flush to the post. You might also rabbet the top of a support post to receive a beam.

Kerf the Cut. To make a dado or rabbet, first set your circular saw blade to the exact depth of the cut; experiment on a piece of scrap wood to make sure you've got it right.

The side of a notch that cuts across the grain is called the shoulder—the cut parallel with the grain is the seat. A rabbet at the end of a piece of lumber will have a seat cut and one shoulder cut. A dado has two shoulders and a seat. Mark the shoulders of the dado (or the rabbet's single shoulder) on the piece of lumber (usually a post). Cut the shoulders; then make a number of closely spaced kerfs through the waste area. **1** Use extra caution when making these shallow cuts—the saw's body and handle are higher than usual, which makes the saw less stable.

Clean up the Seat. Use a hammer or your chisel with the flat side up to knock out the bulk of the waste. **2** The closer together you made the kerfs, the easier it will be to remove the waste.

Finally, use your chisel flat side down to clean up the seat of the dado or rabbet. **3**

CUTTING NOTCHES

A notch is essentially a dado or rabbet, but in a board instead of a post or beam. The most common reason you'll need to cut notches in deck building is to fit a decking board around a railing post. The first step is to mark for the notch.

Mark the Notch. Start by putting the board you need to notch on top of the last full board you installed next to the post. Then slide the board over against the post, and mark the width of the notch, defined by the edges of the post, on the face of the decking board. Now measure how deep the notch needs to be, and lay out the notch with your square. Remember to include the spacing between your decking boards as you lay it out. Keep the board in position while you make your marks so that you can visualize as you go, and you will be less likely to make the common mistake of measuring on the wrong side of the board.

Make the Shoulder Cuts. Start the shoulder cut or cuts by cutting in with a circular saw until the kerf just hits the

SMART TIP

USING A WATER LEVEL

A water level is a low-tech tool that uses a basic principle of physics: that water always seeks its own level. The inexpensive tool consists of a clear, flexible plastic tube and a couple of clips to fasten the tube in place. To use it, simply fill the tube with water (and a dye to make the level easier to read), and wait for the water to stabilize at the ends of the tube. The center portion of the tube can snake up and down over the site in any direction, and the water at each end will still be dead level.

Find level over distances.

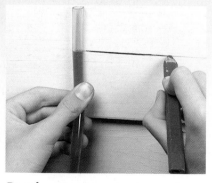
Dyed water is easier to read.

CUTTING RABBETS AND DADOES

TOOLS & MATERIALS
- Sawhorses
- 4x4 Post
- Square
- Pencil
- Circular Saw
- Hammer
- Chisel
- Mallet

One step beyond simple butt-joint carpentry, but still short of mortise-and-tenon joinery, lapped or dadoed joints will give your deck a sleek appearance.

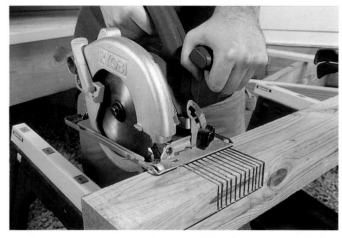

1 Cut a series of closely-spaced kerfs with the blade set to the depth of the dado.

2 Use a hammer to break down the strips of wood. Closely-spaced kerfs make this step easier.

3 Clear the wood shavings, and smooth down the ridges with a sharp chisel.

RIGHT Complex deck designs are attractive, but they usually require the know-how to make a variety of cuts. Practice on scrap lumber before making a new cut.

124

SMART TIP

LEDGER CHECK
To check the flatness of a ledger or house wall, nail two same-thickness blocks at each end and string a line between them. A third same-sized block should just tuck under the string. Where it doesn't fit, you'll see the margin of high and low spots.

Attaching a Ledger

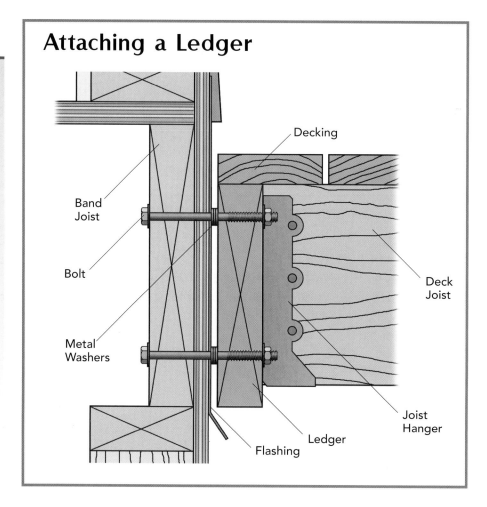

Band Joist

Bolt

Metal Washers

Decking

Deck Joist

Joist Hanger

Ledger

Flashing

LEFT Cutting notches around posts and making connections with dadoes and rabbets leads to a well-built deck that has crisp, clean-looking joints.

SMART TIP

CUTTING POSTS

Most do-it-yourselfers don't have a circular saw with enough capacity to cut through a 4x4 support post in one pass. That leaves two options. You can use a handsaw to cut straight through, or make two passes (from opposing sides) with a standard circular saw. Take the time to make square marks around the post to serve as a guide. And because posts typically are treated lumber, remember to wear a respirator mask, gloves, and safety glasses.

seat cut layout line. Because the saw's circular blade cuts a curved path through the wood, there may still be some wood to remove at the bottom of the cut. You'll need to finish the shoulder cuts using a handsaw, reciprocating saw, or saber saw. If the cut is a little uneven when you're finished with the notch, try smoothing the cuts with a chisel.

Finish the Notch. For a notch at the end of a board, make the seat cut in the same way. If the notch is in the middle of the board and the wood is straight grained with no knots in the way, make the seat cut with your chisel. Place the chisel along the seat cut line with the flat side facing away from the waste. Make sure the chisel is perpendicular to the board, and give it a sharp hammer blow.

Otherwise, make the seat cut with a saber saw or reciprocating saw. Another option is to nibble away the waste with repeated circular-saw cuts into the seat cut as you did for the shoulder cuts; then clean it up with a chisel.

MAKING A PLUNGE CUT

Occasionally you have to cut a hole in the middle of a board. You could drill a pilot hole and use a saber saw, but for a straighter line, use your circular saw to make a plunge cut (sometimes called a pocket cut).

Make sure your power cord is out of the way, and grasp the saw with both hands. Position the saw, and raise up the back, using the front of the foot plate as a fulcrum. Now hold the blade guard so that the blade is exposed, and lower the saw until the blade is just above the right spot. When you are sure everything is safe and

aligned, squeeze the trigger, and slowly lower the blade down to make the cut. If you do not twist as you go, you will be able to move forward with the saw after you have plunged through the board, but be sure the foot plate is resting fully on the board before you do so.

CUTTING 4X4S

A 7¼-inch circular saw will not cut all the way through a 4x4 in one pass, so you'll need to cut from two opposing sides. Using a square, draw a line all the way around the 4x4: if the last line meets up with the first, you know your layout lines are square. Then make cuts on two opposite sides. If your blade is square and you cut accurately, the entire cut will be fairly smooth, but don't expect perfection. In nearly every case, the top of a 4x4 gets covered up by other pieces of wood anyway.

If you are cutting off a 4x4 that has a piece of lumber such as a built-up girder or outside joist attached to it, first cut whatever you can get at with a circular saw to remove most of the waste; then finish the cut with a handsaw or reciprocating saw.

BUILDING TECHNIQUES

NAILING

Some contractors have a one-question test for new carpenters: they just hand the prospective employee a hammer and watch how he grips it. If the guy wraps his thumb around the shaft, he's in, but if he extends the thumb up the handle toward the head, he's out. The second grip puts less power in each swing and can result in serious damage to the tendons in the wrist. Good nailing technique, once learned, becomes second nature.

SMART TIP

PREDRILLING

Where you have to make a butt joint between boards, predrill each end at a slight angle to avoid splitting the wood as you drive nails. On a long deck, be sure to stagger butt joints so that they don't line up and fall on only one or two joists.

Predrill each board at butt joints.

Nails won't split predrilled boards.

REDUCING STRESSES AND MISSES

Many handymen and even some pro carpenters do not have good nailing technique. A common mistake is to hold the hammer too stiffly, with the wrist locked in place. Instead, let your wrist flex a little, and finish each stroke with a snap of the wrist. Spend some time practicing; as you gain confidence, you will become more relaxed, and letting the wrist flex will come naturally.

Start with a hammer weight that feels comfortable when you swing it, weighing maybe 16 or 20 ounces. Hold the nail in place, and hit it once or twice until it can stand on its own. Then drive it home with several powerful strokes.

AVOIDING SPLITS

Whenever you are nailing near the end of a board (or near what will be the end once the board is cut off), take precautions to minimize splitting. Remember that any little split you see now will only get larger in time; and some spots that look OK now can develop splits later.

There are two techniques. First, you can predrill each hole. This may seem bothersome, but if you can do a whole row of nails at once, it really doesn't take much time. And the extra 15 minutes you spend now will mean a much better-looking deck for years to come. Use a drill bit that's slightly smaller than the diameter of your nail shaft.

Another less effective but easier technique is to

PNEUMATIC NAILING

To make sure your compressor can handle a framing nailer, check out the specs. A nailer needs 3 cubic feet per minute (cfm) of air at 90 pounds per square inch (psi).

1. Air-powered nailers speed work by firing nails from a clip that you slip into a slot below the handle. An air compressor powers the tool.

2. The most important safety feature on a pneumatic nailer is a lock-out safety tip. This keeps the tools from firing accidentally, even if you squeeze the trigger.

SMART TIP

TOENAILING

When you can't nail through the face of one board into the end of another, drive toenails. Start the nail at a slight angle, and after a few blows, increase the angle to drive the nail in. Don't rely on toenails alone to make structural connections.

Start a toenail at a slight angle.

Increase the angle as you nail.

blunt the nail before driving it. Hold the nail upside down against a solid surface, and tap the tip a few times with your hammer to blunt it. This reduces the outward strain that the nail puts on the board.

SKEWING

If you're driving two nails through a decking board and into the joist below, skew the nails, or angle them toward each other a little. This creates a stronger connection by hooking the boards together and reduces the possibility of splitting.

TOENAILING

Most of the time, when two boards need to be joined at a right angle, you drive a nail through the face of one board into the other.

But sometimes the face into which you would prefer to nail is inaccessible, or the piece you have to nail through is too thick. In cases like this, toenail the pieces together.

Toenailing means nailing at an angle through the end of one board into the face of another. Position an 8d or 10d nail about 1½ inches from the end of the board. Get the nail started; then adjust it to a steep angle so the tip will come out near the center of the board's end grain. If possible, drive two nails on each side of the board.

Toenailing works well for nonstructural connections and positioning boards temporarily, but don't depend on toenails to secure a joint that carries loads. Reinforce the joint with framing hardware whenever possible.

DRILLS AND SCREW GUNS

Though nailing has its advantages, there's a lot to be said for fastening with screws. They hold more firmly than nails and are easier to remove or tighten. Screws generally cost more, but the extra expense is usually a small part of your materials budget. And once you get the hang of using them, screws can actually be easier to use than nails.

With practice, anyone can master the art of driving screws. A screw gun or a special attachment for your drill can help: it sets the depth automatically and makes it difficult for the driver bit to slip completely off the screwhead.

A screw gun is different from a regular drill, either corded or cordless. The chuck will only drive screws—you can't put a regular drill bit in it to drill holes. The depth of drive is adjustable.

Drive all your screws to a uniform depth, just below the surface of the lumber. A deeply sunken screw head is a place for water to collect, leading to decay.

DECAY-RESISTANT DESIGN

In addition to choosing the best wood possible, construction methods such as those that follow will help reduce decay and minimize the effects of wood shrinkage over time.

FASTENING TIPS

Nailing decking boards requires some delicate work with the hammer to avoid damaging the wood. A nail set eases the process, but also slows it down. The best bet with screws is a screw gun with an adjustable depth-of-drive feature. Various types of hidden fasteners leave the face of the board untouched.

When driving nails, the final blow should seat the nail without leaving a mark. (1) Dents create pockets that hold water. (2)

When using a pneumatic nailer, the force of the gun should match the density of the wood to seat the nail flush. (3) Too much force can cause splits that will trap water. (4)

As with nails, screws should seat flush. (5) Use a drill/driver with torque control for best results. A poorly driven screw will damage the surface. (6)

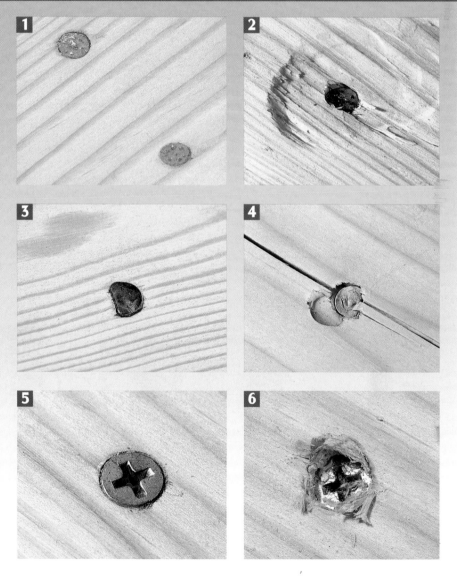

PROTECTING OPEN GRAIN

When you look at the end of a board, you are looking at the open grain, also called end grain. Open grain soaks up rainwater—and any other liquid—like a sponge, making it the most vulnerable part of a piece of lumber.

For this reason, cover up open grain whenever it is possible. This is especially important when the open grain is horizontal, or facing up, so that water can sit on it. Plan your deck railings carefully to eliminate exposed horizontal open grain whenever possible.

Avoiding Trapped Water. Of course, a certain amount of open grain is unavoidable—the ends of decking boards typically have exposed end grain. This usually isn't a problem as long as the boards can dry out quickly after they get wet. In fact, covering vertical open grain with wood or butting it against the house often increases the likelihood of decay. Unless the wood stays tightly butted against the house for years, which is unlikely, there will be small gaps in which water can collect and sit.

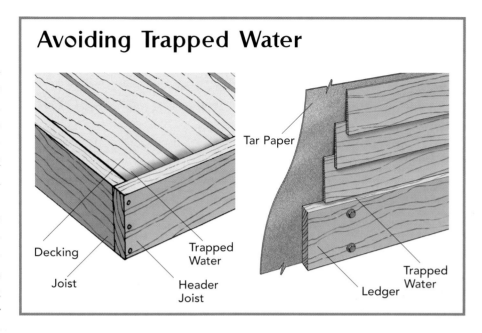

Avoiding Trapped Water

Tar Paper

Decking

Joist

Header Joist

Trapped Water

Ledger

Trapped Water

TIGHTENING BUTT JOINTS

If possible, plan your decking pattern to minimize butt joints. This may mean spending extra money for longer boards, but you will end up with a deck that has fewer problem spots.

When you make butt joints, take steps to ensure that they will remain tight for years. Choose dry lumber to minimize shrinkage. After you have installed the first board, firmly tap the second toward the first before you fasten it. Drive your nails or screws at an angle so that they pull the decking boards tightly together.

TREATING OPEN GRAIN

If you are worried about open grain exposure, apply preservative/water repellent to the problem areas.

For boards that will get a lot of contact with moisture, the most effective way is to set the end of the board in a container of preservative and let it soak for a few minutes. A more common solution is to brush it on. Plan ahead: in some places you can brush on preservative after the deck is built, but in other places, such as where the decking meets the house, you won't be able to get at it.

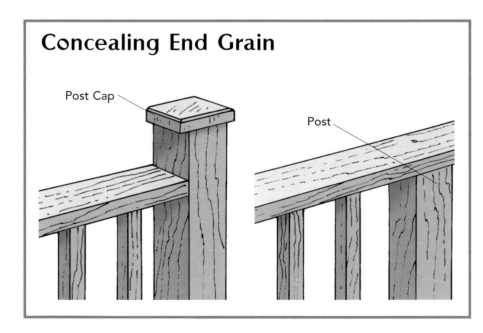

Concealing End Grain

Post Cap

Post

LAYING OUT AND CUTTING CURVES

For short curved edges, mark the cut line with a compass—don't just eyeball it and expect it to come out right. For longer curves, make your own compass out of a pencil, a length of string, and a nail driven into the deck.

Experiment with centers and compass openings until you find the curve that pleases you. **1** Tack a nail at that point, and tie your string to it. Tie the other end to your pencil, and experiment to be sure you've got it right. It's easy to make mistakes, so do a dry run without making any marks on the deck boards. Be sure to hold the pencil at the same angle at all times. **2**

When cutting out a curve, be sure you have a heavy-duty saber saw, one that cuts with ease and does not wobble. **3** Spend some time practicing on scrap pieces of lumber first—a mistake here might be difficult to correct. Don't force the saw through the cut—let it proceed at its own pace. Pushing too hard could deflect the blade and leave you with a bad cut.

SMOOTHING AND ROUNDING

It's a good idea to spend time smoothing rough spots and rounding off sharp edges of decking and railings. For a small amount of time and effort, your deck will take on a more finished, handcrafted look. And your family and friends will be less likely to encounter splinters.

The best way to round-over decking and other parts of the deck is with a router and roundover bit. **4** If set properly, this is a nearly mistake-proof method of rounding. But the router will probably not be able to reach every part of your deck that needs rounding, and you will have to finish some spots by hand using a file.

Some good places for rounding are the edges of decking, rail caps, built-in benches, and exposed posts and girders. You can do most of the rest of your smoothing with a sander or sanding block. **5** You may have to start with a rough-grit sandpaper and then go over it all again with medium-grit paper. (80-grit is fine for finishing; a finer paper is rarely needed.) Whenever possible, use long, smooth strokes rather than short quick ones. And it doesn't pay to press down hard; a moderate amount of pressure usually lifts off just as much. Usually, the only areas on a deck that you should consider smoothing are those places that people often handle or against which they rub, such as rail caps, seats, tables, and play areas.

For rounding off, the trick is to decide how much you are going to round off, and then stick with the same pattern. If some parts are only slightly rounded while more wood is removed from other places, the deck will look sloppy and haphazardly built.

For softer woods, the sanding block will do a moderate amount of rounding off. Though it may take some fairly heavy work, the advantage of a sanding block is that you can't make a big mistake. For more extensive jobs, consider a belt sander. But be careful—it's easy to make a deep gouge very quickly if you hold a belt sander in one place for too long.

SMART TIP

WHEN TO CAULK

Most decks require little if any caulk because they are designed to drain. But you might need some caulk where elements of the deck meet the house—for example, where a railing joins the house siding and where a ledger board or ledger flashing meets the foundation. If you do apply caulk, choose a type that combines long life with good adhesion, either straight silicone caulk or a siliconized latex caulk.

Caulk covers nailheads on flashing.

CUTTING CORNER CURVES

TOOLS & MATERIALS
- Measuring tape
- Pencil
- Nail
- Hammer
- Saber saw
- Router & bits
- Sander

Curved edges on a deck add lots of visual interest but require careful framing. (See page 192.) A perfect layout is crucial, so take your time with the setup and the cutting.

1 *Think of the curve you want as part of a circle. Find the center by measuring the radius from each edge.*

2 *The intersection of the lines is the center. Use the nail, string, and pencil to draw a curve on the deck.*

3 *Use a saber saw to cut the corner curve. Support large waste pieces while cutting.*

4 *For a finished appearance, smooth the edges with a router fitted with a roundover bit.*

5 *Sand the edge for a final finishing. You can use a random-orbit sander or a sanding block.*

BUILDING TECHNIQUES

FOOTINGS
AND
FOUNDATIONS

7

Footings are like masonry tree trunks supporting a network of timbers above. If the footings are strong, the joists, decking, rails, and stairs they support are likely to stay where you put them. Footings are the basis of every good deck, and building them begins with some heavy-duty digging.

DISTRIBUTING THE LOAD

A deck's footings must support not only the dead load of the deck—the total weight of the framing, decking, railings, benches, and planters—but also the nonpermanent weight called live load—things like snow, people, and furniture. Building codes typically mandate that a deck support 10 pounds per square foot of dead load and 40 pounds per square foot of live load. So your footings must be strong enough to handle 50 pounds per square foot of deck (8,000 pounds for a 10 x 16-foot deck.).

This load is distributed through the framing structure to the footings set in the ground. The ledger will easily shoulder its portion because it's bolted to the house and transfers its percentage of the load to the house's foundation. If your deck cantilevers out beyond a girder, the girder will carry more than the ledger. (See "Maximum Cantilevers," page 140.)

Loose soil may not be able to support much weight—perhaps as little as 500 pounds per square foot—which can mean that you will need more footings or wider footings than you would with firmer soil. By increasing the area of the footpad—the base of the footing where it sits on the undisturbed soil—you can compensate for loose soil. If your soil carries 800 pounds per square foot, a 12 x 12-inch footing can carry only 800 pounds, while approximately the same size footing with a 24 x 24-inch pad, at 4 square feet, can carry a whopping 3,200 pounds.

Some soils, especially those with a lot of clay, may be quite firm when dry but will lose strength when they get wet. If you suspect a problem, ask your town's building department engineer or inspector to assess the situation and make suggestions.

SITE WORK

The shade provided by your deck will usually discourage plant growth, but to be safe, lay down plastic or landscaping fabric and cover it with gravel because it will be difficult to do so after the deck is built. Landscaping fabric is usually a better choice than plastic because it does not trap moisture. If you live in an area where vegetation is extremely

LEFT Deck height plays a role in the type of piers and posts needed. Check with the building inspector for code requirements in your area.

lush and tenacious, consider removing the grass, plants, and roots from the site by digging up all of it and hauling it away. Then fill the area with landscaping fabric and gravel. (See "Removing Sod" and "Preparing a Gravel Bed," pages 136 and 137.)

SOLUTIONS FOR WET SITES

You may find that your chosen deck site presents you with some extra challenges, usually in the form of water. Here's a list of common problems and typical solutions:

A Site That Is Already Wet. You can build over a moderately soggy site, once you provide drainage to prevent standing water under the deck. The deck may reduce the amount of rain that falls on the ground, but a deck also puts the site in shade, so water will evaporate more slowly, especially if your deck is very near the ground. Any water standing under a deck for more than a few days breeds mosquitoes and can start to smell horrible on hot summer days.

The simplest way to deal with this problem is to grade the site—to make sure it is sloping uniformly away from the house with no valleys or pits. This can usually be handled simply by shifting dirt with a shovel and rake, although it is back-breaking work. You may find it useful to measure the slope using a tape measure and line level.

REMOVING SHRUBS

TOOLS & MATERIALS
- Shovel
- Burlap
- String
- Wheelbarrow

You may need to remove vegetation to make way for your new deck. Save valuable shrubs and other plants by transplating to another area.

1 Use a shovel to dig under the root of the shrub. Mature plant roots can be difficult to remove.

2 Lift the plant and roots free of the hole, and place the root ball on a piece of burlap.

3 Tie the burlap with string to protect the root area, particularly if the new planting site is not ready.

Another method is to build the deck so that the deck boards all slope a bit in one direction so that most of the water runs off one edge of the deck. Of course, you'll need to deal with the water at that edge, but you can do this after the deck is built and you have a good idea how big the problem is.

For more severe problems, dig a drainage ditch to collect water and carry it away from your site. Dig the ditch about 12 inches deep at the high end, and angle it down about 1 inch for each 10 feet of trench. Put approximately an inch of gravel in the bottom of the ditch; install a perforated drainpipe (with the holes down); cover with more gravel; and top it off with soil. The far end

of the pipe can emerge from the ground if you have a good slope on your property and somewhere to direct the water, or it can pour the water into an underground dry well—a large hole filled with stones and topped with gravel and soil.

Runoff from Heavy Rains. If you have downspouts that dump water on your deck site, plan to change your gutter system so that it will empty out elsewhere.

As a heavy rainfall runs off the deck, you may end up with a little water-filled moat all the way around. This is a problem that's hard to predict before you build, but it's also fairly easy to fix. For minor puddling, try ringing your deck with

REMOVING SOD

TOOLS & MATERIALS
- Square-bottom shovel
- Work gloves
- Wheelbarrow

You can reuse sod if you are able to replant it in a day or two. Keep rolls of sod moist.

1 *Score 16-in.-wide strips of sod with the shovel. Sharpen the blade with a file.*

2 *Roll the sod out of the way. Include about 2 to 3 in. of soil as you roll.*

3 *Sod rolls can get heavy, so work with sections that you can easily manage.*

plants in a wood-chip bed. For larger problems, you may need a bed of gravel 6 inches deep, or you may even need to install a drainage ditch as described previously.

Erosion from Water. On a very hilly site, you might have erosion problems; little gullies left where the rain has carried away soil are the usual telltale signs. Severe erosion can undermine your footings, causing them to sink, tip, or fail completely.

Limit erosion by planting suitable foliage to stabilize the site. Check with a local nursery for the best type of plants to use. Or you may need to provide drainage: simple trenches might solve the problem, or you may need to dig a drainage ditch.

Unstable Soil. Any concrete footings or posts sitting in a posthole must sit on undisturbed soil, which is almost always reached by the time you dig down 16 inches or so. Footings placed in unstable or loose soil will settle along with the soil, sometimes unevenly. Swampy soil is likely to be unstable, as is any area that's recently been excavated and backfilled. A yard with a significant amount of fresh topsoil may also need time to settle. If you are unsure about your soil's stability, talk with a local soil engineer, an architect, or the local building department. Experts such as these should know a good deal about local conditions and what sorts of foundations work best in the kind of soil on your site.

PREPARING A GRAVEL BED

TOOLS & MATERIALS
- Rake
- Shovel
- Perforated plastic or landscape fabric
- Gravel
- Wheelbarrow

This method will stop weed growth, but you can also use a general herbicide in addition to these steps. Be sure to follow the instructions on the label.

1 *Clear away rocks, roots, and other debris. The ground should slope away from the house.*

2 *Roll out the plastic. Overlap the edges by 6 in. shingle-style so that water runs away from the house.*

3 *Dump the gravel in several piles around the site. Rake it out to create an even surface.*

LAYING OUT THE FOUNDATION

The footings will be the least visible element of your deck, so there is a temptation to treat them with nonchalance. But if footings are not set accurately, correcting those mistakes during the rest of the job could be a colossal pain. So take the time to check, cross-check, and recheck every step of the way.

It's best to have a helper for this, not only because you need someone to pull strings taut, hold one end of the measuring tape, and help make adjustments, but also because two heads are usually better than one when working.

Locate the Ledger. The ledger board is usually the primary reference point for the deck. You may even want to install the ledger first and then go on to laying out and digging the foundation. (See "Preparing the Ledger," pages 154-158.) In any case, to lay out the footings, you first need to mark the ends of the ledger. Account for the outside joists and the fascia board, if there will be any. If you will be applying one-by fascia, for example, your ledger board will need to be 2¼ inches shorter than the finished deck on each end (1½ inches for the framing lumber plus ¾ inch for the fascia).

Draw a Reference Line. Once you have marked the ends of the ledger on your house,

LAYING OUT LINES

TOOLS & MATERIALS
- 1x4 lumber
- Saw
- Drill-driver
- Layout strings
- Measuring tape
- Level
- Plumb bob

You can tailor the 3-4-5 method for determining a square corner to suit your project: use multiples of those number, such as 9-12-15.

1 Construct batter boards from the 1x4 lumber. Make pointy ends to drive the boards into the ground.

3 Measure up one leg 3 ft.; measure up the other 4 ft.; in a square corner, the connected points equal 5 ft.

4 You could also measure the diagonals. If they are equal, the corners are square.

use a level or a plumb bob to bring the line down to a place on the house near the ground. If your yard slopes appreciably downward from the house, place this mark near the ground. If the yard is fairly level, make the mark a foot or so off the ground. Attach a screw or nail to this spot so that you can tie a string line to it.

Assemble Batter Boards. For each outside deck corner you will be locating, construct two batter boards. **1** Make these by attaching a 36- or 48-inch-long crosspiece squarely across two stakes. You can buy premade stakes at the lumberyard, or simply cut pieces of 2x4 or 1x4 to a point on one end. Although they are temporary and will be used only to hold string lines, the

2 *Set the batter boards in pairs a few feet outside of the actual contruction zone. Attach lines.*

5 *Use a plumb bob or level at the intersection of your lines to determine the location of the corner pier.*

batter boards must be sturdy—there is a good chance they will get bumped around.

Lay Out the Perimeter. Measure from the house to determine the location of your posts, and roughly mark lines, using a string or long pieces of lumber. You want this line to run through the center of the posts, meaning that you have to take into account thicknesses of beams and outside joists: a two-by is 1½ inches thick, and the center of a 4x4 is 1¾ inches from each edge. Pound a stake into the ground or otherwise mark the location at the (again, rough) intersections of the lines.

Establish Centers at Corner Footings. Firmly pound two batter boards into the ground 16 inches or so beyond the stake in each direction. Run string lines from the house to the batter boards and from batter board to batter board in the other direction if necessary. **2** On the ledger, the string line will usually be run 1¾ inches in from the outside ends of the ledger locaton.

Now check for square using the 3-4-5 method: measure along your house or ledger board, and mark a point 3 feet in from the nail holding the string. Now measure along the string and use a piece of tape to mark a spot 4 feet from the house. Finally, measure the distance between the two marks. If this is exactly 5 feet, then you have a square corner. **3** If you have the room, you can be more accurate by using multiples of 3, 4, and 5 feet—for example, 9, 12, and 15.

Double-check the layout for square by taking three pairs of measurements: the two lengths of your rectangle should be equal to each other, as should the two widths and, most importantly, the two diagonals. **4** Once you have established that your lines are square, attach them securely to the batter boards using a nail or screw to make sure that they cannot slip sideways when someone bumps into the string.

Mark for Postholes. Use a plumb bob or chalk-line box, which can double as a plumb bob, to mark the spot on the ground that will be the center of each post—and therefore, the center of each posthole. For the corner posts, bring a plumb line down from the intersection of your lines. **5** Hold the line until the bob (or chalk-line box) stops swaying, and mark the spot with a small stake.

Maximum Cantilevers

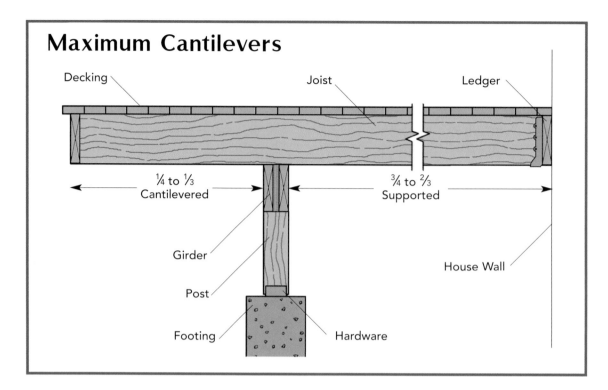

Decking   Joist   Ledger

¼ to ⅓
Cantilevered

¾ to ⅔
Supported

House Wall

Girder

Post

Footing   Hardware

BELOW You don't see it, but a well-designed foundation will provide years of reliable service.

MARKING FOR UTILITIES

Before you start digging piers for your deck, check into the location of underground utility lines, such as a natural-gas main or sewer line. On a big job where you're using a contractor to do the digging, the excavation contractor should plot the exact location of underground utilities. But even then it pays to check on them yourself with the local utility company. In most areas, a company representative will come to the site and locate the lines so you can mark them with flags.

FOOTINGS

Most likely you will need to pour concrete and make new footings. Consult local codes and ask the following questions when choosing a footing:

- Is it massive and stable enough?
- If you want to avoid having a floating deck, does it extend well below the frost line?
- Is it raised above the ground high enough to keep the post dry?
- Do local codes require reinforcing bar?
- Do you need to provide drainage?

Precast Piers. If you have a stable site with little sand and no wintertime frost or you don't connect the deck to the house, you might get away with simply setting precast concrete piers directly on top of undisturbed soil instead of using footings. Remove loose soil, and provide a spot where the piers can rest on level, undisturbed soil. Make sure that this system is code-approved in your area.

DIY OPTIONS: TYPES OF FOOTINGS

PRECAST PIER

HOLE-DUG PIER

HOLE-DUG PIER WITH FORM

HOLE-DUG TUBE FORM

HOLE-DUG PIERS

No Frost Line. In stable soil, you can simply dig a hole that will act as a concrete form. For areas with little frost, a hole that is 12 inches in diameter and 8 inches deep, for instance, will yield a substantial footing. Fill the hole completely with concrete, and taper it upward so that the center is an inch or two above the ground. Insert an anchor or bolt directly into the concrete.

Below the Frost Line. Another option is to dig a cylindrical posthole that extends several inches below your area's frost line, and fill it with concrete. Flare the bottom of the hole a bit for stability. This method works best for footings with wide diameters.

ABOVE **Plan pier locations carefully.**

HOLE-DUG FORMS

The top of a footing formed by pouring concrete into a hole is usually flush to the ground, which means that the bottom of the post is near ground level and subject to moisture. You can modify this technique by extending the form above the ground using 1x6s or pieces of plywood.

Precast Pier on Concrete. You can purchase a precast concrete pier and set it into your bed of concrete. It is a good idea to paint the bottom of the pier with concrete bonding agent before setting it 1 to 2 inches into the concrete.

Pouring into a Tube Form. This is an easy and accurate way of pouring a footing. The tubes come in a variety of sizes, though 8 inches in diameter is the most common. The forms are made of fiberboard and are easy to trim to the exact length you need. A tube form has great advantages over just digging a posthole and filling it with concrete: it can be easily extended above the ground to whatever height you desire; it makes inspectors happy because they know the exact dimensions of your footings; and it makes your job easier because you don't have to mix extra concrete. The tubes are waxed, so you can easily strip away the part that shows above-ground after the concrete has set.

POST ANCHORS

With most anchors, you embed one part of the metal in the concrete while it's still wet. Often you just insert a J-bolt or an anchor strap and attach the rest of the anchor later, but some anchors come in one piece and you embed just the lower portion. Look for an anchor that you can adjust laterally. Adjustable anchors give you

DIY OPTIONS: POST HARDWARE

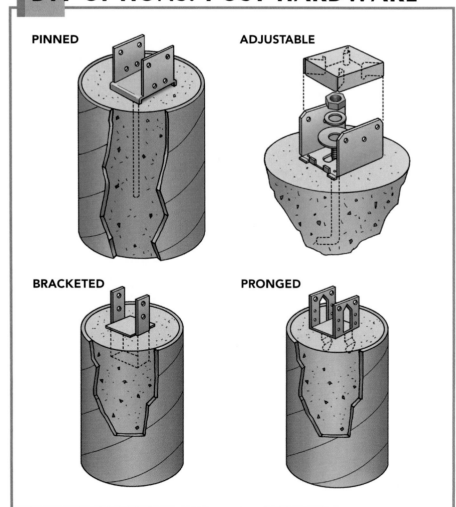

PINNED

ADJUSTABLE

BRACKETED

PRONGED

SMART TIP

ALIGNING PIER HARDWARE

When you set and pour concrete piers, you may set the anchoring pin slightly off line. That's one good reason to use adjustable post hardware. Most types have a slot in the base instead of a hole. That allows you to adjust the hardware slightly in any direction to place the base of the post exactly where you want it.

DIY OPTIONS: FOUNDATIONS

There are several prefab products that can help you build footings and piers faster. Dek-block piers (right) simply sit on the ground, and the deck frame tucks into cuts in the tops of the blocks. The system meets many codes because the deck floats. It's not actually attached to the house and may even be considered a temporary structure. Be certain to check this kind of sys-

tem with your local building department. The Bigfoot form (far right) is a high-density plastic form that attaches to prefab pier tubes.

It adds strength and stability by forming a bell-shaped foot under the pier, and sheds water away from the footing.

an inch or two of play in either direction so that you can compensate for small layout errors.

CONTINUOUS POSTS

You can also extend posts down into postholes. It may seem that doing this adds a lot of strength to the structure, but in the case of a mostly horizontal structure such as a deck, that is rarely the case. Nearly all the lateral strength of your deck—what will keep it from swaying—comes from the way it all ties together. Every nail, screw, and bolt you install makes it a bit firmer. In addition, you will probably gain rigidity by tying the deck to your house. So unless you are building a freestanding deck that is raised more than a couple of feet above the ground, concrete-set posts do not add significant lateral strength.

And there are drawbacks to posts sunk in concrete or gravel: first, there's no correcting of mistakes. Second, posts set into the ground are more likely to rot. And third, they are very difficult to replace in case they get damaged. So unless you have special reason to use them elsewhere, use this type of post only for the stair rails, which often need a little extra lateral support.

However, continuous posts are required in some areas subject to earthquakes. They are also sometimes called for when the deck is

SMART TIP

CONTINUOUS POSTS

In some situations you can set posts directly into a concrete form—for example, to help support the end of a stairway railing where it's not practical to pour another pier. But the most durable design is to set posts in hardware on top of piers.

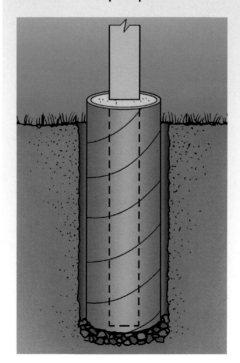

DIY OPTIONS: DIGGING

Working in rocky soil, you will find it handy to have a pickax, or at least a heavy-duty wrecking bar to help dislodge rocks.

1. Using a shovel is the basic and sometimes back-breaking way to dig piers. But you'll wind up moving more dirt than you need to.

2. A posthole digger has two handles that work in a scissors action to cut and scoop dirt. They make a neater hole with a smaller diameter.

3. The power auger is a tool you can rent. There are one- and two-person models that churn through the dirt. Both are a handful to operate, but they are efficient.

raised high above the ground to make sure the post bottoms won't move. Continuous posts are often simply set into postholes that are back-filled with concrete. They can also be inserted into a large-diameter, concrete-filled tube form.

DIGGING POSTHOLES

If there are just a few holes to dig, you can do the work yourself using a posthole digger. For larger projects, however, you'll thank yourself for renting a power auger to speed up the job. Some are designed for one-person operation (though it certainly wouldn't hurt to have a helper), and the larger ones require two fairly brawny people.

Dig the Holes. Once the marker stakes are all firmly established, remove the string lines to give yourself room to dig. Whether you are using the auger or a posthole digger, if you run into a rock, you'll need a wrecking bar (also called a breaker bar or a crowbar) to break up stones or pry them loose. If you run into roots, chop at them with your posthole digger or shovel, or use branch pruners. In extreme cases, you may have to go in there with a handsaw.

Tamp the Bottom and Reattach String Lines. The bottom of your footing hole should be firm. Even if you have reached undisturbed soil, an inch or two of dirt crumbs will be left over from the digging process, so tamp the soil down with a piece of 4x4. Put your string lines back in place; recheck them for square; and double-check your footing locations.

Install the Forms. Once you have dug the holes, install the concrete forms of your choice, making sure they are secure. If you are using a fiberboard tube form, you can usually just back-fill it with dirt to keep it stable. Some designs call for leveling all the footings with each other. To do this, first backfill all the tubes; then mark them with a water level; and cut them off with a handsaw.

Add Gravel and Rebar. Pour 2 to 3 inches of gravel into the bottom of the concrete form.

If your building inspector requires reinforcing bar, this is the time to add it. Usually, this means pounding a long piece of the rebar into the ground at the bottom of the hole so that it runs through the center of the form. Do it carefully, so the rebar will be at or near the center of the concrete. Be sure it does not stick out of the form and will not interfere with the part of your post anchors that you'll embed into the wet concrete. Ask the inspector to specify a size for the rebar; also inquire about rebar spacing.

POURING CONCRETE

Now it's time to begin forming a permanent part of your deck. Though backfilled footings aren't too impressive looking, they are important to the overall stability of your deck.

ESTIMATING

Concrete is sold by the yard; a cubic yard is 3 feet by 3 feet by 3 feet, or 27 cubic feet, and there are 1,728 cubic inches in a cubic foot.

For box forms, multiply the inside length times the inside width times the depth, all measurements in inches. Divide the result by 1,728 to convert into cubic feet; then divide by 27 to convert into cubic yards.

To find the volume of cylindrical footings, the formula is: volume = $\pi r^2 h$. That means that you multiply pi (3.14) times the radius squared times the height to get cubic inches. Then you convert that into cubic feet by dividing by 1,728; then divide by 27 to obtain cubic yards.

MIXING CONCRETE

TOOLS & MATERIALS
- Concrete mix
- Work gloves
- Wheelbarrow
- Hoe
- Bucket
- Water

To make this dusty work go smoothly, pour in about two-thirds of the water to start; then mix and add the rest slowly.

1 *Whether you use premixed ingredients or combine them yourself, do the mixing in a wheelbarrow.*

2 *Mix the dry ingredients with a hoe. Create a crater in the center of the pile.*

3 *Pour in the water slowly, following the directions on the bag. Too much water ruins the mixture.*

GETTING CONCRETE

There are two basic ways to get concrete ready to pour on site: you can add water to premixed bags or mix your own from piles of raw materials. (See the "Smart Tip" opposite for dealing with large amounts of concrete.)

Using Premixed Concrete. You can buy bags that have the cement, sand, and gravel already mixed. A wheelbarrow makes a good container for adding water and mixing. Each bag yields about ⅔ cubic foot, so a typical 8-inch-by-42-inch cylindrical footing will take two bags, and ½ cubic yard will require about 20 bags.

Mixing Your Own. For in-between amounts or for sites where truck delivery would be difficult, consider mixing your own concrete in a wheelbarrow or on a sheet of plywood. Or, for larger amounts, you can rent an electric mixer.

MIXING AND POURING

The basic technique is the same here whether you are using premixed concrete in bags or combining your own dry ingredients. You can build or buy a mixing trough, but the easiest method is simply to mix right in the same wheelbarrow you will use to transport the concrete. (See "Mixing Concrete." page 145.)

Mix Dry Ingredients. If you're mixing your own dry ingredients, shovel them right into the wheelbarrow. Use three shovelfuls of gravel, two of

BUILDING PIERS

TOOLS & MATERIALS
- Form tubes
- Level
- Concrete
- Trowel
- Post anchor hardware
- Wrenches

Backfill fiberboard forms once they are in the hole to hold them steady, eliminating the need for braces.

1 Place a cut tube in the hole. The top of the tube should project 6 in. above grade.

3 Pour concrete into the form. Insert the J-bolt that comes with the hardware into the center of the form.

4 After the concrete cures, attach the rest of the post anchor hardware.

sand, and one of cement. Mix the dry ingredients thoroughly with a concrete hoe even if you are using premixed bags. If you have a large wheelbarrow, try mixing two premixed bags at once.

Add Water. Hollow out a hole in the center of the dry ingredients, and pour in some water. Mix thoroughly; then slowly add more water, testing the concrete as you go for the right consistency. Don't make it soupy, even though more water makes mixing easier. It should be just fluid enough to pour into your form.

Pour and Strike Off the Concrete. Pour the concrete directly from the wheelbarrow, or scoop it into your forms with a shovel. Clean up any excess as you go. Poke a 2x2 or a piece of rebar

2 Level the tube, and backfill to hold the tube steady. Check for level while backfilling.

SMART TIP

DELIVERY BY TRUCK

If you need ¾ cubic yard or more, you may be better off having it delivered in a truck, even if the concrete yard's minimum is 1 full yard. You need to be completely prepared before the truck arrives. Map out where the truck will park and where the chute of the truck will reach to fill the wheelbarrow.

deep down into the concrete in several places to get out any air bubbles. Once you have filled the form, strike it off with a scrap piece of 2x4 to obtain a smooth, level top surface.

Install Post Anchor Hardware. Install your J-bolt or post anchor immediately. Wiggle it a bit as you place it to get rid of air bubbles. Then line up the hardware with your string line and a plumb bob to ensure it will be in the center of the post. Be certain that it is sticking up the right distance out of the concrete, and use a torpedo level to make sure it's plumb. Loosely cover the top of your footings with plastic, so they won't dry too quickly. You can start to build on the footings after 24 hours. But remember that concrete takes three weeks to fully cure, and it will be prone to chipping if you bang into it during the first few days.

INSTALLING POSTS IN POSTHOLES

If you choose to sink your posts into the ground, give the buried section an extra dose of preservative, especially the open end grain.

Dig Flared Holes. For additional stability, flare your holes so that they are 3–4 inches wider at the bottom than at the top. Throw 2–3 inches of gravel in the bottom for drainage. Another option is to use a large-diameter concrete tube form and put the post inside before pouring the concrete. This makes more efficient use of concrete and makes it possible to bring the concrete several inches above grade.

Check and Brace the Posts. You will let the posts run wild and cut them to their exact height after the concrete is set. For now, however, use a line level to make sure that all the posts are sitting high enough. Align them with your layout strings, and plumb them in both directions. Then attach two braces to each post.

Pour the Concrete. As you pour, poke a long pole or piece of reinforcing bar into the concrete on all four sides of the post to release any air bubbles. This is especially important when the post extends down inside the footing and the concrete forms a long, narrow ring around the post. Use a trowel to slope the top of the concrete upward, so that rainwater drains away from the wood.

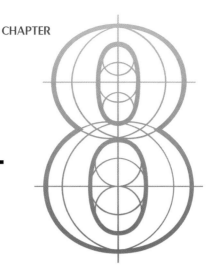

FRAMING SUPPORT MEMBERS

The ledger, posts, and girders are the components that secure the deck to the house and the ground. They carry the structural load of your new deck. In most cases, looks are not important, but what is important is selecting the right materials to do the job and installing these elements correctly.

FRAMING BASICS

In nearly every case, two-by or four-by treated lumber is the best choice for framing a deck, though in some situations redwood or cedar is a reasonable but expensive alternative. Treated lumber generally costs only a little more than standard construction grades of fir or hemlock and will last much longer. For highly visible areas such as outside joists, you may want to pick the best-looking board in the pile. Or you can do away with the treated look altogether by cladding the frame with a more finished wood— for example, the same kind of redwood or cedar you use on the railings.

A basic deck frame is made of posts, a girder, joists, and a ledger. Posts rest on your footings and are usually made of 4x4s; for a raised deck, 6x6s may be required. The main girder usually rests on top of the posts, although to create a ground-hugging deck, it can also rest directly on level footings. This main support beam can be a solid four-by or two or more two-bys. Joists that support the decking usually rest on top of the main girder on one end, and are attached to the ledger board at the other end. Joists and ledgers are made of two-by lumber and are generally of the same width. The ledger is attached to the house.

SIZING AND SPACING FRAME MEMBERS

The recommended span for a piece of lumber is the distance it can safely traverse without being supported underneath. If you exceed a recommended span—for instance, if you use 2x6 joists, spaced 16 inches apart, to span 10 feet— your deck will feel flimsy, and there is a good chance it will sag over time.

The span chart listed for reference on page 173 is on the conservative side. The listings can help you plan the deck—for example, to decide whether you want a massive girder with only a few post supports or a smaller girder with more posts. But remember that you will need to follow local codes concerning lumber sizes and spans. Local codes may vary, and it's not unusual for neighboring towns to have different standards. For instance, the deck projects included at the end of the book were approved by the building inspector in the municipalities in which they were built. But some of those decks do not comply with the charts in this chapter and may not be legal in your area. Even if you are sure about sizes and use lumber that is generally larger than the sizes you see on other decks in your neighborhood, be on the safe side and check the sizes and other aspects of the plans with the local building department.

Also remember that the same sizes of different wood species can have different requirements.

ABOVE **Connections at the ledger, posts, and girders**

Not all 4x12s have the same ratings. Generally, stronger woods such as Douglas fir can span greater distances than weaker woods such as cedar.

You'll also find that the suggested spans in this book (and in literature from your building department) are based on normal loads. If you plan to place heavy objects on your deck, such as soil-filled planters or a hot tub, you'll need to reduce the spans or beef up the lumber sizes, or both.

You will need to determine the span of the girder and the span of the joists. Then you can select the right materials for the job.

will determine the stability of your new deck.

FRAMING SUPPORT MEMBERS

SMART TIP

SPACING OPTIONS

Final spacing of framing members is up to the building inspector. But you have a lot of leeway in the design stage. Generally, if you use fewer piers and posts, you will need a larger girder to span the spaces between them. This approach can be an advantage on sloping sites and where digging even two

piers is a difficult job. Conversely, if you use more piers and posts in the design, a smaller girder will be strong enough to span the shorter distances between supports. Practical issues such as lumber costs can have a big impact on spacing, but you can alter the framing plan based on looks, too.

SAFETY

SAFE HANDLING OF MATERIALS

Get product data sheets for any of the materials you use on your deck. Many materials, such as treated lumber, require extra precaution when cutting, sanding, and disposing of the material. The data sheet should outline any special requirements.

JOISTS

In planning your joists, keep in mind the size and lumber type of the joists, as well as how far apart they will be spaced. This is called the on-center, or o.c., measurement.

Cantilevering. If you plan to cantilever your joists over a girder—that is, let them stick out beyond the main support beam—the amount of the cantilever should not be excessive. The rule of thumb for cantilevering is to create a maximum unsupported span of no more than one-third of the joist length, while two-thirds is supported. (See "Maximum Cantilevers," page 140.) But to create a deck that feels solid, don't project more than one-fourth of your joists. These rules of thumb apply to joists, but may not be possible on a girder. Codes often call for a support post at or very near the end of a girder.

As a practical matter, there is usually no good reason for a lengthy cantilever. But an extension of a foot or so often will help hide the main girder and posts. When you cantilever your deck, you may also have to make provisions for an uplift force at the house end of the joists.

BEAMS

House framing may contain several types of major beams, although on almost all decks there is only one, generally called a girder, that supports the outer ends of the joists.

You can sometimes reduce the girder size by adding a post or two, thereby saving money in lumber. But that savings is likely to be overshadowed by the extra labor of digging and pouring additional piers. Allowable girder spans depend on the size and type of the lumber, as well as the span distance of the joists that rest on it.

Bear in mind that the building department may consider a beam made of two 2x8s to be just as strong as a 4x8, or they may consider it weaker. Built-up strength also depends in part on how the built-up girder is constructed.

Posts. Unless your deck will carry an unusual amount of weight, 4x4 posts will work if your deck is 6 feet or less above the ground. Larger 6x6 posts may be required for decks over 8 feet high. If the deck is between 6 and 8 feet, consult your building department or use 6x6s.

REMOVING SIDING

TOOLS & MATERIALS
- Water level
- Pencil
- Circular saw
- Wood shims
- Gloves
- Hacksaw blade
- Prybar or hammer

You have some leeway in how high you place your ledger on the wall. The step down from house level to deck level can be anywhere between roughly 1 inch and 6 inches. The best plan is to set the ledger where you can bolt it securely to the house framing.

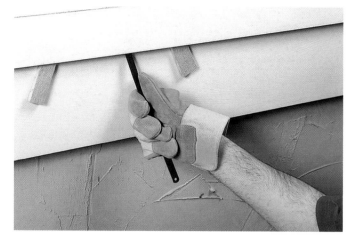

3 Pry the siding up, and insert wedges to hold it up. Use a metal blade to cut nails.

SMART TIP

CHECKING LEDGER LOCATION
The connection between the ledger and the house is crucial. That means fastening the ledger to the structure of the house, not the siding alone. To locate the framing, measure its position off the foundation inside and transfer the location outside. Then double-check by cutting out a piece of siding, stripping the tar paper or house wrap, and testing for hollow areas and solid framing with a nail. The ledger bolts should reach into or through the house framing.

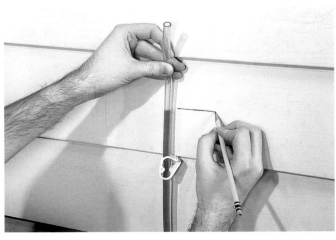

1 *Establish the ends of your ledger; then find level points at each end and snap a chalk line.*

2 *Set your saw to cut through the siding but not the sheathing. Make cuts at each end of the ledger.*

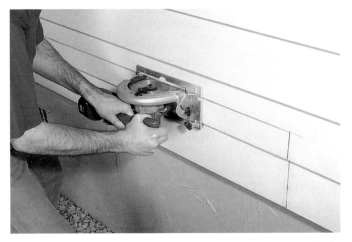

4 *Make the horizontal cut with your saw. Set the blade to siding depth to avoid cutting the sheathing.*

5 *The siding should come out easily. If it does not, use a pry bar and hammer to ease it out.*

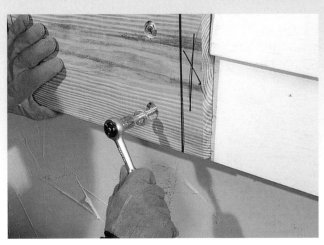

FRAMING SUPPORT MEMBERS

DIY OPTIONS: LEDGERS

No matter what kind of siding you have, there is a way to attach a ledger board securely. But you need to be sure that water will drain past the ledger, and not into the house. Do this by flashing the ledger so that water drains off the front face or by adding spacers between the ledger and the house so that water drains straight through. You also need to be sure that the ledger is solidly connected to the framing of the house.

DIRECTLY ON SIDING

FLASHED ON SHEATHING

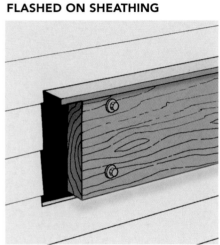

PREPARING THE LEDGER

The ledger usually makes the best starting place for laying out the whole deck, so you may want to install it before you dig your footing holes. It is a major supporting member, so it must be firmly attached to the house. Make your ledger of the same two-by material as your joists. Pick a straight board that is not cupped, so the joist ends can fit snugly against it. This piece of lumber is crucial because it does two jobs. It carries a lot of weight and connects the deck to the house. There are several ways to install a ledger,

but the most important consideration is safety. You must be sure that the ledger is securely bolted to the house framing, typically to the system of floor joists. You can't secure deck ledgers to siding or sheathing alone.

LEDGER DESIGN OPTIONS

The ledger can be a trouble spot because rain and snow can collect between it and the house and damage both. In particular, if you have beveled horizontal siding or shingles, simply attaching the ledger onto the siding is an invitation to trouble because water will collect in the V-shaped channel between the siding and the ledger. To prevent these problems, consider one of five common methods for attaching a ledger. (See above.)

If you will be attaching to a flat surface (either siding or masonry), simply attach the ledger tightly against the house so that water cannot seep behind it. This is the simplest solution, and it works well if you can really squeeze the ledger tightly to the house. However, there is a good chance that your

DIY OPTIONS: LEDGER INSTALLATION

LEAK-PROOF DESIGN

WEATHERPROOF DESIGN

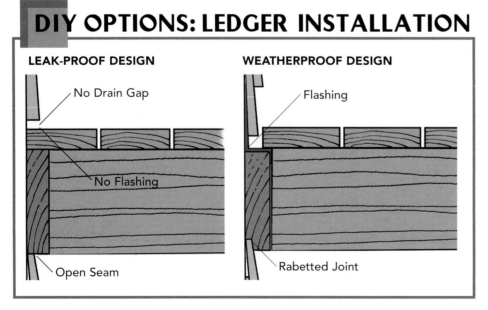

LEAK-PROOF DESIGN: No Drain Gap, No Flashing, Open Seam

WEATHERPROOF DESIGN: Flashing, Rabetted Joint

WEDGED ON CLAPBOARDS

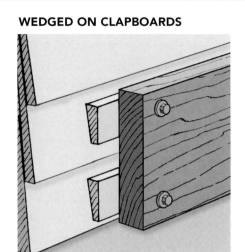

WASHER STAND-OFF

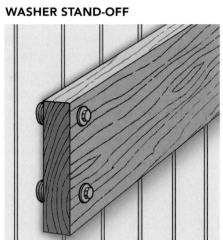

PLYWOOD STAND-OFF

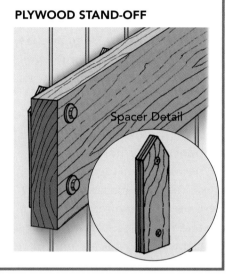

Spacer Detail

SMART TIP

LEDGER SETUP
You can tack joists to marks on the ledger and install hangers later or set hangers ahead of time.

ABOVE Deck height determines the size of the posts for a deck.

inspector will want a more water-resistant detail with flashing.

For joining a ledger to a wall with siding (either flat or beveled horizontal), cut out a section of siding, and fit the ledger into it. In this case, you need to provide flashing that keeps water out of the opening in the siding and forces it to run down the face of the ledger.

For stucco or masonry surfaces, cut a channel above the ledger where you can tuck in the upper edge of flashing.

If you are attaching the ledger to a surface with beveled horizontal siding, you can also take a piece or two of cedar siding of the same shape as the house siding, and install it upside down, thereby producing a plumb house surface. You can then install the ledger against this plumb

SMART TIP

LEDGER BOLTS

When you lag the ledger to the house frame, recess the washers and lag heads so

that they are flush with the ledger surface. This way it won't matter if one of the joist hangers falls in the same location. Drill the counterbore first. Then drill the pilot hole for the lag screw or bolt shank through the ledger. Be sure to check local codes about attaching ledgers.

surface, and either flash it or just let it be.

Against a flat surface, another option is to install several washers or shims of treated lumber behind the ledger at each lag screw, thereby providing a space between the ledger and the house. This way water runs easily between them and the ledger, and the house wall can dry out between rains.

All these methods have proved successful in various parts of the country. Opinions vary on which solution is best, and your inspector may favor one or another. If he orders you to do it a certain way, it's a good idea to just do what he says. The point is to avoid having moisture trapped against the ledger or the house framing for long periods.

PREPARING FOR THE LEDGER

If any of the following steps do not apply to the method of installing a ledger that you're using, just skip to the next step.

Locate the Ledger. It may sound like a good idea to have your deck surface level with your interior flooring, but if you do so, you will be inviting rain and snow to seep under your threshold and into your house. So plan to have a small step down. Even 1 inch will go a long way toward keeping your home drier in most regions. You can make a larger step, but it should be no more than the step in a standard interior stairway. Anything over 6 inches may feel awkward.

But the main consideration should be to locate the ledger where it will be easy for you to bolt it directly and securely into the house floor framing. This should be possible with a step down of only an inch or two. If the step is much greater, the ledger may line up against the house foundation instead of the floor framing. You can still attach it securely, but the job is much easier when you can bolt wood frame to wood frame.

To locate your ledger, measure down from the level of your house floor to the level of the decking. This is the amount of your step. Then add the decking thickness, which typically is 1½ inches for two-by decking. Mark this level, and extend it along the house wall to mark the length of the ledger. You want this line to be perfectly level. (See "Smart Tip" on page 158.) For purposes of drainage, you usually want the deck to slope away from the house rather than alongside it.

To make marks that will ensure that your ledger is level throughout its length, either use a water level or set your carpenter's level atop a straight board. (Because few boards are perfect, it is best to place the level near the center of the board.) You can also use one of the newer electronic levels. Some of these project a beam of light that is easy to mark.

Once you have made several marks, snap chalk lines between them, and double-check those lines for level.

Mark for Outer Joists, Fascia, and Decking. It helps to visualize all the dimensions of your finished deck, so mark for every lumber piece that will go up against your house. This means adding 1½ inches for the outside joist, plus ¾ inch for fascia (if any), plus the distance you plan to overhang your decking (if any) on each side of the deck.

Cut Out the Siding. If the ledger installation requires removing some of your siding, mark an outline for the cutout, taking into account everything that will fit into it: the ledger, the end of the outside joists, an extra ⅛ inch in width for the flashing (if any), and possibly the end of the fascia—but not the decking. Marking will be easier if you tack a piece of ledger-width material in place and draw a pencil line around it.

Cut the line with a circular saw. If you have aluminum or vinyl siding, follow manufacturer's directions; often it works best to reverse your circular saw blade when cutting these materials. Set the blade so that it cuts just through the siding and not much more. You will need to make a plunge cut to start. For wood siding, use a hammer and chisel to neatly finish the cutout at the corners. For vinyl siding, finish the corner cuts with a utility knife. Use snips for aluminum. When making a vertical cut across horizontal beveled siding, it may help to tack on a piece of 1x4 to provide a level surface on which your circular saw can rest.

Seal up the area you have just cut out with felt (tar paper) or house wrap so that no bare wood

sheathing is exposed.

Check for Straightness. Check the surface against which you will be placing the ledger by holding a string against its length. If, anywhere along the length, there is a gap of more than ¼ inch between the string and the wall, tack shims to the house so that when you attach the ledger it will be straight. You can also use a string with blocks to check the flatness of your ledger once it's installed. (See "Smart Tip" on page 158.) Remember that unless you cut every joist to fit (a job that you don't want to do), the front edge of your deck will follow the contours of your ledger.

Install Flashing. If you have cut out a section of siding, install flashing that is the same length as the cutout. (It will cover the top of the outside joists as well, so snip the front edge to make it fit

SMART TIP

FLOATING DECKS

Some decks don't have a ledger and aren't connected to the house, although they might look as though they are. An island deck, built right next to the house, gives the illusion of a standard deck but skips the ledger work and adds an extra girder near the house. Be sure to check local codes about floating decks.

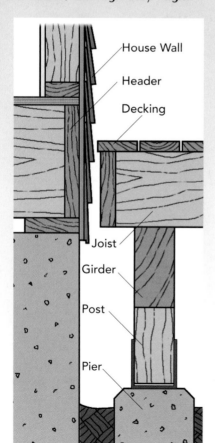

over them.) Tuck the flashing up under the siding. Before you slide the flashing in, make sure you have a clear path for it by prying the upper siding piece loose and removing all nails in the flashing's path. Handle the flashing carefully because it bends easily. Gently renail the siding back into position to hold the flashing in place.

For noncutouts with flashing, it is possible (but definitely not recommended) to attach the flashing to the house simply by first installing

SMART TIP

LEDGER CHECKS

You need to check for level, of course, but also for flatness against the wall. Do this using three blocks. Tack one at each end connected by a tightly drawn string. Use the third to check the margin between the string and the ledger. If the ledger is flat, the margin will be the same all along the ledger.

*Check the ledger for **level**.*

*Check the ledger for **flatness**.*

the ledger, then setting the flashing on it and gluing it in place with roofing cement or caulking. But this will leave you with a problem spot: the cement will probably come loose over time, and it will be difficult to repair because decking will be in the way. So it is best to find a way to tuck in the upper flange. For beveled horizontal siding or shingles, you may have to buy extra-wide flashing, depending on how far above your ledger the next piece of siding or row of shingles is located.

For stucco or masonry, buy or make flashing that has an extra bend so that a lip can be tucked straight into the side of the house. Using a masonry blade on your circular saw, cut a straight line into which the flashing can be inserted.

Depending on the hardness of your siding material, this may require several passes. Be sure to wear protective eyewear. Over stucco or masonry, it's often easier to put the flashing in place after the ledger is installed.

A variety of ready-made flashing is available. One of the most practical has a Z-shape that bends twice—once to slide up under the siding and once to cover the face of your ledger. This last, front-most portion of the flashing need not be wide as long as it is wide enough to keep water from wicking between the flashing and the top of the ledger. Remember that the joists will be smashed up against it, so it is best if the flashing comes down the ledger at a right angle to protect the horizontal surface of the ledger.

Cut and Mark the Ledger. Cut the ledger, which runs at one end of the joists and the header joist which runs at the other, to the same length. If your deck is not rectangular, they will not be be the same length, of course.

Because the ledger and header joist run parallel to each other, and the joists are perpendicular to them both, it makes sense to cut the header joist and ledger at the same time, and to mark them both for the joist locations before you install the ledger. After marking the tops, use a square to extend the lines down the faces of the ledger and header. Don't forget to make an X indicating on which side of the line the joists will be installed. (See "Smart Tip" on page 155.)

INSTALLING LEDGERS ON WOOD

TOOLS & MATERIALS
- Ledger board
- End joist
- Clamps
- Combination square
- Pencil
- Saw
- Flashing
- Drill and bits
- Props
- Ratchet wrench
- 4-in. lag screws

For the most secure connection, bolt through or lag into framing.

1 *Transfer the layout marks for the joists from the ledger to the end joist.*

2 *Predrill and countersink holes for fasteners. This will guarantee clearance for joist hangers later.*

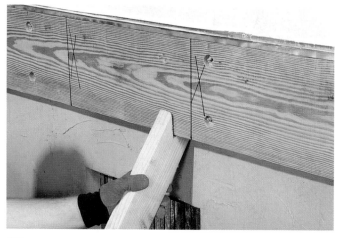

3 *Prop ledger into position, and drive lag screws with a ratchet, or install carriage bolts if possible.*

ATTACHING THE LEDGER

Whether you are attaching to wood, masonry, or stucco, it is important to fasten the ledger securely. Remember that the ledger bears a lot of weight. While about half of the entire deck load away from the house may bear on the main girder and support posts, the remaining load bears on the ledger. Without a beefy beam and a row of posts for support, the ledger must be strong enough to transfer the load to the house foundation. It is a critical connection.

Proof of its importance is found in the investigation of deck failures. Most of them occur because of a faulty connection at the ledger.

ATTACHING THE LEDGER TO WOOD FRAMING

Whether your wood-framed house is sided with wood, aluminum, vinyl, or stucco, you need to attach the ledger through the siding material into the wood framing. Attaching a ledger to a frame house at the level of the floor frame (or just below it to allow for a small step) is the safest approach. (See "Installing Ledgers on Wood," above.)

Depending on the direction of the floor framing, you are most likely to find one of two conditions. If the joists run parallel with the house wall, there will be a solid joist running the length of the deck. If the joists run perpendicular to the

INSTALLING LEDGERS ON STUCCO

TOOLS & MATERIALS
- Ledger
- Circular saw
- Clamps
- Combination square
- Pencil
- Saw
- Flashing for stucco
- Drill and bits
- Props
- Ratchet wrench
- 4-in. lag screws
- Scrap wood
- 1½-in. concrete or deck screws
- Caulk

For stucco over concrete, use lag shields in predrilled holes. For stucco over wood, use bolts.

1 Use a temporary guide board to cut a level line where the top edge of the flashing will fall.

2 Insert the flashing into the groove. Note the lip on top of the flashing.

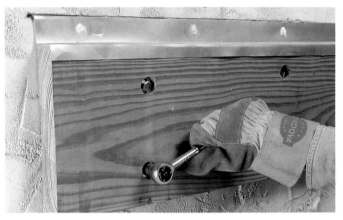

3 Predrill holes in stucco and in ledger. Fasten ledger to the house with lag screws.

house wall, you still should find solid material because the joists ends are covered with a rim joist, also called a belt or header joist.

If you are putting the ledger elsewhere on a frame house—for example, on a raised deck—you will be able to tie into the wall studs. In any case, you should verify the location of solid framing and be sure that your lags or bolts fall directly over them. You may get a tipoff from siding nails that are driven every 16 inches. But to be safe, you should strip off a piece of siding, a section of tar paper or house wrap underneath, and a section of sheathing if need be to be certain of the framing pattern.

Most codes allow you to use ⅜- or ½-inch lag screws. Select screws that are long enough to pass 1½ to 2 inches into the framing member.

PLACING RAISED-DECK

TOOLS & MATERIALS
- 2x4
- Level
- Pencil
- String
- Batter boards
- Posthole digger
- 4x4s
- Clamps
- Drill & bits
- Stakes & braces
- Sledge hammer
- 1½-in. screws

Ground contact can foster rot; use treated wood.

Use a washer for each to increase the strength at the lag head and to keep the head from digging into the wood. It's also wise to countersink all the lags (or bolts) so they will not be in the way when you install the joists and joist hangers.

If you have access to the framing inside, in a basement, for example, you may be able to use bolts instead of lags. This allows you to be absolutely certain of the connections, and to lock up the ledger with a bolt head and washer outside and a nut and washer inside.

If you have horizontal beveled siding and want to make a flat surface for your ledger, cut pieces of siding to the right width and length, and nail them in place. It's wise to brush some preservative on this piece. Always make provision for water draining down the house wall—for instance, with flashing or a spacer system. You don't want to create a water-trapping detail that fosters rot.

Position the ledger; check again for level; and drill pilot holes every 24 inches or according to code. Drill pilot holes for lags and clearance holes for bolts. Then install the fasteners, and be sure that they have locked into solid wood framing.

ATTACHING TO MASONRY

If you will be attaching to a concrete or masonry wall, drill your pilot holes through the ledger; hold it in place; and transfer the hole locations. Next, use a masonry bit to drill holes for lag

shields that are ¼ inch or so deeper than the length of the shields. You often need to back out the bit periodically to clear dust and avoid overheating.

Tap the lag shields in place. They should fit snugly, but you should not have to bang them into the hole. That could deform the shield and prevent the lag from fastening properly.

Then you can reposition the ledger and attach the lag screws and washers with a socket wrench. If you are using a standoff method with a drainage space between the ledger and the house, insert every lag screw into the ledger so that it pokes through ½ inch or so, and place the washers or lumber spacers on the screws.

POSITIONING THE POSTS

There are two basic ways to attach your posts—top and bottom. On the bottom, you can either sink posts into holes the way you might with fence posts and secure them with concrete, or you can set them on concrete piers. Local codes may specify one method over another, and that's the decision that counts. But using concrete piers generally provides more stability and durability. It's the way most houses are built, with a concrete footing and foundation to support the structure above. Concrete piers also keep the

FRAMING SUPPORT MEMBERS

POSTS

1 To locate the posts, start from a reference point on the house and plumb down.

2 Extend layout strings from plumb marks to batter boards. Mark the hole locations.

(Continued on page 162)

post a few inches above ground, which reduces the possibility of rot.

On the tops of your posts, you also have two basic choices. One is to let the post run long and bolt your girder and other beams to it. The other is to cut off the tops of the post so that they form level supports directly under the main girder. The latter method is the most common type of deck construction.

Both methods are strong. But the on-top method can be slightly more resistant to downward pressure on the deck, while the screwing or bolting method is better at keeping the main girder from twisting. The on-top method also may be quicker because it avoids a lot of drilling and fastening. However, it is less forgiving of mistakes because you must cut the top of posts accurately before you install the beam. And you can deal with the twisting problem, in part, by installing galvanized hardware that bridges the joint between the post and the girder.

Here is a rundown of the basic procedure for the most common and probably the most durable system.

GIRDER ON PIER-SUPPORTED POST

Check for Rough Length. In most situations you will cut the post to exact height later. But first make sure that every post will be tall enough. Use a line level, water level, or long piece of lumber with a level on top to find out how high each post needs to be. (It is best to slope your deck slightly down coming away from the house, but this measurement is too small to worry about at this point.) Give yourself at least a few extra inches, and you won't have to worry.

Locate and Attach Post Anchors. If you are using adjustable post anchors, now is the time to fine-tune their positions. Most hardware has a slot or some other way of making an adjustment. This way, if the threaded anchors fixed in the concrete piers are not exactly in line with each other, you can slide the post hardware one way or the other before fastening them in place.

The best way to do this is to confirm your measurements from the house wall, and double-check for square. Then string a line or snap a chalk line between the outermost piers. Center one post anchor (which may not be exactly centered relative to the anchor bolt), and tighten it in place. Most hardware has a platform inside the bracket, which keeps the post slightly elevated and out of standing water. Typically, you fasten down the base plate before inserting the platform. But you should follow the manufacturer's directions. Then repeat the process at the other end, and use your string line to make sure that any intermediate anchors fall into line.

Insert and Fasten the Posts. Make a square cut on the bottom of each post to be sure that it

PLACING RAISED-DECK POSTS (Continued from page 161)

3 Remove the strings, and start digging the hole. Dig below the frost line.

4 The type of footing that supports the post will be determined by the local building code.

seats firmly in the anchor. If you are not using pressure-treated lumber, even though that is the best policy on posts, it will help to flood the freshly cut end grain with wood preservative.

If the posts are short, they may stand by themselves in the hardware. But on most projects you'll need to attach a few temporary braces. You don't need to plumb the posts exactly at this point; just keep them roughly plumb and stable as you fasten the anchors.

The procedure may vary from one manufacturer to another, but a typical anchor has one open side (so you can slide in the post). When the post base is in position, you simply bend up that metal flap with a pliers. Then drive a few nails through the perforated holes in the hardware flaps to lock the post in place. Even though the post is roughly in place, you may want to wait until it is set and braced before driving all the nails. (See "Anchoring Posts," page 164.)

You don't want to pound away on the nails and possibly dislodge the anchor or, worse yet, crack the concrete pier. To guard against this, you can use the old carpentry trick of backing up the post with a heavy hammer as you nail on the other side. The extra weight, say, from a sledgehammer that you hold in one hand, absorbs a lot of the impact and keeps the post from shifting as you use a standard hammer in your other hand.

SMART TIP

PLUMBING POSTS
Plumbing posts can be challenging because you need to manage a level, a brace, and a

clamp at the same time. In most cases, you must adjust a pair of braces while adjusting the posts and the level. A handy tool called a post level clips onto the post and reads in both directions at once, so you can make adjustments and add braces with both hands free.

FRAMING SUPPORT MEMBERS

5 To brace the post, attach a 2x4 to a ground stake and clamp it to the post.

6 Brace the post in two places to keep it steady. Plumb the post.

ANCHORING POSTS

TOOLS & MATERIALS
- 4x4 post
- Sawhorses
- Square
- Circular Saw
- Post hardware
- Wrenches
- Hammer
- Nails

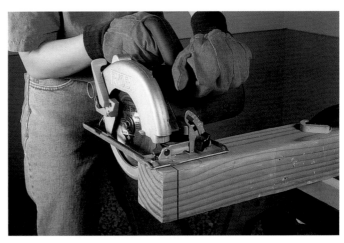

With piers and post anchors, wood stays off wet ground that can cause rot.

1 *Square off the bottom of the posts so that it seats securely in the post anchor.*

2 *Set the post in the anchor. Adjustable hardware provides some play in the anchor position.*

3 *Close the anchor around the post, and drive nails through the anchor into the post.*

SMART TIP

BRACING
Even short 4x4 posts for a deck girder near ground level need to be braced securely in two directions. Drive pointed stakes into the ground about 2 feet away from the post as shown. Attach a 2x4 to each stake, and extend it up the sides of the post at a 45-degree angle. Secure with clamps.

Plumb and Brace the Post. This job is easiest with two people because there is a lot to do at the same time. You need to release the temporary braces; fine-tune the plumb position of the post, checking and rechecking in two directions; and lock up the final position with a clamp before securing the braces.

Ideally, you can have one person check the level and, once the post is perfectly plumb, tell the other person to drive in a screw attaching the brace. Do this again for the other brace, and then recheck the first direction. Don't be surprised if you have to redo things once or twice. But once you have achieved perfect plumb, drive in more screws for stability—at least two for each attaching point. Then you can drive in the rest of the nails to hold the post anchor to the post.

If you are working solo, set up ground stakes and 2x4 braces at 90 degrees to each other. Drive a screw through the base of the 2x4 into the stake, pivot the brace onto the post at about a 45-degree angle, and secure it with a clamp. The idea is to use the clamp as your helper. Keep enough tension on the clamp to prevent the brace from falling, but not so much that you can't tap the post slightly one way or another as you make minor adjustments to bring the post plumb. When the post is plumb, tighten the brace; work on the other side; and finally lock the braces with several screws to hold it secure. Remove the clamps. (See "Smart Tip" on page 164.)

SMART TIP

POST ALTERNATIVES
The most common setup is a series of posts topped with a girder. But there are other options. For example, you can make a sandwich with the girder by attaching boards to opposite sides of a post. With the boards level, you can drill through the sandwich and bolt the components together.

In this design, you need to cut the post flush with the tops of the boards. Another approach is to let the post run long. You can use the extension of several feet to support other parts of the deck, such as railings and built-in benches.

FRAMING SUPPORT MEMBERS

DIY OPTIONS: Y-BRACING

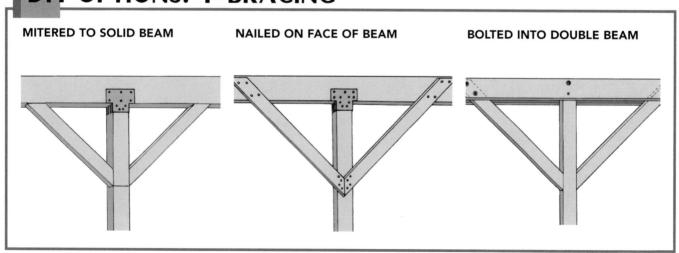

MITERED TO SOLID BEAM

NAILED ON FACE OF BEAM

BOLTED INTO DOUBLE BEAM

ESTABLISHING POST HEIGHT

TOOLS & MATERIALS

- 2x4
- 4-ft. level
- Joist & girder stock
- Pencil
- Combination square
- Circular saw
- Post-cap hardware
- Drill & bits
- 1¼-in. deck screws or 8d nails
- Hammer

Few homeowners have levels long enough to span from the house to the posts. Extend your 4-ft. level by placing it on top of a straight board.

1 Use a straight 2x4 and level to mark the elevation of the ledger on the posts.

2 Use a section of joist stock to measure down from the mark to find the bottom edge of the joist.

3 Using girder stock, measure down to find the bottom of the girder. This will be the top of the posts.

4 Mark a cutline with a square. Use a circular saw to cut the posts. You will need to make two passes.

5 Install the post caps to each post, and secure with screws or nails. Predrill nailholes.

MAKING AND INSTALLING GIRDERS

There are several things to consider when you choose the main girder for your deck. Sometimes one characteristic outweighs all others. For example, if it will be difficult to dig through rocky soil on your site, you may want the largest possible girder and only two piers. More often, several factors go into the final decision about how big and what kind of girder to use.

Girder Size. First, think about space, particularly the amount of vertical room that the girder and joists will use together. If your deck is built close to the ground, you may not have room to put a large girder on top of posts with a layer of joists on top of it. If you need to save room, it can make sense to use more posts and a smaller girder or to bolt the girder to the posts.

Another option is to use the girder itself as the header joist. You might need a large beam made of several 2x12s, for example. But instead of resting the joists on top of it, you can use framing hardware and butt the joists into its side. This way the girder is at the same level as the joists. You'll save almost a foot of vertical space.

Girder Appearance. Next think about whether the girder will be visible, and if so, what it will look like next to a stairway or an entrance to the house. No matter what type of wood you use, an evenly spaced layout and nicely installed bolts on a built-up beam can look good. A massive timber can have a classy yet rustic look. But availability comes into play. It may be that you can't get a good-looking 4x8, for instance.

But you have many ways to dress up a girder. You can cut a 45-degree angle off the bottom corners to create a floating effect or chamfer or rout the edges in a decorative detail. You can coat the lumber with stain to dress up the appearance of treated wood or cover the rough construction lumber altogether with a finished fascia board.

If the girder needs bracing but you don't want to use galvanized hardware in an exposed location, you can add 2x4s or 2x6s to the sides of the support posts and extend them up along the sides of the girder. This makes a neat structural sandwich that you can lock up with bolts.

Girder Weight. Lastly, consider weight. A 16-foot length of treated southern yellow pine 4x12 can be a real back-breaker. And things can get downright dangerous if you have to lift the girder high in the air. So in some cases, it is simply easier and safer to use a built-up beam.

TYPES OF GIRDERS

You can use several types of beams as a main support girder under deck joists. Here is a run-down of some of the most common types.

MAKING AND SETTING A BUILT-UP GIRDER

TOOLS & MATERIALS
- Girder stock
- Clamps
- 10d nails
- Hammer
- Level
- 2x4 braces
- Stakes
- Drill & bits
- 1¼-in. deck screws

Find the crowns on your lumber, and assemble the girder with the crowns up.

1 Sight down the stock and locate the crown. Place the crowns side by side.

(Continued on page 168)

Solid. This is a beam made of a solid piece of four-by lumber, generally set on top of 4x4 posts. This has a classic, clean look, but there is little leeway for correcting mistakes, and it can be difficult to find a straight, good-looking piece of four-by lumber.

Built-Up. This is a beam made of two two-bys (photos below), sometimes with spacers sandwiched between (photos opposite). (Before you add spacers, be sure to check the thickness of the posts on which the girder will sit. With pressure-treated wood, actual sizes are sometimes a bit smaller than the sizes of wood that is not treated.) This built-up assembly can actually be stronger than a solid-timber beam and is usually less expensive. But it does take some extra time to fabricate. Once you assemble the pieces, it may be just as heavy and difficult to maneuver as a conventional solid beam.

Spaced. This is another two-part beam consisting of two pieces of two-by lumber attached to opposing sides of the posts. (See "Making Spaced Girders," page 170.) Though time-consuming to build, this beam may be best for the do-it-yourselfer because it involves little heavy lifting and is easily correctable during construction.

Laminated. This is likely to be a special-order item because the beam is made of many two-by boards that have been joined together with screws or nails and glue. You can build one

yourself, of course. But this option is best reserved for special load conditions where you need a very large girder that is easier to assemble board by board than to buy in one piece.

There are other types of manufactured beams—for example, large timbers made from interwoven strips of wood. Because they are built and not grown, you can order one in almost any size.

Let-In. This is a beam set into notches in a post. The system of letting-in the beam, called dapping, is often used on rough structures such as log and pole houses. It is rarely used in modern deck construction because notching adds some support to the beam but takes away some from the post. To use this method you ought to be using 6x6s for posts. Also, the notches must be cut cleanly and accurately, with no gaps, or you will be inviting water to seep into newly cut lumber, which is always a bad idea.

GIRDER LOCATIONS

Joists can either rest on top of a girder (usually the simplest solution because you can hide the beam by cantilevering the deck) or be attached to the side of the girder with joist hangers. All girder types discussed above can accommodate either method. Both attachment approaches will meet codes if you use large enough lumber with the proper spacing.

MAKING AND SETTING A BUILT-UP GIRDER

2 Screw or nail the boards together; use groups of 3 fasteners 12 in. on center.

3 Put the girder in the posts caps crown side up. You may need a helper in some cases.

PACKING OUT GIRDERS

TOOLS & MATERIALS
- Girder stock
- ½-in. treated spacers
- Clamps
- 10d nails
- Hammer

Some codes require girders to be the same thickness as a 4x4 post.

1 Cut spacers from treated wood. Use treated lumber even if the girders are not treated.

2 Tack the spacers to one side of one girder. Set the spacers 16 in. on center.

3 Place the other board on top to create a spacer sandwich. Secure with 10d nails.

(Continued from page 167)

4 Plumb the girder. Braces help keep the posts from shifting.

5 Secure the girder with a series of braces. Drive screws through the post caps into the girder.

FRAMING SUPPORT MEMBERS

MAKING SPACED GIRDERS

TOOLS & MATERIALS
- Level
- Braces
- Stakes
- Clamps
- Drill & bits
- 2-in. screws
- 7-in. carriage bolts
- Washer
- Rachet wrench
- Handsaw

A sandwich girder can be easier to make than a built-up one.

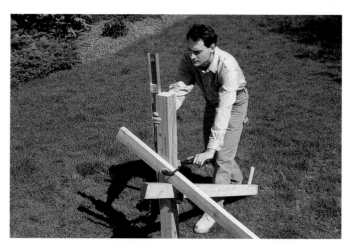

1 Start with plumb posts. Use braces and a level to make sure the posts are plumb.

3 Drill pilot holes through the girder stock and the posts about 1 in. from each edge.

4 Insert carriage bolts (check with building department for bolt diameter). Use washers under nut and bolt.

Attaching to the Top. Where joists cross the top of a girder, you can space them out on your layout lines and tack them in place with a few toenails. This keeps them from shifting, although being attached to a ledger, header, and bridging makes it difficult for them to shift at all.

But there are small pieces of hardware (galvanized straps with a twisted shape) that you can use to tack the joist to the girder without toenails. In some areas, your building department may require these tie-downs to help resist special loads.

Attaching to the Side. By attaching joists to the side of the girder, you can run the joists at the same level as the girder. In fact, the girder takes the place of the header joist and so will be cut to exact length and marked for joists in conjunction with the ledger. As always, make sure the girder is crown side up when you mark for the joists. All beams have a tendency to sag when they are loaded, and installing the crowns up provides some extra resistance to sagging.

GIRDER ASSEMBLY
You can use lag screws and washers to assemble the components of a girder, or predrill and bolt all the way through. But most carpenters simply nail them, and reserve lags and bolts for attaching the ledger and connecting sandwich-style girders to posts.

2 *Use props and clamps to hold the girder stock in position as shown. Level the boards.*

5 *Use a handsaw to trim the posts. The top of the post should be flush with the girder.*

Some inspectors will look closely enough at your work to see how many fasteners you're using for a particular job. In most cases, if you drive nails with a hammer (or screws with a drill-driver), you'll be fine with rows of three fasteners about 12 inches apart. For even more strength, you can flip over the girder and install some fasteners through the other face as well.

Be sure to use nails or screws that penetrate all the components without poking through on the other side. For example, you could use 8d (2½-in.) nails on a basic two-piece girder that is three inches wide. [Some carpenters use 10d (3 in.) nails and drive them at a slight angle to keep them from protruding.]

DIY OPTIONS: CONNECTORS

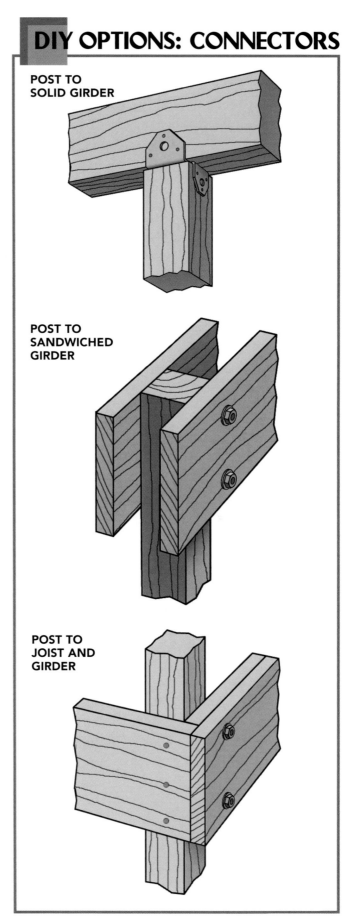

POST TO SOLID GIRDER

POST TO SANDWICHED GIRDER

POST TO JOIST AND GIRDER

FRAMING SUPPORT MEMBERS

INSTALLING A GIRDER

The following is the basic sequence you can use to place your main girder in the right position.

Mark the Corner Posts. Use a level and a long, straight piece of lumber, a line level, or a water level to mark the location of the girder on the posts. It's wise to mark the two corner posts first, and check and double-check your marks from the ledger and between the posts themselves. Once the corner posts are marked, you can string a line between them to mark any other posts in line under the girder.

You want to find the spot on the post that is level with the top of the ledger. If you want the deck to slope slightly for drainage, measure down from that mark $\frac{1}{16}$ inch for every foot of joist travel. But most builders do this only on decks with closed surfaces, for example, tongue-and-groove boards you might be more likely to use on a porch floor. Because typical decks have spaces between the boards, there is more than enough area for water to drain.

From the mark that indicates where the tops of the joists will be, measure down the depth of a joist to find the top of the girder. Follow these steps on both corner posts, and check the post marks for level.

If you plan to butt the joists into the main girder, remember not to make the last measurement. When you level across from the top of the ledger, you will be marking the tops of the joists and the top of the girder at the same time.

Mark the rest of the posts. Use a chalk line to extend lines between the marks you made on the corner posts. You might double-check the line marks with a level to be sure you will be cutting in the right place.

In case of a mistake, you can add a shim to the top of a post. But if you take the extra time to verify your level lines, shimming the post should not be necessary.

Once you are certain of the marks, use a square to extend lines onto all the faces of your posts. You'll need these when you cut because most circular saws can't cut deeply enough to go through a 4x4 post in one pass. (See "Smart Tip" on page 125.)

Cut Off the Posts. To make your cuts safely and accurately, be sure that the posts are securely braced. Double-check your circular saw to make sure it cuts at a perfect right angle.

Because this is an unusual cut and you have to hold the saw sideways, get into a comfortable position with solid footing. Try to keep the same margin along the marked lines—for example, leaving the pencil line on and cutting just up to it. This will help you get a flat surface on the post even though you need to make two passes.

Cutting the Girder. If the girder will be low to the ground, you don't want to let the piece run long and cut it in place. You should probably recheck your measurements. But at this point your posts should be locked in proper plumb position in a line that is squared up with the ledger on the house.

If you are using a spaced-type beam and plan to build it up in pieces along several posts, be sure that the splices will fall over the centers of the posts. You'll need to be careful making these connections. Predrilling is essential to avoid splitting the girder pieces and the post.

SMART TIP

CLAMPING CROWNS

While most structural lumber has a crown, or slight hump along one edge, it's not likely that you will find two with exactly the same curved shape. Even if you nail together a girder with both crowns up, one board may be a little higher than the other. To bring the top edges into alignment and provide a uniform base for the joists, you can drive a few toenails. But you are likely to get better results with a

clamp. Set one end on the low board, the other end on the high board, and tighten to bring the two boards into line.

DIY OPTIONS: GIRDER SPANS

Southern pine or Douglas fir		
Size of girder	With joists spanning up to	Girder can span up to
4x6	6'	6'
4x8	6'	8'
4x8	8'	7'
4x8	10'	6'
4x10	6'	10'
4x10	8'	8'
4x10	10'	7'
4x10	12'	7'
4x10	14'	6'
4x10	16'	6'
4x12	6'	11'
4x12	8'	10'
4x12	10'	9'
4x12	12'	8'
4x12	14'	7'

Hem-Fir		
Size of girder	With joists spanning up to	Girder can span up to
4x6	6'	6'
4x8	6'	7'
4x8	8'	6'
4x10	6'	9'
4x10	8'	7'
4x10	10'	6'
4x10	12'	6'
4x12	6'	10'
4x12	8'	9'
4x12	10'	7'
4x12	12'	7'
4x12	14'	6'

Redwood, Ponderosa pine, Western cedar		
Size of girder	With joists spanning up to	Girder can span up to
4x8	6'	7'
4x8	8'	6'
4x10	6'	8'
4x10	8'	7'
4x10	10'	6'
4x10	12'	6'
4x12	6'	10'
4x12	8'	8'
4x12	10'	7'
4x12	12'	6'
4x12	14'	6'

Note: Be sure to check allowable spans between supports and all lumber requirements with your local building department.

FRAMING SUPPORT MEMBERS

If you need to make multiple splices on your girder, plan the lumber lengths so that you splice one side of the girder on one post and the other side on another.

Attach the Girder. If you have a heavy girder to set, arrange for plenty of help and be sure that any ladders you use are stable. There is an extra step you can take to be sure that the girder won't topple off your posts during assembly.

The idea is to temporarily but securely screw a piece of 2x4 or 2x6, called a scab, onto the corner posts with at least 6 inches projecting past the top. As you get the girder into position, it will bear down on the posts, of course, and now it won't tip because of the scab. You can have a clamp at the ready and use it to pin the girder to

the scab as soon as you set the heavy timber in place. This approach can help even if you install galvanized hardware connectors on the posts. This hardware may be required by local codes unless you install permanent wooden cleats or braces to keep the girder from tipping.

A typical connector has two flanges that fit over the post, and two that rise up around the girder. When the timber is in place, you can tack through perforated holes in the fastener to lock the pieces together.

If you prefer to use wooden cleats, you can clad opposing sides of your 4x4 posts with 2x6s. If you extend them all the way down to the piers, you will end up with a very strong built-up post, plus a reinforced pocket past the top of the post.

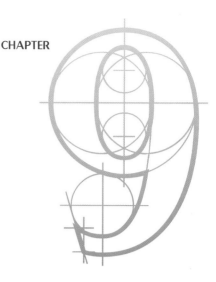

DECK
JOISTS

Once you have the ledger and girder in place, the deck's joists should go down smoothly. Install a solid layer of joists, and the decking that rides across them will be solid underfoot. You may need to coax a few slightly twisted timbers into place to be sure the frame is square and true.

MODULAR LAYOUTS

Every part of a deck needs a careful layout, of course. But when it comes time to plan out and install the joists, you need to be sure to account for the decking that will cover them. Because you will most likely be using lumber in stock lengths, generally in 2-foot multiples, you want to make a modular layout that makes the most efficient use of the materials you buy.

Modular framing layouts for most decks (and for most house frames), work in multiples of 16 inches. That's the distance from the centerline of one joist to the centerline of the next one in line. Two units make 32 inches, and three make 48 inches, which is another basic building block of construction that matches the width of drywall panels, plywood, and other sheet materials. Multiply out that 48-inch unit, and you'll come up with many of the standard sizes of joists.

As a practical matter, if you didn't maintain the 16-inch module, there wouldn't be a joist where you needed one at the end of a deck board. You would wind up wasting a lot of wood.

Spacing the Supports. In most locations, a long deck board gets the support of a full joist everywhere except at the ends, where two boards meet and have to share a joist. That's why the modular layout is from center to center—so that one-half of the joist width supports the edge of the previous board and the other half supports the next one in line.

But there is a glitch in the system that can trip up novice do-it-yourselfers. Because you start the layout at one edge of the deck and fully cover that first joist, you have to shorten the overall layout by ¾ of an inch, or one half the thickness of a joist. If you don't, the leading end of the board will fall short of a joist.

Layout Measurements. Here's the math: a joist is 1½ inches thick; from the center of one to another you want 16 inches, which leaves a 14½-inch space, or bay, between joists—the 16 inches minus half a joist (¾ inch) on each side.

To start the layout correctly, just shorten everything by one-half a joist, which makes the first bay about 13¾ inches across. From then on, you can step ahead in 14½-inch blocks.

JOIST SPANS

Size	Lumber	Spacing	Span
2x6	S. pine or D. fir	12" O.C.	10'4"
2x6	S. pine or D. fir	16" O.C.	9'5"
2x6	S. pine or D. fir	24" O.C.	7'10"
2x6	Hem-fir	12" O.C.	9'2"
2x6	Hem-fir	16" O.C.	8'4"
2x6	Hem-fir	24" O.C.	7'3"
2x6	Redwood	12" O.C.	8'10"
2x6	Redwood	16" O.C.	8'
2x6	Redwood	24" O.C.	7'
2x8	S. pine or D. fir	12" O.C.	13'8"
2x8	S. pine or D. fir	16" O.C	12'5"
2x8	S. pine or D. fir	24" O.C.	10'2"
2x8	Hem-fir	12" O.C.	12'1"
2x8	Hem-fir	16" O.C.	10'11"
2x8	Hem-fir	24" O.C.	9'6"
2x8	Redwood	12" O.C.	11'8"
2x8	Redwood	16" O.C.	10'7"
2x8	Redwood	24" O.C.	8'10"
2x10	S. pine or D. fir	12" O.C.	17'5"
2x10	S. pine or D. fir	16" O.C.	15'5"
2x10	S. pine or D. fir	24" O.C.	12'7"
2x10	Hem-fir	12"O.C	15'4"
2x10	Hem-fir	16" O.C.	14'
2x10	Hem-fir	24" O.C.	11'7"
2x10	Redwood	12" O.C.	14'10"
2x10	Redwood	16" O.C.	13'3"
2x10	Redwood	24" O.C.	10'10"

Maximum length of joists between beams and/or ledger
(S. pine is southern pine; D. fir is Douglas fir.)
Note: *Be sure to check allowable spans between supports and all lumber requirements with your local building department.*

OPPOSITE **No matter how beautiful the finished project looks, all well-built decks start with a carefully constructed post, girder, and joist support system.**

SMART TIP

JOIST ASSISTS

When large joists are too heavy to set yourself, this add-on makes the job possible. Temporarily screw on a strip of wood that overhangs the joist. When you wrestle the joist into place, the strip rests on the ledger and carries the weight.

SAFETY

CARRYING EXTRA LOADS

While a fiberglass or acrylic tub might be light enough to pick up by yourself, a large spa or hot tub can contain hundreds of gallons of water and weigh 1,000 pounds or more. Check the manufacturer's installation specs and the local building department to be sure that you adequately support this kind of heavy-duty, concentrated load. You may be able to double up the adjacent joists. But you may need to add secondary posts and girders to carry the extra weight.

USING PRACTICAL TOOLS

Up to this point on a typical deck project, there has been no production work where you have to turn out dozens of members. You had to set a few posts and hammer some nails, of course. But setting joists is different. On most decks there are a lot of them, which means creating a DIY version of contractor-style production work when it comes to cutting and fastening them in place.

Saws. A handsaw will work, naturally, and you will need one to finish some cuts. But a circular saw is easier and faster. A 7¼-inch model is good for overall framing work. Smaller saws can't cut through a 2x4 in one pass, and larger ones are unwieldy. Use a combination blade for cutting with and across the grain—a blade with about 24 teeth is included with many saws when you buy them.

Hammers. With hammers, the reverse is true for most people: the hand-powered version works best. Air-power is nice but impractical for most do-it-yourselfers, who are better off using a tool with which they are familiar.

In most cases, a 16-ounce claw hammer is the right choice. It's maneuverable in tight spaces and light enough to use for more than a few minutes. Heavier hammers pack more punch—on mishits as well as on nails—but a big hammer with a straight ripping claw can be cumbersome and wear you out if you're not used to hammer-

ing. Try handles of fiberglass or steel with special inserts and grip rings and rubber sleeves—whatever feels best.

Even many contractors who routinely use pneumatic tools also carry the old-fashioned version.

Drill-Drivers. Another option is using a drill-driver to fasten your deck with screws instead of nails, at least in most places. A compact cordless model can really help in tight spots where you don't have enough room to swing a hammer. Also, screws have more holding power than nails.

You can fit the drill with a screwdriving bit, or a boring bit to drill pilot holes for screws if you have trouble driving them. One way to simplify the operation and get a taste of production work is to use a quick-change accessory. It fastens into the chuck of the drill and has a snap-in and snap-out sleeve that accepts boring bits and screwing bits. You don't have to loosen the chuck and refit a new bit every time you switch from drilling pilot holes to driving screws.

Another handy option is an extension sleeve that fastens into the chuck around a screwdriving bit. The idea is to fit the screwhead onto the driving head of the bit, then slip the sleeve over the screw so that you can drive it in a straight line. The little gadget keeps the bit from jumping off the screw—and maybe onto your finger. There are also drill attachments that feed strips of screws into a standard drill so that you don't have to reload. But the preloaded strips are much more expensive than buying screws by the box.

FRAMING HARDWARE

Before you get started installing your joists, it's also wise to plan on using framing hardware as an assist to your nails at each end of each board. (Many types of galvanized fasteners help tie together many other framing connections as well.)

Most framing connections are held together with nails. They do a good job where you can drive them through the face of one board into the end grain of another. Nails have much less holding power when toenailed—driven at a steep angle

SETTING THE INNER JOIST

TOOLS & MATERIALS

- Joist material
- Gloves
- Hammer
- 16d galvanized nails
- Framing square
- Corner bracket
- Joist-hanger nails
- Twist fasteners

On decks that tuck into a corner, you need only one ledger, generally on the long side of the deck. The inner joist might look like a ledger from a distance, but it actually is the first joist and is not attached to the house.

1 When you set the first joist in place, sight down its length to find the crown. Install it crown side up.

2 Tack the edge of the joist to the ledger by toenailing the two together.

3 Make sure the corner is square. There should be about 1 in. of space between the joist and house.

4 Because you won't be able to reach both sides of the joist, secure it in place with a corner bracket.

5 To provide added strength, nail on a twist fastener where the joist crosses the main girder.

ABOVE A simple deck becomes an intimate seating area in this garden. Even simple designs require a good support system.

through the side of one board into another.

On new framing work, of course, most timbers can be face-nailed. But there will be some tight spots where you may have to toenail. That's okay to tack a joist in position, but to make a secure connection that bears up under loads, it pays to rely on framing hardware. You'll probably find that the local building department will insist on fasteners in addition to nails

The most common piece is a U-shaped metal bracket that fits around the end of a joist where it butts up against a second board. On the sides of the U-shape are flanges, perforated for nailing like the rest of the fixture.

You can install the hardware where you need

SMART TIP

STRAIGHTENING JOISTS

Given the conditon of lumber today, it's likely that you will get a few twisted timbers in a load of deck joists. You may be able to return the worst of them. But there will be some twists and turns that won't line up with your square layout lines. To get rid of a small twist, secure a clamp near the end, and use the handle for leverage. This is not what clamps are made for, but it works. To increase your leverage, use several clamps to attach a 2x4, and use it as the handle.

A twisted joist won't square up.

Pulling on a clamp can fix a twist.

SETTING THE OUTER JOIST

TOOLS & MATERIALS
- Joist material
- Measuring tape
- Pencil
- Framing square
- Circular saw
- Hammer
- 16d nails
- Corner bracket & nails

It's important to have a good, clean, square cut on the outer joist—if only because it will probably be the most prominent on the deck.

3 Cut the outer joist using a circular saw. This is usually a prominent area, so make a clean cut.

to nail a connection; then fit the joist into the bracket. If you're not sure exactly where the joist will go, toenail it temporarily, and then fit the bracket around the joint. Once you face-nail through the bracket into the first board and through the flanges into the second board, the connection won't be able to shift.

SPECIAL CASES

Some decks may have to step over an existing set of concrete steps or change levels to accommodate a sloping yard. (See "Changing Levels," page 188.)

Demolishing concrete steps with a sledgehammer and hauling away the rubble is a lot of work. As long as the top step is lower than the top of the deck joists, it's usually easier to leave the steps in place and frame around them. Before you do, be sure that you see no evidence that the steps have heaved due to an improper footing.

If the concrete is sound, stop the ledger at both sides of the steps. Treat the end grain of the ledger board with water repelant before setting it in place. Notch the joists to fit over the top step and rest on the second step. If necessary, insert cedar shims between the joists and second step. Bridge between the joists. (See "Framing Over Steps," page 182.)

DECK JOISTS

1 *Measure out from the girder to determine the amount of overhang.*

2 *Use a framing square to draw a cut line on the joist. Leave girder and post braces in place.*

4 *Before nailing, make sure the deck frame is square and the two outside joists are equal.*

5 *Drive a toenail through the joist into the girder. Reinforce this with a twist fastener.*

Framing Over Steps

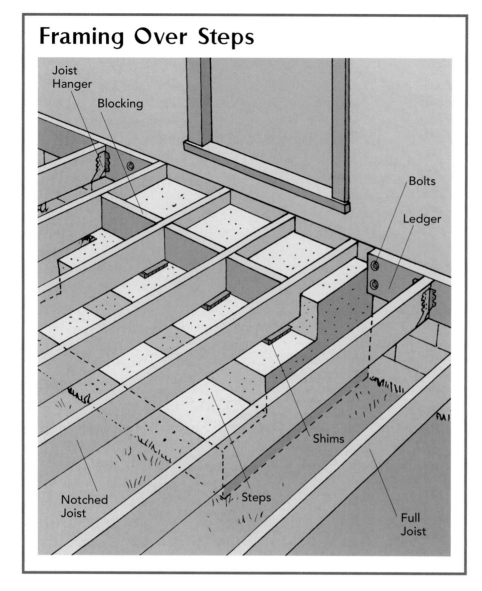

Joist Hanger
Blocking
Bolts
Ledger
Shims
Notched Joist
Steps
Full Joist

INSTALLING JOISTS

There are many ways you can go about the process. But one of the most basic is to install the innermost and outermost joists first, square up the overall areas, and fill in the rest of the joists. Once the boundaries are established, the bulk of the joists will go in quickly. (See "Setting the Inner Joist," page 179 and "Setting the Outer Joist," page 180.)

Joists are usually attached to the ledger on one end. There is a joist or a beam on the other end. Where it is possible—at the header joist, for example—you can attach the joists by face-nailing, that is, by nailing through the face of the header into the end grain of the joists. Use 3-inch deck screws or 16d galvanized nails, three

per joint. But joist hangers are preferred, and probably required, in all locations by building departments.

Build the Box. It is usually easiest to start by assembling the outside members into a box. Assemble these carefully because they will probably be the most visible. Predrill for all screws or nails that come near the end of a board. If your outside joists sit on top of the beam, attach them flush to the ends of the beam. At the corners, attach the header and outside joists together with 16d galvanized nails or 3-inch deck screws driven through pilot holes. Reinforce these joints with angle brackets attached to the joists with 1¼-inch deck screws.

Remember that stock-sized lumber generally does not have a square cut at each end. You also may find some rough spots or cracks that can be trimmed away to create tight joints at the critical corners of the basic box.

Install Joist Hangers. You can install each joist and joist hanger as shown in "Setting Joists," opposite, or you can install all of the hangers and then go back and install the joists.

Take a short block of joist material, and hold it in place: it should touch the line and cover the X, but most importantly, its top edge must be flush with the top of the ledger or header. Slide the joist hanger up against it so that it touches on one side only. There are pointed tabs on the hanger; pound them in, and they may hold the hanger in place. Drive two nails in to hold the hanger in place. Double-check to make sure the block is still accurately in place, then close the hanger around it and fasten the other side with the recommended number of hanger nails.

At the inside corners of your box, install angle

SETTING JOISTS

TOOLS & MATERIALS

- Joists
- Square
- Pencil
- Gloves
- Horses and saw
- Hammer
- Scrap wood
- Joist hangers
- Twist fasteners
- Measuring tape
- 1x4 brace

Make the joists and ledger flush; then install joist hangers.

1 Make a square cut on the ledger-end of the joists. Allow the other end to run long for now.

2 To help support the joist, nail a strip of wood with a small overhang to the joist.

3 Slip the joist hanger around the joist. Check for level and drive nails through the joist hanger.

4 For added stability, add a twist fastener where the joist crosses the girder.

5 Copy ledger layout lines to a brace. Tack to joist at midspan, bringing joists to your marks.

DECK JOISTS

TRIMMING JOISTS

TOOLS & MATERIALS
- Measuring tape
- Pencil
- Chalk-line box
- Framing square
- Circular saw

Snap a line, and the cut joists will form a dead-straight line.

1 Measure out from the ledger on each of the end joists. Mark the top of the end joists.

brackets. You can make your own angle brackets by cutting standard joist hangers with aviation snips.

Slide the Joists in Place. The joist ends must butt tightly against the ledger or header at all points. So before you measure for cutting the joists, be sure that the end you are measuring from is cut square. (Sometimes the lumberyard will give you ten that are square-cut and one that isn't, so look at them all.) Cut the joists to length.

Right now you're probably itching to make some real, visible progress in a hurry. But at this point it's a very good idea to take a little time first to seal the open grain of the cut ends with some sealer/preservative.

Install each joist crown-side-up. This is a two-person operation. If things are tight, you may have to slide both ends down at the same time. A little pounding is fine, but if a joist is so tight that it starts to bend, take it out; measure again; and recut it.

If you have the kind of flashing that makes a 90-degree turn to cover the face of the ledger, just set the joist against the turned edge. If your flashing makes only a slight downward turn, you could tuck the joists under the leading edge. But don't dislodge the metal (or tear it) by bending the flashing up as you install joists.

Finish Fastening. Eyeball the framing to see that everything looks straight and parallel. Finish installing the screws or nails in the joist hangers—put one in every hole. Where joists rest on a beam, toenail or drive a screw to minimize twisting. Hurricane ties provide extra hold-down strength. Although they are not generally required by code, those building in hurricane-prone areas should check the requirements.

BRACING

Decks that are raised above the ground—more than 4 feet for 4x4 posts; more than 8 feet for 6x6 posts—need extra lateral support to keep them from swaying. An on-top solid girder has less lateral strength than a bolted-on girder and may need bracing even if it is lower.

If you will be installing solid skirting (siding panels that enclose your deck below the deck surface), that will provide a good deal of lateral support and can take the place of bracing. Lattice skirting, however, is much less effective. Guidelines on bracing vary greatly from area to area, so check with your inspector if you think you may need it. In most cases, bracing can be added after the deck is built.

Bracing can add a classic, handcrafted look, and for less work than you might think. The only tricks are making accurate 45-degree cuts and

2 Line up the chalk line; the string should touch each joist. Snap the line.

3 Draw a cutting line with a framing square. Trim each joist using a circular saw.

making sure that the braces are in symmetrical relation to each other and are exactly the same size, for a uniform look.

Y Bracing. In most cases, simple Y bracing is sufficient. To brace a solid girder on top of a post, cut pieces of post material (4x4 or 6x6) to go under the girder and against the sides of the post, or use 2x4s or 2x6s and attach them to the face of the post and girder. For girders attached to opposing sides of a post, sandwich the braces between the girders, and secure them using lag screws, bolts, or carriage bolts.

Other Bracing Patterns. Larger projects may require more-elaborate bracing patterns. These are all best done with 2x4s or 2x6s on the face of the post and girder. When building these sorts of structures, first make marks on the posts and girders; then hold up the braces for marking rather than using a measuring tape.

Braces that will span 6 feet or less can be made of 2x4s; for longer spans, use 2x6s. Consider traffic patterns when deciding on your bracing. If you need to walk under the deck, a simple Y may be the best way to go; if you need more elaborate bracing, you

may be able to leave one section unbraced if you really beef up the other sections.

RAISED DECKS

If you are building a deck that's 8 feet or more above the ground, most of the layout will be the same, but your work methods might differ dramatically. Most operations will take twice as long to perform, as you spend lots of time wrestling with ladders, carrying things up and down, and being extra careful.

Decking, ledgers, joists, and girders have all the same requirements as decks built low to the ground.

However, there are a few key differences that

SMART TIP

REMOVING BRACES
As the deck takes shape and the job progresses, it's natural to want to remove the hodgepodge of braces and clean up the working area. Resist the temptation. On the 4x4 support posts, for example, it's wise to wait until they are completely locked in their final position by the main girder and joists.

BELT NAILING

When you box in the free ends of the joists, you may find that some are a little high or a little low, even though they all sit on the same girder. Help bring them into line by working with a helper who can raise or lower the free end of the belt as you work down the row. Even a small amount of leverage will help you align the tops of the opposing timbers. And the tops need to be flush for your decking to

lie flat. You will lose leverage as you connect more joists, but this trick can save you some planing or trimming work.

you should take into account. For example, decks near the ground may not need a railing, which could alter your plans for post and joist placement. You should check with the local building department to be sure, but decks within 30 inches of the ground often do not require railings to prevent falls. (Of course, you may want them for looks in any case.)

A deck raised high off the ground also may require a more substantial system of post supports. You might need to use 6x6s instead of the standard 4x4s. That will require adjustments in your footings and post hardware. To prevent shifting, you also may need lateral bracing, such as an X-pattern of 2x4s or 2x6s, that ties together several long posts.

Bracing the Posts. Generally, concrete piers that extend below the local frost line offer the most solid and durable support for deck posts. And with this system, the posts sit a couple to several inches aboveground (locked in place with galvanized hardware), which basically eliminates the possibility of rot due to ground contact. (See "Anchoring Posts," page 164.)

Use 2x4s or even 2x6s for temporary bracing. Pound the stakes deep into the ground. If you don't have a high stepladder, it will make building the deck much easier if you can confidently lean your ladder against a temporarily braced post—something you will have to do when you cut the posts to height, when you install the girder, and when you begin the framing. You may even want to use four rather than two braces.

If your inspector will allow it, wait until the framing or even the entire deck is completed before pouring the concrete around the posts. This will make your footing stronger because it will not get banged around during the construction process, which could loosen the concrete's bond with the post or with the earth. Also, doing it this way gives you the luxury of being able to make small adjustments to the posts, if necessary.

Notching the Post. Though not recommended elsewhere, notching the post for a girder is the best method when you have 6x6 posts. Unless your beam is also a six-by, setting the girder on top of the post will leave open grain exposed on the post and will have a sloppy appearance.

After you have cut the post to height, use your angle square to mark for the beam; the best design is to notch it completely in, so that the face of the beam ends up flush with the face of the post. To do this, first set your circular-saw cutting depth to equal the thickness of the beam—for example 3 inches for a beam made of doubled two-bys. Make the seat cut first. Then set your saw to maximum depth and, cutting from top to bottom, make the shoulder cuts on the top and both sides. Finish the shoulder with a handsaw.

Attach the beam with through-bolts such as carriage bolts rather than lag screws. Apply siliconized latex caulk to the joints, and give the exposed end grains of the post a healthy dose of a preservative-sealer.

STEP DECKS

Some decks can have several levels, which means you'll have at least one step where deck platforms meet. These steps must be comfortable. Generally, each step should be no greater in height than a normal 7½-inch stair rise. Because the actual width of a 2x8 is 7¼ inches,

SETTING THE HEADER JOIST

TOOLS & MATERIALS
- Joist material
- Clamps
- Scrap wood
- Hammer
- 16d nails
- Corner brackets
- Joist hangers
- Joist hanger nails

Adding a header joist, often called a belt for short, is the last step before installing bridging. Save time and keep an accurate layout by marking the ledger and the belt at the same time. They should be the same size.

1 *The header, or belt, holds the ends of the joists in place and helps maintain proper spacing.*

2 *Create a temporary shelf for the header by clamping strips of wood to the bottom of three or four joists.*

3 *Making sure the top edge of the header and the tops of the joists are flush, nail the header in place.*

4 *Install corner framing hardware where the header meets the end joists.*

5 *To reinforce the deck framing, install a joist hanger where the joists meet the header.*

DECK JOISTS

DIY OPTIONS: CHANGING LEVELS

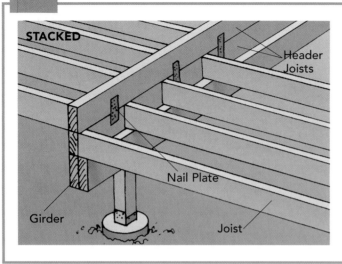

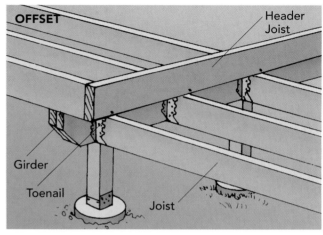

often the easiest way to accomplish a level change is to place a 2x8 joist on top of the frame below. Remember that even a simple step-down between two large platforms can count as a step and be governed by building codes. As always, be sure to check the specifications for level changes with your local building department.

When planning and building a change in level, take care that no decking pieces will be left unsupported at their ends. One approach is to make a second framing box. For small raised areas, the simplest method is to first build the main deck, then construct a box of framing that sits on top of it. This is not cost-effective for larger raised areas, however, because double framing is under the raised section.

Another approach is to create shared girder support. This way the upper level partially overlaps the lower, so that they share the support of the same girder on one end. The end joists of the upper platform can fall directly over the end joist and girder below or it can overlap the level below by about 12 inches. Each level will have its own support at its other end. (See "DIY Options" above.)

BUILDING AROUND TREES

Before you frame in a tree, find out how quickly your tree will grow, and leave enough room for the next ten years at least. But remember that

trees can blow in the wind, too. The point is not to crowd the trunk too much. Instead, frame a roomy square or octagonal opening. Add extra bracing; you can cut a circle in the decking if you'd like.

The framing plan is relatively simple. When a joist in the basic framing structure is interrupted, you have to build a structural bridge to carry loads around the opening. It is one of the most basic operations of construction.

Start by laying out the rough opening and seeing where the joists in your modular layout fall. Chances are, you'll have to add at least one more joist to make an even box around the tree. You may have to add two.

But instead of adding a full joist, even if the tree isn't in the way, add two headers at right angles to the deck framing. (As always, check these header requirements with the local building department. You may need only single headers, but in some cases you might need to double them up.)

Once you have set the headers in place and secured them with galvanized hangers, you can fill in the layout with two pieces of joist lumber. Where the load that would have been carried on one continuous joist is interrupted by the tree opening, the load is shifted by the headers to the adjacent joists. In some cases where you make a large opening, you may also need to double up both full-length joists beside the opening.

You need to pay particular attention to loads if you are building an opening in the deck for a tub or spa. A tree sits in the ground. But tubs and spas sit on the deck. The units themselves don't add much weight to joists and headers that box them in. But even a small tub becomes extremely heavy when you fill it with water. Doubling up headers and adjacent joists may suffice. But be sure to check the manufacturer's specs on loaded weight. You may need to make provisions to support it with special framing hardware, a larger girder, or with additional piers and posts.

BRIDGING

The joists will be pinned at each end but float freely between the house and the outer edge of the deck. On all but the smallest decks, this can cause problems. Eventually, of course, you will nail down decking and have a chance to bring the joists into line. But you may want to treat the deck like a floor frame inside the house, and add bridging. This is a series of short boards or metal braces, typically set along the midspan of the joists.

There is some disagreement about just how much strength and stability bridging adds to a floor frame. Some reports suggest that it isn't really necessary. But those findings generally refer to indoor framing where the joists are covered

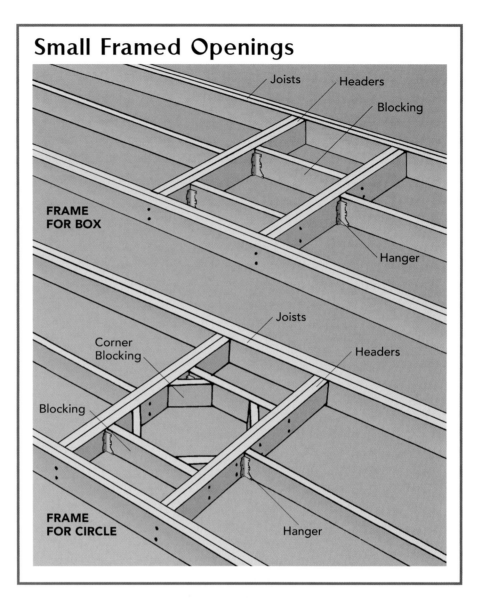

Small Framed Openings

Joists   Headers   Blocking   **FRAME FOR BOX**   Hanger

Joists   Corner Blocking   Headers   Blocking   **FRAME FOR CIRCLE**   Hanger

LEFT
Framing to allow a tree or shrub to grow through the deck adds design interest to the project. It also eliminates the need to remove large trees, an expensive and difficult process.

DECK JOISTS

INSTALLING BRIDGING

TOOLS & MATERIALS
- Measuring tape
- Pencil
- Chalk-line box
- Combination square
- Saw
- Joist stock
- Hammer
- 16d nails

The best material for bridging is often the material used for the joists.

1 Find the centerpoint of the two outer joists. Snap a chalk line between them.

2 Transfer the marks to the sides of the joist. Use a square that will reach the bottom of the joists.

3 Each joist bay will get a section of solid blocking, but you will need to offset them for nailing.

4 Cut bridging from joist stock, and install between joists. The brace helps maintain proper spacing.

5 Drive two nails into each edge of the bridging. Remove the brace when bridging is installed.

with a plywood subfloor, tying the joists together.

Outside on a deck, most people find that bridging does stiffen the frame. The top edges of the joists will eventually be secured with deck boards, but the bottom edges won't be. That's another area where bridging can help: it helps to keep joists from twisting.

Several types of bridging include old-fashioned wood cross braces installed in an X-pattern, the same basic setup in metal, and solid bridging cut from the same lumber as your joists. On decks, solid bridging often is the most practical system, particularly if you have cutoffs from your joists.

BRIDGING LAYOUTS

Solid bridging cut from floor-joist material is easy to install. In a nutshell, you snap a chalk line across the center of the joist span and add bridging in a staggered pattern, alternating from one side of the chalk line to the other so that you can drive end nails instead of toenails. (See "Installing Bridging," opposite.)

When you measure to find the midspan, remember not to include the entire joist if part of its length is cantilevered. Measure from the ledger on the house to the main support girder, and split that distance in half.

In theory, every piece of bridging should be the same length. But you may find small discrepancies in the joist layout. If you simply add the same size piece of bridging in each bay, you might build in an accumulation of errors.

That's one good reason for temporarily tacking a brace across the tops of the joists. You can use a long 1x4, for example. The idea is to set the brace along your ledger and transfer the joist layout. Then set the brace near your chalk line and bring each joist into line on your layout marks.

You should be able to rely on the measurements, but it pays to take a look down each joist from the outer end of the deck to make sure it's straight. You need only one nail through the brace into each joist, and you don't need to drive it home.

The next step is to pencil in square lines on the sides of the joists where the bridging will fall. This will help you set the bridging correctly. Remember that in one bay the bridging needs to

ALIGNING JOISTS

TOOLS & MATERIALS
- Square
- Pencil
- 1x4 brace
- Hammer
- 10d nails
- Clamp

Instead of laying out a new series of marks on your brace, transfer them from the marks on your ledger.

1 When you attach your brace (page 183), you will probably find some joists out of alignment.

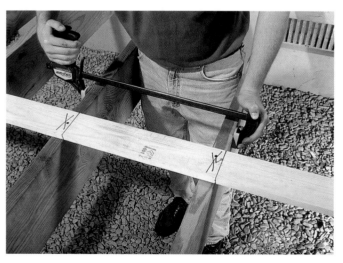

2 Push or pull the offending joist into alignment. Use clamps or spreaders for this job.

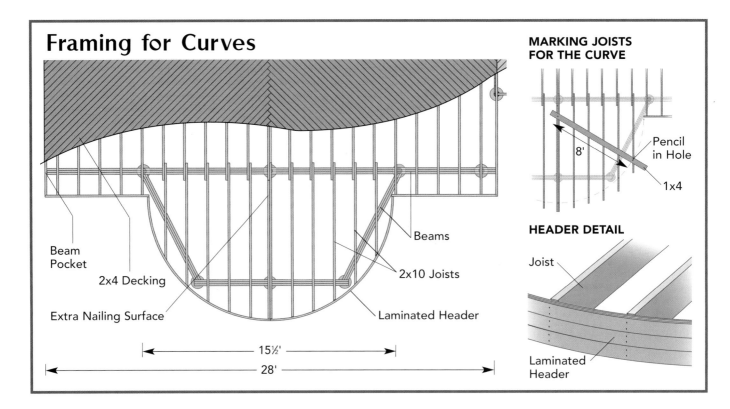

Framing for Curves

Beam Pocket

2x4 Decking

Extra Nailing Surface

Beams

2x10 Joists

Laminated Header

15½'

28'

MARKING JOISTS FOR THE CURVE

8'

Pencil in Hole

1x4

HEADER DETAIL

Joist

Laminated Header

ride on one side of the lines, and in the next bay it needs to ride on the other side.

The final step is straightforward once you have prepared the job. Just cut the blocks; tap them into position on your marks; and drive at least two nails into each end. If you find that the bridging blocks are not exactly the same size as the joists, keep the tops flush with the tops of the joists. That's where the decking will ride, so you want all the framing components to be in one flat plane.

MOVING JOISTS

There may be one or two joists that have a big twist that is difficult to correct. You probably should have left them at the lumberyard, but sometimes a crooked board or two slips by, and you have to find a way to use it.

To push or pull a joist into place on the layout marks of your temporary brace, you can use other joists as a backstop for a 2x4 and force the crooked timber into place. In extreme cases, you can use a handy tool called a come-along, or winch. This ratchet-action cable tool will even pull a series of joists into place as long as the other end of the cable is solidly anchored.

If you need to untwist a joist, say, to line it up

with your square mark on a header, use a lever to help with the untwisting. One approach is to securely clamp on a short 2x4 and simply pull it to one side or the other until the joist corrects. You may need a helper to hold the position while you drive several screws or nails. With a minor twist, you may be able to use the clamp itself as a lever. It's a good idea to overcorrect slightly because the joist will likely slip back slightly. (See "Aligning Joists," page 191.)

FRAMING FOR A CURVED SECTION

After installing the beams, let the joists run wild at the curved section. Mark them for cutting only after you've secured all of them in place. You'll need a laminated header for the curved section.

For V-pattern decking, lay out the joists, as shown above. Start in the middle. Establish the joist where the tip of the V-shape in the decking will fall. Next, measure 16 inches on center to either side of this joist. Install the joists using joist hangers secured to the ledger. Install the two short header joists, allowing them to run longer than needed. For the curve, splice the

LEFT A curve adds an interesting design element. Finish with a curved fascia, or leave the end open for low-level decks.

table saw. Then laminate five or six of these strips together. Cut the 2x4s longer than you'll need so that the fascia won't end up short.

To make a gluing form, cut pieces of plywood that match the curve of the deck. Then laminate the strips together using epoxy, clamping them to the curved form every 6 inches. You'll need to use lots of clamps. Cover every strip thoroughly with epoxy, or the slats may delaminate. Allow the assembly to dry for 24 hours; then belt-sand the edge to produce a finished appearance.

Set the pieces in place, and fasten them to the ends of the joists, driving two nails into the edge of each joist. Once you've stacked three of these assemblies on top of one another (for 2x10 joists), you'll have a strong laminated fascia.

joists over the beam, and allow them to run wild past where they will be cut. Double the thickness of the center joist by scabbing on pieces of 2x4. Make sure that you attach the joists firmly in place.

If your deck will contain decking running in one direction only, there is no need to add the doubled-up center joist.

Mark the Curve. To mark the joists for the curve, make a beam compass, or trammel. For the dimensions shown here, drill two holes exactly 8 feet apart in a 10-foot length of 1x4. Use a $\frac{3}{16}$-inch bit for one hole and a $\frac{1}{4}$-inch bit for the other. To establish the centerpoint of the radius, tack a nail through the smaller hole and into the center of the doubled-up joist. Place a pencil into the other hole, and then swing your compass around the arc to mark the top of each joist. Adjust the size of the compass to fit the dimensions of your deck.

Use a square to mark plumb lines down from the compass marks, and cut each joist with a circular saw. Note: adjust the bevel of the saw for each cut to make sure that it follows the compass mark on top of the joist.

Curved Fascia. To make a curved header/fascia, resaw 2x4s into $\frac{5}{16}$ x $3\frac{1}{2}$ inch pieces using a

SMART TIP

RECESS BOLTS

On some parts of a deck project, extra steps pay off later on. For example, when you bolt the main ledger to the house framing, it's

wise to drill shallow counterbores that can accommodate the bolt heads. When you install joist hangers, the bolts won't be in the way.

DECKING OVER A SLAB

Concrete patios have two problems. Many slabs eventually develop so many cracks that they basically look broken. And after you patch the cracks, the repairs stand out, making the slab look even worse. You could keep patching, or jackhammer the slab into oblivion and start from scratch with more concrete. Here's another alternative: covering the cracked concrete with wood decking. This approach uses sleepers—supports that serve in place of conventional joists.

DESIGN ADVANTAGES

You'll see many advantages to this approach. First, you don't have to remove the slab, which is quite a job physically, and can add considerably to the cost of the project. That's mainly because concrete is heavy, and carting costs are generally based on weight.

Second, even an old slab with an unsightly surface can serve as the foundation for the deck. It won't matter if the surface is pitted or cracked on the surface, because you won't see it under the new layer of wood.

Third, the deck boards, generally 2x4s in this kind of project, are more flexible than concrete. That makes them more comfortable to walk on and provides a little resilience that can absorb some seasonal heaving in the slab. With concrete, even slight movement can cause splitting. And once a crack opens, water can enter, freeze up, and expand in winter, and make the split even wider, which lets in more water in a cycle of ever increasing deterioration.

The basic plan is to install wooden nailers on the concrete and a finished deck surface on the nailers. To prevent rot, use pressure-treated wood on the slab. To fasten the nailers, a contractor uses a special nail gun that fires a small explosive charge to drive a hardened nail through the wood and into the concrete. Using one of these tools can be dangerous if you're not experienced. It's not really a do-it-yourself tool, and you may have trouble even finding a dealer who will rent one to you. But you can get by without one, and use a manual-powered hammer. The job may take a little longer, but it will be safer. Here's how to safely install sleepers to a concrete pad.

ABOVE **Ground-level decks work well with adjoining patios.**

NAILING SLEEPERS

Once you establish your layout, including boards around the perimeter and interior boards spaced about 16 inches on center, determine the material you'll use. You could use 1x4 nailers, but 2x4s provide more nailing substance for the surface boards. Thin nailers offer plenty of support but split too easily as you nail.

It's also wise to lay out the sleepers perpendicular to the main house wall. This will allow water to drain away from the house.

Remember that it's a good idea to use a respirator mask when cutting treated wood, particularly when you use a power saw. Even outdoors, this operation makes a lot of sawdust. (Some newer brands of treated wood are less toxic than the traditional treatment.)

Also be sure to wear safety glasses while nailing. Because the concrete is so much harder than wood, nails sometimes can snap, and pieces of metal can fly up unexpectedly. You may not stick to safety glasses for odd jobs around the house, but this is one case where eye protection is essential. Unlike nailing in wood, where the force from a misdirected blow causes a bend, a mishit concrete nail can snap and ricochet off the slab into your face packing quite a wallop.

Use hardened nails, often called cut nails, or masonry nails to fasten the sleepers. You'll find that standard common nails used on wood framing will bend over before penetrating the slab.

Be aware of another phenomenon peculiar to concrete nailing called hammer rebound. The hardened nail may hit a piece of stone in the slab, at which point all the force from your hammer blow comes right back off the nailhead and makes the hammer jump up in your hand. Try a few nails to get the feel of it—notice when the nail is penetrating and when you've hit an immovable object and are forced to move over an inch or so.

With those caveats in mind, simply proceed to attach the nailers, say, 16 inches from center to center across the slab. Keep nails a few inches away from the edges of the concrete to avoid splitting off small chunks.

Here's one more reason for using 2x4s instead of 1x4s for your nailers. Although it may take more time to fasten the larger lumber (and cost

Decking over a Slab

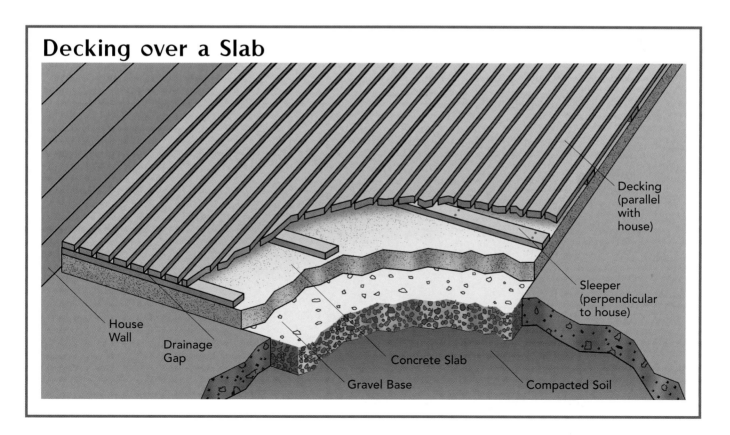

Decking (parallel with house)

Sleeper (perpendicular to house)

House Wall

Drainage Gap

Concrete Slab

Gravel Base

Compacted Soil

a bit more, too), you can level out some irregularities in the slab. While thinner boards would bend up over the rises and dip a bit into the low spots as you nail, pressure-treated 2x4s will bridge most of the gaps.

If you have a few major depressions in the slab, nail the sleepers at the high spots and insert shims (wedge-shaped pieces of pressure-treated wood or cedar shingles), to keep the 2x4s level as they ride over the low spots.

Roof Decking

Drainage Gap

Hidden Panel Seam

Deck Boards

Panel Section

Roofing

Sleeper

Overlapped Boards

Removable Panel

Drainage Bay

FASTENER DETAIL

Sleeper

Deck Board

Scews (brass or stainless steel)

Overlap   Sleeper

TWO-PANEL OVERLAP

PLANNING THE DECK SURFACE

Now comes the nice part of the job—installing the surface decking. Because the surface 2x4 (or 2x6 if you like) decking doesn't sit directly on the concrete, air will circulate around the wood. That means you don't have to use pressure-treated wood, even though treated boards are likely to last longer than fir, redwood, or cedar out in the weather.

Some people just don't like the look of wood after it has undergone the chemical treatment. Most treated products loose their original look over time; others will keep their original look. You can use treated boards and coat them with a semi-transparent wood stain to kill the tinge, or use standard construction framing timbers and apply a water-resistant surface sealer to protect the wood.

NAILING THE DECK

To make the surface look really nice, take care with the spacing between boards needed for drainage through the deck surface and nail placement through the surface timbers into the sleepers. The old-fashioned and reliable system is to use the shank of a common nail as a spacer between boards. Or you can insert any convenient spacer that will allow something like ⅛-inch clearance to start with. (Some products shrink considerably. Check product data sheets or with the manufacturer for specific nailing instructions.)

Each surface 2x4 or 2x6 should get two nails. Be sure to select a galvanized common nail that reaches through the deck boards and most of the way into the sleeper but not into the concrete.

ROOF DECKING

There is another, more exotic application where sleepers take the place of conventional joists: on a flat or very low-slope roof. If you don't have much of a view or a breeze in the back-yard, why build a deck at ground level when you might have an airy perch on the roof? This is not a great idea for turreted Victorians or steeply sloped Capes. But almost any flat or very low-slope roof can be covered with a wood platform that is more durable and more inviting than asphalt.

The first concern, of course, is safety. Although you can build or rent a scaffold and work from the edge of the roof, it's generally easier (and safer) to haul materials and tools through the house. This leads to the first step in most roof-deck projects: building an opening and installing a door.

ABOVE Roof-top decks afford views and privacy that ground-level decks cannot. Here a dormer window was replaced by French doors to connect the deck with the bedroom inside.

Door Location. Many factors can influence the door location. You want an opening that creates easy access, say, from a second-floor bedroom or hallway right out to a garage or first-floor roof. But you also want a stretch of wall free of pipes, wires, and ducts. Rerouting these mechanical systems can make a straightforward door installation much more complicated. Often, changing out an existing window for a door is the most practical approach.

Door height is another wrinkle. Most doors are just under 7 feet high, which poses no problem in standard, 8-foot-high walls. But the floor level inside usually is too close to the roof level outside, and creates a leak-prone seam that is almost impossible to flash. So instead of cutting the opening down to floor level, roof access doors generally are installed on a curb, which is simply a narrow section of the house wall that you don't remove. Construction details will differ depending on the type of roof you have and how it joins the house wall. But if a well-flashed curb winds up creating an awkward step, build raised landings inside and outside the door.

The most practical deck system over roofing is a series of interconnecting panels, called duck boards, that are 4 or 5 feet square. The platform sections have boards about a foot apart that rest on the roof (the sleepers that serve as joist supports), and a top layer of closely spaced boards screwed at right angles to the supports below. To prevent your fasteners from puncturing the roof, drive brass or stainless-steel screws up through the sleepers into the surface boards. (See drawing opposite.)

Check Building Codes. Even well-built panels will be a little rickety compared with a ground-level deck with rows of 2x4s nailed or screwed into large joists. Roof panels have to be strong enough to keep foot traffic and chair legs from damaging the roof but light enough to remove.

Check your local building codes for all details on this kind of deck project. All roof decks require a railing. Be sure to observe the rules about railing height and spacing between balusters that enclose the deck space.

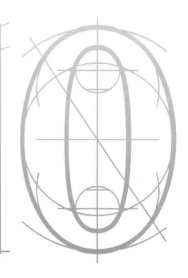

CHAPTER

INSTALLING
DECKING

Now comes one of the most rewarding parts of building a deck: adding the decking. This is the part of your project that will show the most, so take your time. Maintain even spacing between boards, and follow the manufacturer's directions if installing composite materials.

MAXIMUM DECKING SPANS

⅝x6 Southern pine or Douglas fir, perpendicular	16"
⅝x6 Southern pine or Douglas fir, diagonal	12"
⅝x6 redwood or cedar, perpendicular	16"
⅝x6 redwood or cedar, diagonal	12"
2x4 or 2x6 Southern pine or Douglas fir, perpendicular	24"
2x4 Southern pine or Douglas fir, diagonal	16"
2x6 Southern pine or Douglas fir, diagonal	24"
2x4 redwood or cedar, perpendicular	16"
2x4 or 2x6 redwood or cedar, diagonal	16"
2x6 redwood or cedar, perpendicular	24"

Note: Be sure to check allowable spans between supports and all lumber requirements with the local building department.

SMART TIP

WHICH SIDE UP?

Installing deck boards bark side up is a well-known rule of thumb of deck building. The bark side is the side of the board that faced toward the outside of the tree. Because of the round shape of trees, the bark-side grain has a convex shape that would seem to be good for shedding rain.

The idea seems to make sense because if the nonbark or dry side gets wet, the reasoning goes, it will trap water. But there are some major problems with the rule.

First, if you install boards that are still wet, or green, they will shrink as they dry out. And a green board installed bark side up is likely to dry into a U-shape, which means water will be trapped on the boards.

Second, if you use good lumber—especially cedar, redwood, or Douglas fir—there is little chance of significant cupping. And a small cup is not really a problem because no end grain is

exposed to the water. In fact, the United States Department of Agriculture has determined that it doesn't matter whether boards are laid bark side up or down. So unless you are using very wet or very dry treated lumber for your decking, just pick the side that looks the best.

DECKING OPTIONS

Laying the decking is the most gratifying part of building a deck. The work proceeds quickly because most of the layout work is completed at this stage. With a helper or two, you can cover the framing on a deck in a day, even if it has some angles or finishing details at the edges.

These can take the form of trim that covers the rough end grain of deck boards, fascias that cover rough joists or girders, and skirting that conceals the area under the deck and makes the structure blend in with the yard.

You may be anxious to finish the project at this point. But it pays to take the time to carefully space the surface boards and to drive your nails or screws the same way (with the same edge margins) over the entire surface. Of course, you should also take the time to examine boards; discard lumber with excessive twisting, cracking, or other problems; and set the best side up.

PLAN FOR THE RAILINGS

Before you start laying deck boards, make sure that the installation will work with the railings. In most cases, you can install railings after the deck boards are set, even if you have to create notches in the outer board. If the decking overhangs the frame, you'll need notches for the railing support posts to sit flush against the joist. However, in some designs, especially those that incorporate benches, you must install posts or other supports before the decking. But you can take another approach: installing the posts first and notching deck boards around them as needed.

Also take into account the location of the fascia boards and skirting panels if you're using these finishing details. Because these components are generally nailed onto the outer joist or header joist, you will need a generous overhang on the deck boards to cover their top edges.

There are several factors to consider when you think about how to deck over the joists. Some of the options are limited at this point, of course, because you need to use decking lumber and a surface layout that will work with the joist spacing. On most decks, that's 16 inches on center. But there are plenty of choices. You still need to select a species of wood, its width and thickness, the decking pattern, how the decking will be fastened, and in some cases, where and how to install the fascia boards and skirting.

TYPES OF WOOD

The most popular choice for decking today is treated wood of some kind. But many people use a construction grade such as Douglas fir or a more finished wood such as cedar or redwood. Cedar and redwood are more attractive and less likely to split, but they also cost more and are more likely than treated wood to deterio-

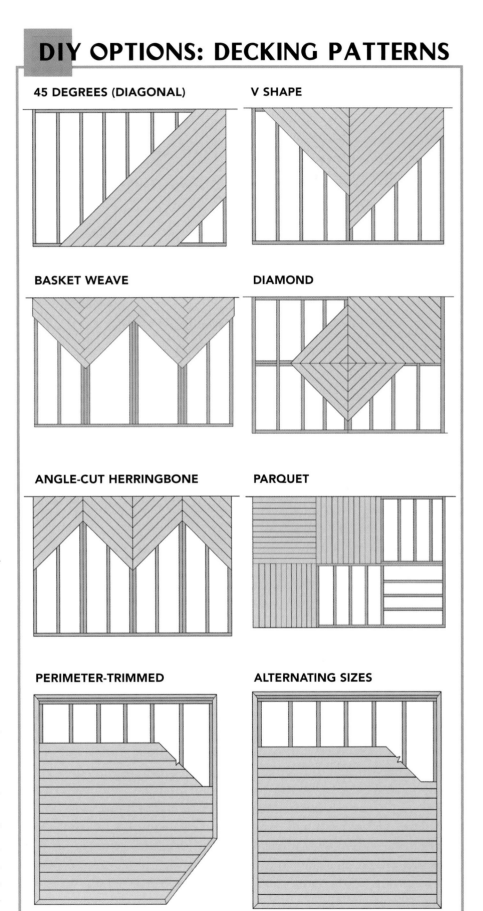

DIY OPTIONS: DECKING PATTERNS

45 DEGREES (DIAGONAL)

V SHAPE

BASKET WEAVE

DIAMOND

ANGLE-CUT HERRINGBONE

PARQUET

PERIMETER-TRIMMED

ALTERNATING SIZES

LAYING OUT DECKING BOARDS

TOOLS & MATERIALS
■ Decking
■ Pencil
■ Scrap plywood
■ String
■ Measuring tape
■ Common nails

Measure the deck using board width plus the spacing, if any.

1 Set a ½-in. strip of plywood against the house, and set the first board in place. String a chalk line.

2 Use a scrap piece of decking to make sure that there will be a gap between the first board and the house.

3 Set out the boards and spacers if necessary. The end board should overhang the framing.

rate in warm, damp climates. Remember that all woods will fade after a few seasons of being out in the weather.

LUMBER DIMENSIONS

Most decks look good and work well with either 2x4 or 2x6 lumber. (Thinner ¾ stock is used more on porches.) Do not use wider boards except as an occasional accent piece. The wider the board, the more it will expand and contract.

Generally, 2x6s cover more ground and make the work go faster. They may be less prone to twisting than 2x4s, which are often cut from smaller, younger trees. When you run into a knot in a 2x4, you've got a nailing problem, whereas a 2x6 is wide enough to give you room to work around a knot.

PATTERNS

Most decks look best with boards running parallel with the longest house wall. Straight runs that cross the joists at right angles are also the easiest to install. There are many pattern options, but they often require extra framing and more cutting and predrilling on the deck boards. If there are a lot of angle cuts or a pattern of mixed sizes, count on ending up with extra waste lumber, too. Some herringbone and parquet designs can eliminate a lot of angle cuts. But bear in mind that these patterns may run wild along the edges of your deck and make the overall pattern look incomplete. If your deck has different levels, you can create a basic pattern contrast by running the decking at a different angle for each level.

FASTENING SYSTEMS

Although 16d nails have more holding power, many carpenters use them only for beams, and attach deck boards with 10d or 12d galvanized common nails. There are also ring-shanked and twisted deck nails. But for maximum holding power, you can't beat screws. Once you get the hang of using a drill-driver, the boards go down quickly—and it's easy to back out a screw in case of mistakes. Also consider hidden fasteners (of which there are several) that attach to the joists and screw up into the deck boards from below. This presents the cleanest deck surface with no nail or screw heads.

FASCIAS AND SKIRTS

Both fascia boards and skirting tuck under the decking that overhangs the outer joists. This method is easy, does not require precise finish carpentry, and is rot resistant because there are no places where water can be trapped against open grain.

ABOVE **On most decks, the decking runs parallel with the house. But installing the decking on an angle to the house often creates an interesting design element.**

DIY OPTIONS: EDGE DETAILS

No matter what kind of deck boards you use, there are three basic choices for fastening them along the edges of your deck. You can cut them flush, box them in with a fascia, or let them extend past the joists an inch or so. You can make a case that any one of them looks better than the others. But to build a durable deck, overhanging boards are best because they shed water and do not create water-trapping seams where wood can rot.

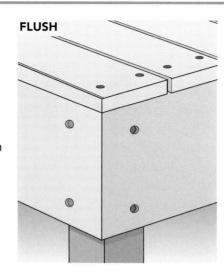

FLUSH

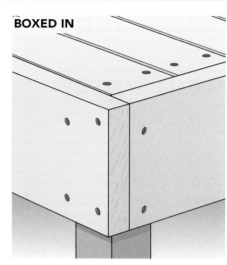

BOXED IN

DECK BOARD SPACING

TOOLS & MATERIALS
- Common nails
- String
- Decking
- Measuring tape
- Fasteners

Spacing requirements vary with the material. Some will follow the directions shown here, but other products require no spacing between boards.

1 A common nail makes a good spacer for kiln-dried lumber. Position the board, and remove the nail.

2 String a chalk line from one end of the deck to the other. Check for bulges and depressions.

3 Measure from the ledger frequently. This helps keep the courses square with the deck frame.

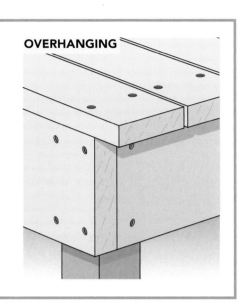

OVERHANGING

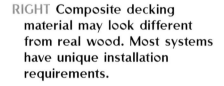

RIGHT Composite decking material may look different from real wood. Most systems have unique installation requirements.

With fascia boards, you might also cut the decking flush to the edges of the joists and cover both the joist and the decking with the trim boards. This detail calls for straight cut lines and high-quality lumber that won't twist or shrink over time. Even then, the seam where the butt ends of the decking meet the fascia can trap water and foster rot.

ESTIMATING MATERIALS

You could just figure out your square footage and then order enough lumber to cover it, plus 15 percent for waste. And the lumberyard would love it if you did because it could unload the lengths that are overstocked. To minimize waste and time-consuming butt joints on the deck surface, though, take the time to make a plan of your deck surface that shows every piece. Then you can determine the lengths that will work most efficiently and result in less waste.

To figure decking that will be cut at a right angle, start with the width of the deck to find out how many deck boards (or rows of deck boards,

if the deck is longer than the longest deck boards you can buy) will be needed. Divide the total width of your deck by 5.6 (for 2x6 or ⁵⁄₄x6 decking) or 3.6 (for 2x4 decking). This figure adds about ¹⁄₁₀ inch for the space between boards. Once you know how many boards you will need, be sure to order the correct lengths to save money.

Estimating is more difficult for angled patterns. Start by calculating how many total linear feet of decking you will need. Divide the deck's square footage by 0.47 for 2x6 decking or 0.3 for 2x4. Add 5 to 10 percent for waste, and you will have a good general figure. Now look at your drawing, and estimate the most-efficient lengths you will need.

Sometimes it's possible to avoid making butt joints by buying extra-long pieces of decking— 18 feet or longer. These may cost more per foot, but they're worth it: you'll have fewer rot-prone butt joints, and the installation will be easier and quicker. Where you do need butt joints, be sure to stagger them over different joists. It looks best to keep the joints at least two joists away from each other.

SMART TIP

STRAIGHTENING BOARDS

To bring a bowed board into line, you can use a specialized tool such as the Bowrench, (1) which locks onto the supporting joist for leverage. Or you can dig a flat bar into the joist and pry against the board. (2)

INSTALLING THE DECKING

Before you start nailing, it makes sense to sort through the boards, and square-cut and seal the ends that will be butted. Then you can set the first board next to the house. Its position is important because it sets the starting point for the other boards. You can then lay down the decking, repeating your nailing patterns and spacing to make a uniform surface. Finally, you make the trim cuts, and add the finishing touches, such as edging that covers exposed end grain, fascia boards, and skirting.

PREPARING THE BOARDS

Sort through the stack of lumber, and choose which side will be up for each piece. Weed out any boards with bad cracks, twists, or other damage. If you have a number of different lengths, stack them accordingly, so it will be easy to find the boards you want.

If the boards are long enough, you can let them run over the outer joist and trim them later. Wherever a board end needs to be butted, you can make the cuts ahead of time or wait to see how the boards fall on the joists and make the cuts as you go. This is the way most carpenters do it. Cutting butts ahead of time seems to make sense, but it can get you into trouble if the on-center measurements are a bit off. You need to be sure that butted boards join in the center of a joist, which is only 1½ inches wide.

Unless you are using treated lumber, you may want to keep a can of preservative handy so that you can coat the freshly cut butt ends.

As you get ready to install the decking, lay out ten or so boards on the deck as they will go down—for example, with the lengths positioned to stagger butt joints. This keeps the work moving and provides a temporary surface to stand on.

INSTALLING STARTER BOARDS

Straight Runs. For decking that runs parallel with the house, pick a straight board and cut it to length, allowing for the overhang. Measure out from the house at both ends of the run, and mark the width of the decking board plus at least ¼ inch to leave a drainage gap. Snap a chalk line or string a line between your end marks, and check at several points along the wall with a block of decking to be sure you have enough room. (See "Laying Out Decking Boards," page 202.) If the house wall bows in or out, you may need to increase the margin. Don't make the mistake of twisting the board to conform to the house wall. You want the deck boards to be straight. For decking butted to the house, you should follow the same basic procedure.

Diagonals. If you are installing a diagonal pattern, don't start with a short piece in a corner. Start with a straight board at least 6 feet long instead, and set it on a 45-degree angle by

INSTALLING DECKING

TOOLS & MATERIALS
- Decking
- Chalk-line box
- Measuring tape
- Fasteners
- Hammer

The house wall may bow in and out, but your first board should be straight. In severe cases, you can cut the first board from a larger timber and scribe it to conceal irregularities.

1 *The decking should overhang the outer joist plus any fascia or skirting by 1 to 2 in.*

2 *Set the first board on the chalk line drawn earlier. Maintain the gap between the board and house.*

3 *For professional results, keep nails spaced evenly. Use the shank to locate each nail from the edge.*

4 *Drive nails an inch from each edge. Protect deck with scrap wood when pulling bent nails.*

5 *Lay out 10 to 12 rows as you work. This will help you keep butt joints several rows apart.*

EDGE TRIMMING

TOOLS & MATERIALS
- Measuring tape
- Pencil
- Chalk-line box
- Circular saw
- Handsaw

To get a smooth cut along the deck edge, use a sharp blade and set the saw depth slightly deeper than the thickness of the deck boards.

1 *The overhang should cover the end joist and the fascia by about 1 in.*

2 *Snap a chalk line from one end of the deck to the other. This will be your cut line.*

3 *Run the circular saw along the cut line with the saw's shoe resting on the deck.*

measuring equal distances from the starting corner. Before you fasten it, measure from the center of the board to the corner, and use blocks to check how the boards will fall. You don't want to end up with a tiny piece in the corner.

Parquets. To keep track of things when you have boards running in both directions, tack at least four starter boards in place, and measure carefully to make sure that all your decking boards will come out right. Then drive the screws or nails home. With complex patterns, you may want to lay out all of your decking boards, including spacers, to see how the pattern will fall on the framing.

Herringbones. With a herringbone pattern,

you need to account for the repeats. Generally, it looks best to use a pattern of full boards centered on the deck and equal-size partial lengths where the pattern meets the edges.

FASTENING THE DECKING

If you nail by hand, expect your arm to tire after a few hours. There's not much you can do about that except use a pneumatic nailer. But because a lot of deck work is best done on your knees, you may want to make the work easier by investing in knee pads.

Position and Cut the Boards. As you place each board in position, make sure the long end hangs over far enough to trim squarely and still cover fascias or skirts. For angled, herringbone, and parquet designs, you will need to measure and cut at least some of the boards as you go. When possible, hold the boards in place to mark them.

You may want to cut a few boards next to the house to length. But when you make trim cuts with a circular saw, you can get pretty close to the house wall and then finish the cut with a handsaw.

Fasten Nails and Screws. You can set all your fasteners as you go (the way most pros do it) or set only a few to locate the boards and come back later to drive the rest. This can be an advantage if you discover mistakes later. But it's not hard to pick the best face of a board as you install it, and take care of spacing and fastening in one shot. (See "Installing Decking," page 207.)

Use nails as spacers. You might try a thicker 16d nail if the wood is dry already, or a thinner 8d nail if it is still relatively wet. You can simply hold the spacer nail against the last nailed board, and tap the head with a hammer to hold it as you set the next board in place. You should then be able to release the spacer by hand and tap it into place on the next spaced edge.

You drive a pair of nails where each board crosses each joist, about ¾ to 1 inch in from each edge. Some people like to angle their nails slightly toward each other. The idea is that it provides increased holding power. But if you need more holding power you should use larger nails, or screws, instead of nailing incorrectly.

Pros generally drive nails or screws straight in to leave a flat head on the surface. An angled head can tear one side of the wood and create a small water trap. It's also difficult to seat an angled nail without digging your hammer into the surrounding wood.

You don't want to mar the deck boards with mis-hits, of course. But deck work is not trim work. Hit the nails hard, giving one final whack to set the heads flush with the surface. Don't tap lightly and use a nail set to seat the heads, or you will be there on your knees forever.

For appearance sake, it's not much trouble to keep your nails evenly spaced on the boards and in a straight line across the deck. You can use a string line for a guide, draw a pencil line, or just

DIY: COMPOSITE DECKING

Composite and other engineered products often have proprietary installation requirements. The product shown here has a tongue-and-groove design.

Most enginereed products require standard lumber posts, girders, and joists. Cut material with a circular or saber saw.

This tongue-and-groove product requires a starter strip at the leading edge of the deck. Install the strip with stainless-steel screws.

Place the tongue of the first board into the groove, using hand pressure only. Secure the groove side of the board with a deck fastener.

SMART TIP

ADDING A HATCH

Create accessible under-deck storage space by adding a hatch in the decking. A hatch can be one joist bay wide or you can extend it to two bays. If you are building a larger hatch, do not remove the middle joist. It will provide needed support.

1. Attach one-bys to the deck. The one-bys should be one decking board longer at each end of your planned hatch. Remove the deck nails. Make a plunge cut parallel with the one-by boards. The one-bys will keep the cut section from falling through.

2. Use decking screws to attach two 2x6 braces to the underside of the hatch. Inset the braces from the edge of the hatch. Remove the original supports.

3. Drill holes for gripping the hatch. Test-fit the hatch. To support it, install joist stock flush with the tops of the existing joists at the front and back of the opening. Install 2x4 supports on the side joists flush with the joist tops.

look up to follow the line of set nails.

Predrilling to Prevent Splits. Even if you use screws, be sure to predrill near the ends of all deck boards to avoid splitting. Screws don't exert as much splitting force as nails because they have thinner shanks and turn their way through the wood, but within an inch or two of the end of a board, it helps to have a pilot hole. One rule of thumb is to use a pilot bit that is two-thirds to three-quarters as thick as the shank of your nail or screw.

If you see a crack start to open as you're working on a butt joint, back out the screw or nail and increase the hole size or move to another location. Any small split that appears now will only get larger with time.

Using Deck Board Hardware. Deck clips or continuous deck fasteners allow you to fasten decking from below and leave the wood surface with no visible nail or screw heads. They are a bit more expensive than screws and take some extra time to install, but they may be worth it if you have beautiful decking boards that you want to show off to their full advantage. Check the manufacturer's recommendations about using the hardware with deck boards subject to substantial shrinkage. And, of course, be sure you have enough room to work on the deck from below.

There are several types of deck-board hardware. (See page 105.) Some require you to put nails into the sides of the deck board and the joist, while others require nailing into the joist only and use a spike on the hardware to lock the deck board in place. The most common type (and probably the most efficient) is a perforated, L-shape strip. You can screw through one side to fasten the hardware to the joist, and through the other to fasten the deck board to the hardware. Some call for toenailing one side of each deck board; others do not. All of them automatically space the boards.

Straightening as You Go. Every third or fourth board, check the run for straightness. You can do this by holding a taut string line along one edge of the board, or by eye. But it's also wise to measure back to your starting row against the house at several points. This keeps the boards square to the frame.

BREADBOARD EDGING

TOOLS & MATERIALS
- Decking
- Table saw
- Construction adhesive
- 8d finishing nails
- Hammer
- Drill & bits
- Belt sander

This detail is a favorite of furniture builders who use it to conceal and secure the end grain on wide planks that are fitted together to make a table.

1 *Rip ¾-in.-wide lengths of breadboard edging from decking material.*

2 *After trimming the deck boards, apply construction adhesive to the board edges.*

3 *Install the trim to the edges of the deck board using finishing nails.*

4 *Predrill nailholes at the ends of the breadboard trim to keep the wood from splitting.*

5 *Because some deck boards may be higher than others, trim the surface with a belt sander.*

You can straighten most bends by pushing them into position. You may need to use a chisel or pry bar for the tougher ones. Start at one end and fasten as you proceed down the board. Keep all your spacer nails in place until the whole board is straightened. Anchor the straightened parts of the board securely with two fasteners at each joist so that the straight part doesn't get bent while you work.

MAKING THE FINAL CUTS
Measure out from the last joist to allow for an overhang of about an inch, and to account for a fascia board or skirting panel if you use one or the other. Measure the overhang at each end;

snap a chalk line as a guide; and make the trim cut with a circular saw. Set your blade about ½ inch deeper than your decking thickness. (See "Edge Trimming" on page 208.)

CUTOUTS FOR THROUGH-POSTS
If your posts continue upward past the decking to become part of your railing system, you will need to cut your decking to go around them. According to one school of thought, you should make these joints watertight by cutting very tight notches to begin with and caulking the seams as well. While a tight fit looks nice, caulking rarely does, and it's easily smeared onto other boards.

INSTALLING FASCIA

TOOLS & MATERIALS
- Fascia
- Measuring tape
- Pencil
- Circular saw
- Sander
- Drill & bits
- Construction adhesive
- 8d finishing nails
- Nail set
- Hammer

Select a fascia board that is one size up from the joists—for example, a 1x10 to clad a 2x8.

1 Set your saw to cut 45-deg. angles, and miter the ends of the fascia boards where they meet at corners.

3 Predrill near the ends of the fascia to avoid splitting the wood. This will be a highly visible joint.

4 Because you will be using finishing nails, apply construction adhesive to the end joists.

And if you think about how the rest of the deck is built, it makes more sense to cut a notch that encourages drainage. At the ledger, for example, you should either flash the inside edge to shed water or leave a gap with washers so that water can run past. The same approach goes for the deck boards: you should fasten them securely so that they don't cup and trap water. So it makes sense to create notches that allow water to drain around posts, as well.

Create a gap by cutting the deck board notches with a good ¼ inch space around the post. You can even run a roundover router bit around the notch edges to finish them.

But in most cases, cut your notches with square edges and just a bit of extra room. That makes it easy to set the board in proper position.

Start by holding the deck board in position against the post to mark the sides. Be sure you have butt joints cut in advance and spacers in place to maintain the layout. Mark the sides; measure in to mark for depth; and square up your marks on the board.

To make the cutouts with a circular saw, you'll need to cut only part way into the notch on the sides; make the beginning of a plunge cut on the back edge; and use a handsaw to finish up the cuts in the corner. You'll find that it's easier (and a lot quicker) to use a saber saw that can cut all the way into the corners.

2 *Before installing the boards, dress the exposed surface with a random-orbit or belt sander.*

5 *Finish the installation using finishing nails. Use a nail set to seat the nails to avoid marks on the wood.*

FASCIA BOARDS AND SKIRTING

If you select good-looking lumber for the most visible joists and install fasteners neatly in an even pattern, the deck frame may look fine. To improve the look of rougher framing, you can add a coat or two of stain or clad the exposed lumber with fascia boards.

The idea is to select a high-quality one-by board, such as cedar or redwood, and apply it under the deck surface overhang. The process is straightforward. First, cut the board to length and miter any corner joints. Then sand the boards as needed; predrill for screws or nails to avoid splits; and fasten the fascia in place. You may want to add construction adhesive and decrease the number of nails for appearance sake. (See "Installing Fascia," opposite.)

ADDING SKIRTING

There are several types of skirting material and a number of ways to close off the space between your deck framing and the ground. Lattice is the most common material, although you can use closely spaced 1x2s or fencing materials to create a similar effect.

One approach is to add a support frame near the ground and set the skirting along the outermost edge of the deck. This requires a fair amount of extra framing work because you have to hang the new supports from the joists. It's often easier to use the supports you already have: the row of piers and posts, and the girder that rests on them.

To avoid rot (even if you use pressure-treated lattice or 1x2s), it's best to keep the skirting an inch or two above the ground.

Assemble the Lattice. One good approach is to buy large sheets of prefab lattice and cut them to size. Then you can build simple frames around the panel sections to strengthen them and dress up the edges. Some lumberyards and home centers sell slotted trim designed to work with lattice, but any reasonably stiff frame will do the job.

To mount the panels, apply them to the front of your posts or add nailers on the sides of the posts so that the panels will tuck between them. (See "Installing Skirting," opposite.)

It's wise to do as much work as possible on the panels, including jobs such as staining and predrilling, before you have to crouch under the deck overhang and finish the installation.

DECKING AROUND A TREE

When you are installing decking at a framed opening in the deck for a tree, take the same approach as you do on the deck edges: let the boards run long, and make the final trim cuts all at one time. This is the best way to get a neat edge, and it saves the time of cutting each board

to the exact length you need as you nail it down.

You may have to slice off the end of a board at an angle just to get it in place, but try to get all the boards close to the tree. Once they are fastened, it's time to figure how to make your final cuts. For most trees, you'll want to leave a gap of at least 2 or 3 inches between the tree and the decking. You can always leave more. Depending on the overall shape of your deck or the area of the tree, you may want to cut a square or a rectangle. Generally, a simple square shape with a roughly even margin around the tree looks best. But you also can use a saber saw and cut a contoured shape that mirrors the tree trunk. In all cases, cut the boards so that they overhang the box framing around the tree.

Cutting a Circle. If you prefer to cut a circle, use the framing that you can see around the tree for reference. (If the tree weren't there, of course, it would be easy to scribe a circle from a centerpoint.) If you want to be precise, establish four or eight equidistant points on the circumference of the circle. Or simply set a hose or extension cord around the tree.

DECKING CURVES

On most decks that have a curved corner, you lay the deck boards to overhang the framing, tack a nail at the radius of the circle, and mark the corner cut with a pencil and string that swings from the nail.

The easiest way to frame supports for a curve is by installing an angled joist at the corner. (See "Framing for a Curved Section," on page 192.)

On small platforms—at the head of a stairway, for example—you can form a different kind of curved pattern by cutting 2x6 lumber on a diagonal. By placing the narrow ends near the radius, the wide ends will spread out in a fan shape. This system also requires extra support framing.

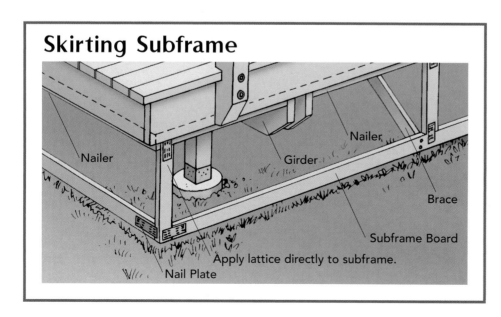

Skirting Subframe

Nailer

Nailer

Nailer

Girder

Brace

Subframe Board

Apply lattice directly to subframe.

Nail Plate

INSTALLING SKIRTING

TOOLS & MATERIALS
- Measuring tape
- Pencil
- Nailers
- Drill-driver & bits
- 2" screws
- Power miter saw
- Framing material
- Exterior glue
- Hammer
- 6d finishing nails
- Lattice panels

Even on a relatively low deck, skirting can conceal the barren area beneath the framing.

1 Measure between the posts to determine the length of the skirting panel.

2 To recess the panel, attach a nailer to the sides of the posts. Install the panel flush to the post edge.

3 Miter the corners of the frame material. The frame stiffens the lattice and hides its edges.

4 Join the frame sections at right angles using glue and nails. Some frames have slots for the lattice.

5 Attach the frames to the nailers on the posts. Use screws for easy removal.

ADDING STAIRS

Although your deck plans may call for new French doors or sliders to connect your house to the deck, you will also need to add stairs to provide a transition between the deck and the yard. Well-built stairs are comfortable and safe to use, and they add a distinctive design element to the deck.

Deck Stairway Components

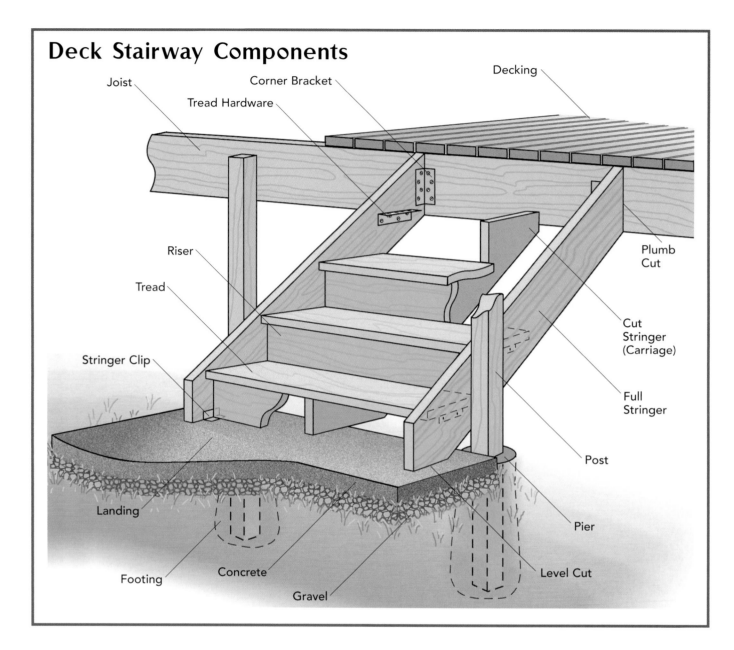

Joist · Corner Bracket · Decking
Tread Hardware
Riser · Plumb Cut
Tread
Stringer Clip · Cut Stringer (Carriage)
Full Stringer
Landing · Post
Footing · Concrete · Pier · Level Cut
Gravel

DESIGN OPTIONS

Building a deck is one home improvement project that many homeowners can tackle because construction is straightforward—until they come to the stairs. Even a drop of a few feet can present a confusing combination of dimensions that account for slope, tread size, and space between steps.

While stairs are an important part of most decks, they are usually left for last when the final details of the deck are in place. Then you can make a practical plan and do the calculations that account for any small changes made during construction.

STAIRWAY COMPONENTS

Figuring stairways takes a bit of calculating, even though there are only a few components. The most important ones are stringers, the angled pieces along the sides of the stairs. They hold the treads, which are the boards you step on. Some deck stairs also have risers, typically one-by lumber installed on edge to cover up the space between the treads. But you don't need risers for strength. In fact, they are often omitted from outdoor stairs because they inhibit drainage and create a joint where water can collect and cause decay.

Once the deck is built, you may find yourself changing your mind about the stairway—how it should look and how you will use it. If all you need is a way to get from the deck to the ground, a simple 36-inch-wide stairway with standard treads will do. And you can generally build it without much trouble using only two stringers.

But whether you stick with a basic, straight-run design or combine your stairs with a platform, you must stay within the limits of building codes, which are stringent when it comes to stairs. Generally, you'll find that codes call for a tread depth of no less than 10 inches, a step up, or rise, between treads of no more than about 8 inches, and a stairway width of no less than 3 feet.

(one of the angled side supports for the treads) in various positions to see how different tread and riser proportions will work with your deck.

Another option is to create very deep steps that can double as seats. For instance, you might use three 2x6s with drainage spacing between for a total tread of about 16 inches (actually about 17 with an inch of overlap). But these low-angle designs may spread the stairs beyond the design capacity of standard 2x12 stringers.

Several rule-of-thumb formulas can help you make a stair layout. One is that rise x run = 70 to 75 inches. Another is that rise + run = 17 to

TREADS AND RISERS

It's convenient to plan a tread depth of approximately 11 inches, which works out to be two 2x6s or three 2x4s. This is a safe and comfortable size that allows the top tread to project a bit over the one below. Also remember to figure in the same drainage spacing between treads that you use between deck boards.

But on outdoor stairs, many people find that it's easier to negotiate stairs that have more ample proportions than typical indoor stairs. That means increasing the tread depth and decreasing the rise from one step to another. This makes the stairs more comfortable and helps raised decks look more anchored to the ground.

You can use a large rise (generally 7 to 7½ inches) to make the stairs as compact as possible. Or you can use a small rise (4 inches is generally considered the minimum), to stretch out the stairs with more treads. These variables are best investigated initially on paper. After that, you should clamp an uncut 2x12 stringer

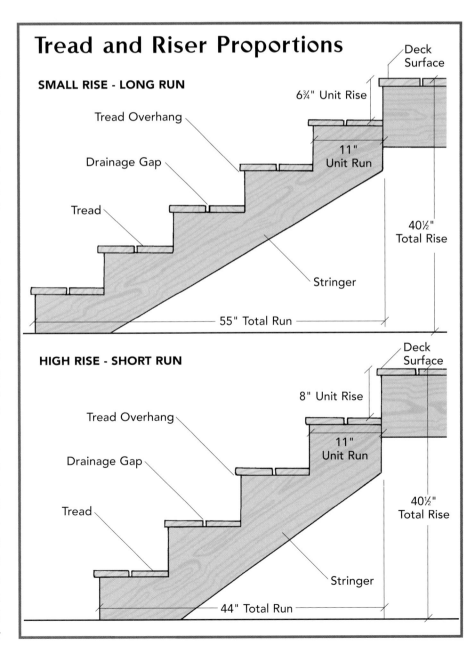

Tread and Riser Proportions

SMALL RISE - LONG RUN

Deck Surface
6¾" Unit Rise
Tread Overhang
11" Unit Run
Drainage Gap
40½" Total Rise
Tread
Stringer
55" Total Run

HIGH RISE - SHORT RUN

Deck Surface
8" Unit Rise
Tread Overhang
11" Unit Run
Drainage Gap
40½" Total Rise
Tread
Stringer
44" Total Run

11

ADDING STAIRS

FRAMING A PLATFORM

TOOLS & MATERIALS

- 2x lumber
- Circular saw
- Square
- Clamps
- Drill-driver & bits
- 1¼" & 2" screws
- Brace
- Hammer
- Nails

Use the same techniques on a stair platform that you use on a main deck, matching the joist size and spacing. Put aside good lumber for the exposed sides, and use screws for extra holding power.

1 *For clean edges, make square cuts on the platform framing lumber. Allow for overlaps on the corners.*

2 *To assemble, check for square and then clamp the frame together. Use a brace if needed.*

3 *Predrill for screws at the corners to avoid splitting the wood. Secure the framing using deck screws.*

4 *Reinforce the corners with galvanized deck hardware. Add joist hangers to interior joists.*

5 *Check the frame for square, and lock it into position using a diagonal brace.*

20 inches. In both formulas, 10-inch-wide treads with a 7-inch step up would qualify. Building departments also have stair guidelines. Most important is to make the stairs uniform. As people approach stairs, going up or down, they generally find the handrail and take a look at the first step to make sure of their footing. But then they look away, assuming that the first stride will work the rest of the way. On your own deck, you would become used to irregular stairs with a surprise first or last step. But building codes have to account for other people, too, including the next owner of your house.

It's also important to see where the last step falls. For example, shorter stairs on the side of a deck may fall within the boundary of the overall construction area, while longer stairs may project into the yard and get in the way. Remember, using fewer treads makes a steeper descent but a smaller footprint. Using more treads makes a more gradual descent but uses up more yard.

PLATFORM DESIGN

A platform can break a long drop into two more manageable sections and serve as a landing beside the main deck. Platforms should be framed like the deck itself, generally with the same-size joists. You can include a platform landing in your deck frame or build it separately and bolt it in position.

STRINGER DESIGN

Use 2x12 lumber for your stringers. If you have two-by treads that are longer than 36 inches, you will need a middle stringer, or carriage. In choosing a stringer, you have three basic options: notched stringers, housed or solid stringers, and for wider stairs, housed stringers with a notched middle carriage.

Notched Stringer. The most commonly used type of stringer is notched, that is, cut into a sawtooth pattern so that each tread has a flat support. You need to be sure of the layout because cuts can't be corrected. Despite the increased area of exposed end grain in the sawtooth pattern, there is a classic look to notched stringers and overhanging treads. And stairs that are wider than 36 inches will need a

DIY OPTIONS: STRINGERS

Most do-it-yourselfers find it easiest to work with solid, or housed, stringers. You simply buy a few straight 2x12s, lay out the tread pattern on the sides, and screw on galvanized metal brackets to hold the treads. Cut stringers are more complicated to lay out, but many home centers and lumberyards sell precut stringers. The proportions are generally set to provide a 10- or 11-inch tread and a 7- to 7½-inch rise. The angle is fixed because the tread supports of the sawtooth pattern must be level; just cut the bottom edges to fit your site.

CUT STRINGER

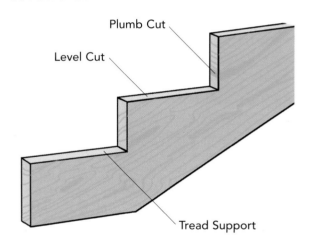

Plumb Cut

Level Cut

Tread Support

SOLID STRINGER

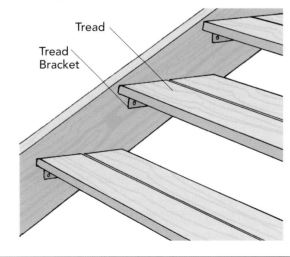

Tread

Tread Bracket

Concrete Landing Pad

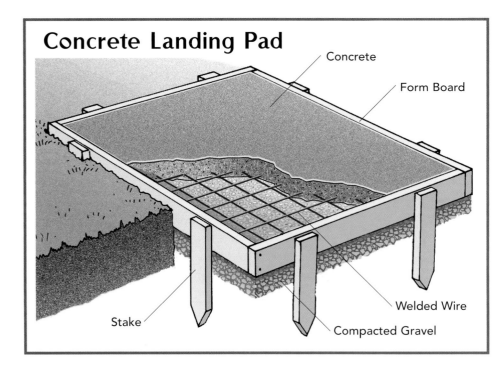

Concrete

Form Board

Welded Wire

Compacted Gravel

Stake

notched middle carriage anyway. With careful work, you can build a stairway with notched stringers that will last for decades.

Many do-it-yourselfers will get the best results using precut notched stringers that are available at lumberyards and home centers. If the exact location of your bottom pad doesn't matter, you can adjust its position to accommodate store-bought stringers. Before buying, figure your rise and run to be sure you won't end up with a bottom step that is more than ¾ inch different from the rest of the steps. Ideally the last step to the landing pad should have the same rise as the wooden steps.

Solid Stringer. Also called a housed stringer because treads are contained within the angled framing, this type of stair support is used with cleats that support the treads. You still have to make a layout with equally spaced steps, but you don't have to cut the pattern into the stringers. And if you make a layout mistake, it's easy enough to shift tread cleats. The best cleats are L-shaped galvanized metal brackets that won't decay the way wood cleats can.

If your stairway is wider than 36 inches, one practical approach is to first cut a notched stringer (carriage), which will support the treads in the middle, and use it as a template for locating your tread cleats on the housed stringers.

(Check your local codes about tread spans on stairs.) Just set it up against the housed stringers, and mark the positions for the cleats, as well as the bottom plumb and level cuts.

To handle unusual stair loads—for example, where stringers are more than 8 feet long—you can use double stringers or laminate a cut stringer to each solid stringer.

LANDING PAD DESIGN

Stringers must have something solid to support them at the bottom and protect them from ground contact. You can provide the support in several ways. On a small stairway, you can build two extra piers (one for each stringer). On a larger stairway, it's often more economical to build a concrete slab. Of course, you also can combine piers with a landing pad made of bricks, gravel, or other material that does not have to support the stringer.

INSTALLING A PLATFORM

There are many ways to include a platform in your stairway. For example, you can support it with four posts and piers to stand away from the deck so that one run of stairs reaches from the deck to the platform and another reaches from the platform to the ground.

Another approach is to attach a platform to the deck to make a step-down landing. This works well if you want the stairs to tuck in next to the side of the deck instead of extending out into the yard. As you climb alongside the deck, you need a transition area, like a landing on indoor stairs, where you can turn and take the last step up onto the deck.

Incorporating a platform landing into your stairs is often easier (and better looking) than extending part of the deck to serve as a landing. This approach also allows you to build the frame

SETTING A PLATFORM

TOOLS & MATERIALS
- Scrap lumber
- Clamps
- Level
- Flashing
- Bolts
- Wrenches
- Measuring tape
- Drill-driver & bits
- 3 in. screws
- 4x4 posts

Attach the landing platform to both the deck and the house for support.

1 Clamp the platform to a temporary post. Use clamps to hold the platform against the deck.

2 Check for level in all directions, and make adjustments as needed.

3 Using lag screws, attach the platform to the ledger board against the house.

4 Attach the platform to the deck framing using long screws or carriage bolts.

5 Install permanent posts as needed. Screw the posts to the frame, and trim the tops of the posts.

independently, complete with joists and fasteners, and bolt the landing frame to the deck frame. In most cases, you will need at least one new pier to support a post at the outer corner of the platform. You may need two, but not if the side of the platform bolts to the deck and the back bolts to the house framing.

PLATFORM FRAMING

The platform needs to be as strong as the deck. You should plan to frame it with the same lumber you used for the main joists, but pick good-looking lumber for the exposed sides. Set the joists with the typical deck spacing, and secure the connections with galvanized frame hardware. In addition to standard joist hangers, also use L-brackets to reinforce the outside corners of the platform frame. (See "Framing a Platform," page 220, and "Setting a Platform," page 223.)

INSTALLING A LANDING PAD

Whatever design and material you choose for a landing pad, it's wise to build it somewhat oversized. This provides a margin of error of several inches in each direction when it comes time to install and bolt down the stringers. If you live in an area subject to frost, you may need to go

PLATFORM POST DETAILS

TOOLS & MATERIALS
- Combination square
- Pencil
- 4x4 post
- Horses
- Circular saw
- Hammer
- Mallet
- Chisel

Rabbeted posts provide support in two ways: the shoulder of the rabbet supports the posts from below and you can screw the joists to the rabbeted end for additional support.

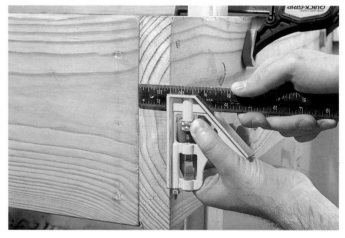

1 Measure the thickness of the platform's outer joist; save the measurement on a combination square.

3 Set the depth of cut on the saw to the layout mark. Make cuts every ¼ in. along the post.

4 Use a hammer to break the thin strands of wood left by the saw cuts. Trim with a chisel.

below the frost line with your pad foundation. Be sure to check local codes for requirements. Here are some of the options.

Concrete. Use this material to make the strongest landing pad. The area is small, so there isn't too much work involved, though waiting for the concrete to set may slow down your job.

First dig out enough sod and topsoil to accommodate at least 3 inches of gravel and 3 inches of concrete. Ideally, the pad should sit an inch or so above grade to help with drainage. It's also important to compact soil at the bottom of your small excavation (or leave it undisturbed), and to compact the gravel bed, as well.

One approach is to construct a frame of 2x4s laid on edge, reinforced with 2x4 or 1x4 stakes.

2 Transfer the thickness mark to the post. Extend the line to equal the thickness of the joist.

5 Repeat the process on the adjacent side of the post. This creates a rabbet for the other corner joist.

This frame can be a permanent part of the pad (using treated lumber) or removed after the concrete has set. Make sure the frame is square and level. (See "Concrete Landing Pad," page 222.)

Place the gravel in the hole, tamping firmly with a 4x4 or a hand tamper. If you will be using reinforcing wire mesh, cut it to fit loosely in the form (so you don't have any wire sticking out after you've poured) and place it in the form, using rocks to hold it up from the gravel.

Pour the concrete, and level it off with a 2x4 that spans across your frame. Finish using a concrete finishing trowel, and use an edging tool where the concrete meets the frame. If you like, give it a final brush stroke with a broom for a skid-free surface.

Brick. Before you install a brick surface, check with your inspector, who may require concrete. (Setting bricks or pavers in a bed of concrete is also an option.) There are two main tricks to getting a nonconcrete landing pad surface that is strong enough. First, tamp the gravel and sand beds (if you're using sand instead of a concrete set). Second, set the landing material so that the load it carries from the stringers is spread over several bricks or pavers. Choose a solid edging to keep the bricks in place, such as pressure-treated landscape timbers or bricks set vertically.

Gravel. The most basic landing pad is a bed of gravel. This is not as stable or as strong as concrete, but it provides excellent drainage, and if installed correctly, can be surprisingly strong. Check with the building inspector before building a gravel pad.

Dig a hole 10 to 12 inches deep; fill part way with gravel; and install a frame made of treated 2x4s or 2x6s secured with stakes made of 2x4s or 1x4s. Lay 3 to 4 inches of gravel; compact it firm with a hand tamper or a piece of 4x4; then lay the next layer. Don't lay the final 1½ inches until the stringers are in place.

When you build your stairs, spread the load so that the stringers will not dig into the gravel, lowering the level of the steps over time. Attach treated 2x4s to the bottom of the stringers, spanning from stringer to stringer. Rest this setup on the gravel, then fill in with the final 1½ inches of gravel.

ADDING STAIRS

11

STAIRWAY LAYOUTS

Before you start figuring out the nitty-gritty details, here's the basic idea behind stair layout. To sort out the different possible dimensions and proportions, start by carefully recording two key measurements. One is the overall drop from the deck surface straight down to the level of the yard or landing. The other is the overall span from the edge of the deck to the end of the stairs.

To work out a preliminary plan, divide the drop into equal segments of *rise* (the vertical distance between tread surfaces), and divide the span into equal segments of *run* (the depth of each tread, including a 1-inch overlap).

If you use precut stringers, the basic proportions are already settled. In that case, you simply make the cuts at the end of the stringer so it rests on the landing pad when the tread support sections of the stringers are dead level.

In stair terminology, the drop is split into increments called *unit rise*, which is the total vertical distance between the top of one tread and the top of the next tread. Horizontal distance is split into increments called *unit run*, which is the horizontal distance traveled by each step. The unit run consists of the width of the tread minus any overhang or nosing.

Most do-it-yourselfers have to experiment with rise and run ratios to find a design that will provide a safe, comfortable, and code-approved stairway. Here is the sequence you can use to come up with a final plan.

Find the Total Rise. If the ground below your deck is level, you can find the total rise simply by measuring straight down from the top of the deck. But the ground may slope away from the deck. In addition, the ground may slope across the width of the stairs. So you need to determine where the steps will land and calculate the total rise from that point. (See "Stringer Layout," opposite.)

Find the Number of Steps. Let's say you would like a unit run of 11 inches and a unit rise of 7½ inches, and your deck is 36 inches off the ground. Divide the total rise of 36 inches by the unit rise of 7½ inches to get 4.8. Round up to find that you will need five steps if the ground is level. One of those steps is the deck itself, so subtract it from the equation when figuring total run. Because you are shooting to make each step 11 inches deep, multiply 11 times 4 to find that your landing should be 44 inches from the deck.

Locate the Stair Width. Make two pencil marks on the edge of the deck to indicate the planned width of the stairway. Let's say you want to build steps that are 36 inches wide, including the thickness of the stringers but not including the overhang of the treads on either side of the stringers, if you are using notched stringers. You'll probably want to make the landing pad a couple of inches wider on each side, so figure the pad will be 40 inches wide.

Locate the Landing Area. From the marks on the deck, measure out the proposed total run, making sure you are running your measuring tape square to the edge of the deck. Drive a long stake into the ground at these points, making sure the stakes extend above the level of the deck. Plumb the stakes. (If these stakes are more than 60 or 72 inches tall, you will need to have a helper hold a level against them as you

Stringer Markup

FIRST PHASE

Rise Mark

Run Mark

Framing Square

Top Plumb Cut

Top of Tread

Tread Thickness

Bottom of Tread (top of cleat)

Base Level Cut

Base Plumb Cut

SECOND PHASE

STRINGER LAYOUT

TOOLS & MATERIALS
- Measuring tape
- 2x4
- Framing square
- Stops
- Horses
- Pencil
- 2x12 stringers

You can lay out stringers with a framing square fitted with stops.

1 Extend a level 2x4 from the platform, and measure the distance down to a level landing area.

2 Set stops on a framing square where numbers on opposite sides match your rise and unit run.

3 Mark the top of the stringer. Slide the stops along the stringer to repeat tread layout lines.

proceed, to be sure they are plumb.)

Have a helper hold one end of a string on one of the marks on the deck. Hang a line level on the string, and run the other end to the corresponding stake. When the line is level, mark the position on the stake. Repeat the process to make a mark on the other stake. Measure from the marks on the stake to the ground, or 1 inch above the ground if you want your landing pad to be an inch higher than your yard. If the two measurements differ, use the shorter measurement as the total rise.

Make the landing pad level so that it rises above grade on the low side to compensate for the difference. Let's say, for example, that the mark on

the left stake as you face the deck is 40½ inches from the ground while the right stake is 42 inches from the ground. The ground slopes away from the deck and down from left to right. Use 40½ inches as your total rise.

Figure the Unit Rise and Unit Run. Round the total rise off to the nearest whole number of inches, and divide by 7. If you know you want short rises, you can start by dividing by 6 inches instead of 7. In the example above, 40 divided by 7 equals 5.7. Round again to the nearest whole number. This tells you that to keep the unit rise and unit run you have in mind, you'll need six steps, including the one onto the deck, to cover the total rise.

INSTALLING SOLID STRINGERS

TOOLS & MATERIALS
- Level
- Measuring tape
- Combination square
- Stair stringers
- Drill & bits
- Stair brackets
- 1¼" screws
- Framing square
- Stair clip
- Lag screws
- Wrenches

Clamp a marked stringer in place to check pencil marks for treads before installing the stringer.

1 *Make sure the landing pad is level before installing the stringers.*

3 *Attach the top edges of the stringers to the platform using corner brackets.*

4 *Screw galvanized tread brackets to the stringer, following the layout lines.*

You can adjust the unit rise or the unit run, or both, to accommodate your true total rise. In most cases, you will not want to change the planned unit run, because it is determined by the lumber you've chosen for stair treads. The easiest thing to adjust is the unit rise. Divide the total rise (40½ inches) by six steps to get a unit rise of 6¾ inches. Remember, two times the unit rise plus the unit run should equal between 25 and 27 inches. In our example, two times 6¾ inches plus 11 inches equals 24½ inches, which is close enough to the general guideline.

Now it's easy to determine exactly where your stairs will land. Again, because one of the steps is the deck surface, your stringers will have five

steps, each traveling 11 inches for a total run of 55 inches. Of course, because you have added a step since figuring the tentative total run, that's 11 inches farther than the original total run of 44 inches.

That's fine, provided the ground is level where the stairs land; simply adjust the position of the landing pad. If the ground continues to slope, you are better off increasing the unit rise so that you can stick with a four-step stringer. To do this, divide the total rise of 40½ inches by 5 (the rise includes the fifth step onto the deck). The calculator says that's 8.1, or for practical purposes, a unit rise of 8 inches. Two times 8 inches plus 11 inches equals 27 inches, which is also within the

2 Mark the location of each stringer on the platform or deck. The edges of the stringer must be straight.

5 Attach a galvanized clip to the pad. See below for other attachment options.

rule of thumb for proper stairway design.

Despite all the figuring, there is no substitute for marking up a stringer, clamping or bracing it in place, and seeing in this full-scale dry run exactly where the treads will fall.

BUILDING THE STAIRS

Here is a look at the basic sequence of building a set of stairs. Of course, you may have to add some construction steps (or skip over a few) if you are building something more complicated or unusual than a relatively short, straight run.

Estimate Stringer Length. To buy the stock for your stringers, you'll need a rough estimate of their length. Here's a quick method. On a framing square, use the stair layout numbers on opposing sides as a guide. The idea is to measure on a diagonal between the number matching your unit rise on one side to the unit run on the other side. This will tell you how far the stringer has to travel per step. Multiply this number by the number of steps you will have, plus one (to be safe), and you will have a good rough estimate of how long your stringer needs to be. For example, a step with a unit rise of 7 inches and a unit run of 11 inches will travel 13 inches per step. If there are five steps, you should buy stringers about 6 feet 6 inches long.

Lay Out the First Stringer. Using a framing square, transfer the rise and run to a 2x12 with

DIY OPTIONS: STRINGER BASE ATTACHMENT

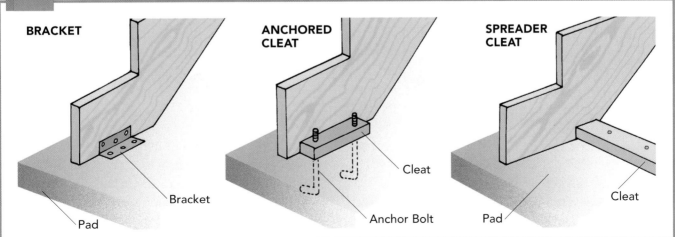

BRACKET

Bracket

Pad

ANCHORED CLEAT

Cleat

Anchor Bolt

SPREADER CLEAT

Cleat

Pad

SETTING CARRIAGES

TOOLS & MATERIALS
- Carriage
- Level
- Drill & bits
- 3" lag screws
- Angle brackets
- 1¼" screws
- Measuring tape
- Square
- 1x brace

On wide stairs, add at least one center carriage for extra support.

1 Tack the center carriage in place, checking for level at each tread location.

2 Use the access space from inside the platform framing to drive lag screws into the top of the carriage.

3 Reinforce the carriage attachment by installing corner brackets.

4 Measure the stair opening and center the middle carriage.

5 Tack a brace across the bottom of the stringers. This secures them as you add fasteners and treads.

the crown side up. It helps to mark your square with tape if you can't find metal stops, sometimes called buttons. The stops are handy because they let you ride the square along the side of a stringer, maintaining the same angle for every tread. Mark the stringers in pencil. Don't be surprised if you get a bit mixed up and have to start over. (See "Stringer Layout," page 227.)

Start at the top of the stringer—the end that will meet the deck. When you come to the bottom step, shorten the rise by the thickness of the stock for the treads.

Make the Stringers. Cut the top and bottom of the stringer—you don't have to cut the notches yet—and hold it up to the deck in the position where it will be attached when you build the stairs. Rest the bottom end of the stringer on the landing pad, or a piece of lumber that simulates the height of your landing pad. Check that the layout lines for the treads are level.

To be safe (as long as you have some extra length in the stringer), you might want to sneak up on the plumb and level cuts at the ends of the stringer. For example, you might leave the mark plus ½ inch or so for the first dry run. You can always trim off the excess and use the margin to correct the angle one way or another.

To make the cuts for a notched stringer, use a circular saw. Because you are entering the board at an angle, you may need to retract the blade guard at the start of each cut to avoid cutting a wavy line. Rest the shoe of the saw solidly and evenly on the surface of the board as you cut. It's okay to go past your lines a little (¾ inch or so), but only if the board face you are looking at will not be visible once the stairway is completed. But instead of weakening a stringer with overcuts, you can finish circular saw cuts with a handsaw.

It's generally neater to finish the sawtooth-pattern stringer cuts with a handsaw, holding the blade at 90 degrees to the board so you don't get overlapping cut lines on the other side of the board.

Brush on a coat of sealer at all your cuts, and let it sink into all of the end grain. Take care not to bump the projecting teeth of the stringer after they are cut and before treads are attached. The stringer teeth could split off.

ATTACHING CLEATS

An alternative to attaching stringers to a pad with galvanized brackets is to attach a 2x4 cleat. Use lag screws and masonry shields to attach the cleat. After cutting the cleat to size, predrill holes for the screws.

Drill holes *for the masonry shields.*

Use a rachet wrench *to drive the screws.*

Screw stringers *to the cleats.*

DIY OPTIONS: TREADS

On solid stringers, do not rely on nails driven into the treads through the stringers to support the step. This weak detail can cause splits and accidents.

A better way to support treads is to attach a nailing block, or cleat, to the stringer, and nail or screw the tread to the cleat. (1) However, with time the wood may decay. Galvanized brackets provide durable support for treads. (2) Fasten treads by screwing through the flange into the bracket. On sawtooth stringers, the sawtooth pattern creates a ready-made support for the treads. (3) If treads extend beyond the stringers, finish treads with curved corners and beveled edges. (4)

After you have cut the first stringer, check it in position to be sure the cuts are correct. Then use it as a template for other stringers. If you are going to have two solid stringers and a notched center carriage, cut the notched piece first and use it to mark the housed stringers.

For a housed stringer, make the top and bottom cuts first. Then position the tread cleats; drill pilots; and fasten the cleats to the stringers with 1¼-inch lags. If you're not sure of the tread layout, you can screw on the hardware after the stringers are installed. This gives you a chance to make corrections. (See "Installing Solid Stringers," page 228.)

Locate the Posts. On some designs, you can install the stringers and treads completely, and then attach the main railing post. On stairs that project away from the deck with two railings, of course, you'll need two posts. If your 2x12 stringers are securely bolted into a concrete landing pad, you may gain enough strength for a railing post by bolting it to the pad and the stringer. It will be even stiffer once you add a substantial railing and balusters.

Another option is to set the stringers temporarily; mark the post locations; remove the stringers; and dig postholes. You might set the posts in concrete or build piers with hardware so that the porous post ends stay off the ground.

Attach the Tops of the Stringers. To make a solid connection, you may have to beef up the deck framing. Depending on its size (and the amount of unit rise), you may not have enough joist material to make a solid connection. In that case you will need to add another support, typically fastened between posts.

To attach a stringer to the face of a joist, you may be able to drive nails or screws through the back of the joist into the end of the stringer. In any case, be sure to secure the face of the connection with angled joist hardware or brackets. You may see some parts of this hardware, but most will be concealed by the treads.

Attach the Stringers to the Pad. The stairway will be quite stable once the treads and railings are installed. But to lock the stringers in place, you can install a small galvanized bracket to the concrete pad. (See "Installing Solid Stringers," page 228.) Another option is to set J-bolts in the concrete while it is wet and attach a treated wood cleat to them. Or you can notch the bottom of the stringers and install a 2x4 cleat attached to the pad with masonry nails, or with lag screws and masonry shields. (See pages 229 and 231.)

Install Treads and Risers. If you will be using risers, install them before the treads. The top of each riser must be flush with the horizontal stringer cut, but there should be a gap at the bottom to allow water to drain. If your rise is less than 7¼ inches, you will have to rip 1x8s to fit.

Risers are often installed flush to the outside of the stringers, but this design can lead to problems if your cuts are not perfect or if the boards shrink. If you let them overlap the stringers by ¾ inch or so, you will avoid these problems. Of course, this works only on cut stringers where you also can let the treads extend by the same margin. On cut stringers, you may like the floating effect that comes from extending the treads 3 or 4 inches beyond the edge of the stringer. If possible, the overlap should be equal on both sides of the tread.

If you're nailing, it's wise to predrill your treads. Driving screws is a better option and provides more holding power. Better yet, use concealed hardware, and drive screws up through brackets into the bottoms of the treads. There won't be any screw or nail heads on the surface of the tread. (See "DIY Options" opposite.)

Driving screws up into treads isn't practical on bottom steps that may be only 6 or 7 inches from the ground. There probably won't be room for a drill. The solution is to attach the L-brackets to the undersides of the treads first, clamp the assembly in place, and then drive screws sideways to fasten the brackets.

SMART TIP

BOX STEPS
If your deck is only a step up from the yard, you might avoid stringers altogether and build box steps. These are easy-to-build rectangular frames, usually made of 2x6

treated lumber and covered with deck treads. For two or more steps, build a large box, placing progressively smaller ones on top.

Positioning Stringers

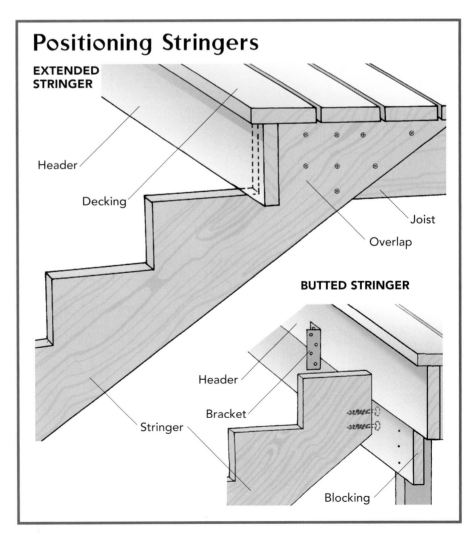

EXTENDED STRINGER

Header

Decking

Joist

Overlap

BUTTED STRINGER

Header

Bracket

Stringer

Blocking

RAILINGS AND BENCHES

12

A railing provides a measure of safety, some privacy, and a place for displaying plants. Local building codes vary, but generally, decks built more than 18 inches aboveground will require a railing. The building code will specify minimum requirements for the design of the railing.

ABOVE **The posts on this railing are boxed in and shingled to complement the house's style.**

RAILINGS: BASIC CHOICES

Whether you are standing on the deck or viewing it from the yard, the railing is the most visible part of the structure. The railing greatly influences the overall appearance of the deck, giving it either vertical or horizontal lines, an open or closed appearance, or a polished or rustic look. But railings must also be designed for safety.

Modern codes typically call for a railing that is 36 inches high with balusters spaced no more than 4 inches apart. (Be sure to check code requirements with the local building department.) But within these limits, you can make many kinds of railing—for example, with vertical balusters and one top rail or several horizontal rails between the main posts. Another option is to incorporate a railing into built-in perimeter benches.

There's no heavy lifting, no messy digging at this stage. And with a few simple techniques,

you can produce a structure that looks professional and handcrafted—something you can point to with pride for years to come.

RAILING MATERIALS

Some lumberyards and home centers now carry prefabricated railing systems. They come with all the components ready for assembly, including railings and factory-milled balusters and newels in several different decorative patterns. You can also use cast metal, steel cables, plastic tubing, clear acrylic panels, and so on, as long as you get the approval of the local building department.

The most popular and easiest-to-use railing materials are stock pieces of dimensional lumber. You can cut and assemble one-by, two-by, and four-by materials in a variety of styles.

LUMBER

It is usually best to have the railing materials match the decking and fascia, but this is not a hard-and-fast rule. Sometimes it works best to think in terms of matching the railing with the house, inasmuch as the railing is a vertical line that is seen with the house as a backdrop. For example, on a Colonial or Victorian house, turned spindles and fancy newels may look best, especially if they can mirror elements on the house.

And there's no rule that says you can't stain or paint all or part of the railing to help it blend in. If you have an unpainted deck against a painted house, you already have wood and paint in combination, and there's no harm in continuing that pattern. In any case, paint the top cap to protect it from the weather.

SELECTING LUMBER

The railing deserves the best lumber you can find. Not only do these pieces get handled, they also provide nooks and crannies through which water can be absorbed. And splinters on a rail can be downright dangerous. You must select railing material carefully. This particular component is important when it comes to appearance, and even more so when it comes to safety.

Cedar and redwood look best and splinter least. However, because they get handled and are exposed to the weather, plan on treating railings made of these materials with a wood preservative at least every other year. Treated lumber of high quality can also work, and there is a variety of composite and vinyl railing systems available.

Precut Components. You can save time using precut components such as decorative 2x2 balusters. But don't change your railing design just to accommodate their size. With a power miter saw and an easily made jig, you can quickly gang-cut 100 2x2s to the length you need. It can sometimes be a problem to find good-looking 2x2s, because they often twist if not stacked well. You may want to select a larger stock and rip it into pieces to make balusters.

In some areas you can purchase lumber that has been milled to accept stock components. For example, you should be able to buy a top cap that has a 1½-inch-wide groove in the bottom to accommodate 2x2 balusters.

FASTENERS

When things come loose on a deck, it is usually at the railing. There's a lot of exposed joinery, and the railing gets leaned on and bumped. So plan for a railing that is as strong as possible at all points.

Unfortunately, there are few specialized railing hardware pieces, and they are not as effective as joist hangers for the framing. In general, the metal connectors for attaching rails to posts are unattractive and provide a place for moisture to collect. And unless they are galvanized, they can rust. There is a post-to-railing clip that is more helpful; it allows you to connect the top cap to the post while concealing the fasteners. Wood cleats that can add an extra nailing surface often look unprofessional and may be susceptible to water damage.

DIY OPTIONS: CAPS AND POSTS

Precut posts are available in many styles and sizes. You can cut them to length and combine them with stock sizes of railing caps and balusters. If you use stock posts, you can dress up the tops with flat or shaped caps. Many have a screw end, so you can drill a pilot hole and easily turn them onto the posts.

The upshot is the need to make the most of standard fasteners. Start off by attaching the support posts to the outermost joists with either lag screws or through-bolts. Through-bolts offer maximum support. It's also wise to drill pilot holes for all nails or screws that are near the end of a board. Use 3-inch deck screws or 16d galvanized nails for plenty of holding power. Try to avoid driving nails or screws at an angle (toe-nailing), and driving more than two fasteners at railing connections. For example, where you need to piece a horizontal rail over a 4x4 or 2x4, use a lap joint and one pair of fasteners driven through both boards. This is less likely to cause splitting than driving two pairs.

RAILING BASICS

All railings use some, but not necessarily all, of the following components. *Posts* are structural members, usually made of 4x4s or 2x4s turned on edge for lateral strength. They keep the railing from wobbling and provide the main support that counteracts the weight of someone leaning or falling against the assembly.

Balusters are the numerous vertical pieces, often made of 2x2s, that fill in spaces between the posts and provide a sort of fence. *Bottom rail* and *top rail* pieces run horizontally between the posts, and are either flat or on end. On many designs, the balusters are attached to these rails. Some railings do not have vertical balusters, and use several horizontal rails instead. (Check local codes.)

Other designs use a *top cap*, a horizontal piece of lumber laid flat on top of the post and top rail. It covers the end grain of the post and can provide a flat surface that serves as a shelf.

COMPLYING WITH CODE

The railing is one part of your deck that an inspector will check closely. You'll likely find that any deck more than 18 inches from the ground requires a railing that uses vertical components and must be at least 36 inches high. Some codes may specify a height of 42 inches.

If the deck is more than 8 feet high, you may want to build a 42-inch railing for extra security.

When you're planning the railing system, consider one of the most limiting codes: the minimum space between components. Commonly, this dimension is 4 inches, based largely on the idea of preventing very small children from falling through or getting their heads stuck between rails or balusters. Some codes may call for a smaller maximum opening at the bottom of the railing.

There also may be specific requirements about posts and fasteners to ensure that your railing is strong. But there are many design variations that you can use and still comply with code.

RAILING DESIGN CHOICES

One approach to railing design is to work from two lists of dimensions: one that includes stock-size lumber, such as 2x4 and 4x4 posts, and another that includes code requirements, such as 4-inch spacing between balusters. You'll find that there are many ways to put the pieces together.

Here is a quick look at some of the other factors that can affect your choice of materials and the overall design.

Matching Deck Overhangs. The first thing to think about in selecting a design is how you will attach the railings and posts to the deck. There are several possibilities. For example, if you have balusters but no bottom rail so that the balusters are attached to the joists or fascia boards, you may want to cut the decking flush to the joists. Otherwise you would have to make hundreds of little cutouts to make room for the balusters. But if you are using several rails instead of balusters or if you have a bottom rail to which you'll attach the balusters, then the decking can overhang the joist.

Choosing a Cap Width. If your top cap will butt between the posts, it should be the same width as the post—which usually means it will be a 2x4. If you want a wider cap (handy as a shelf), use a design that places the cap on top of the posts. This style looks best if the cap overhangs the posts by ¼ to 1½ inches on each side.

Most railing designs allow you to choose either a 2x6 or a 2x8 for a top cap. The 2x8 may look a little clunky, especially on a small deck, but has a lot of shelf space. Whatever design you choose, select the very best pieces of lumber for your top cap.

Setting Posts. There are three basic approaches to post-setting. One is to attach the decking boards flush with the edges of the outermost joists. This allows you to fasten the railing posts to the deck frame without cutting any notches. But most decks look better (and drain better) with an overhang.

Another approach is to notch the posts to accept the deck overhang. This allows the bottom section of the posts to rest against the joists where you can secure them with lag screws or bolts. This works well if the overhang is small and you're using large posts, such as 4x4s. But with a large overhang, you'll need a big notch, which can weaken the posts. The best approach often is to notch the deck boards where they overhang the joists. This leaves a full-thickness post where you need maximum strength.

Corner Posts. You can install a single corner post or two posts near one another on opposite sides of a corner. Single corner posts should be 4x4s or better.

RAILING OPTIONS

Here is a look at several design options. If you want to create your own design, you can mix and match ideas.

Balusters and Top Rail Only. This is the simplest design. But it is suitable only for smaller railings because it lacks posts and a flat-laid top cap, both of which give lateral strength to other designs. Of course, the closer the balusters are to each other, the more strength you gain. On a long deck this railing can have a monotonous appearance because all the vertical lines are the same width.

To build it, install the balusters for each end of the rail, and attach the rail. Then fill in the middle balusters. Screws work better than nails. The uncompleted railing will wobble a bit if you

ABOVE **Decorative top rails and post caps provide distinctive details to your deck.**

pound on it.

Cap with No Rails. This has the vertical feel of the first design, with the added strength of posts and the usefulness of a top cap. The easiest way to build this railing is to use a cap with a factory-milled groove to fit the 2x2 balusters. But some outlets offer these caps only in 3½-inch widths. If you want to set out some flower boxes, use a 2x6 for the top cap, and attach a 2x2 nailer underneath it. Screw the balusters to the nailer.

Install the posts every 72 inches or so (but within code limits), and lay the top cap on them. Install the nailer between the posts if you're not using the cap with a groove, and attach the balusters.

DIY OPTIONS: POST AND RAILING

FLUSH

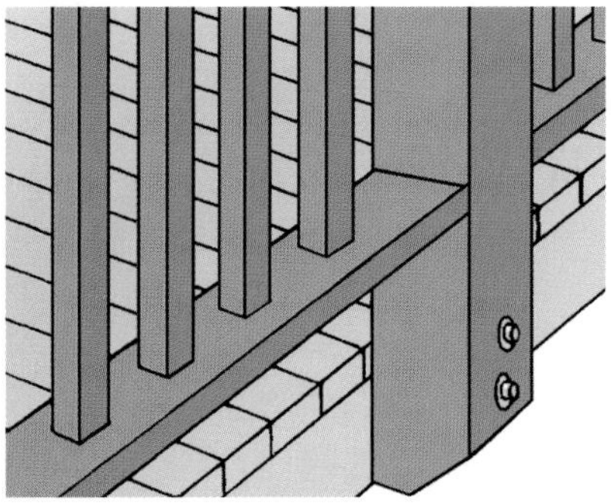

DOUBLE CORNER

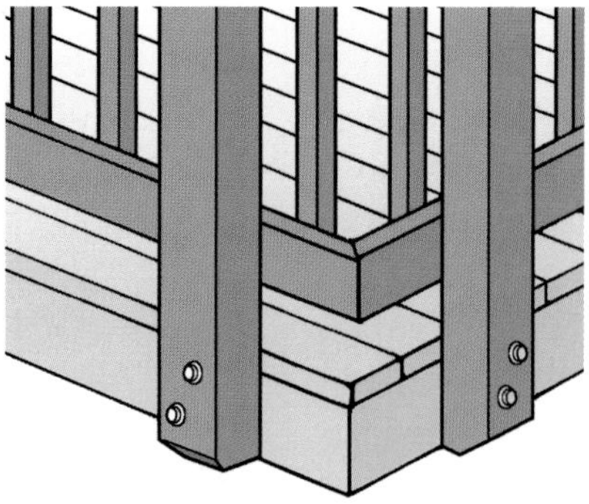

NOTCHED

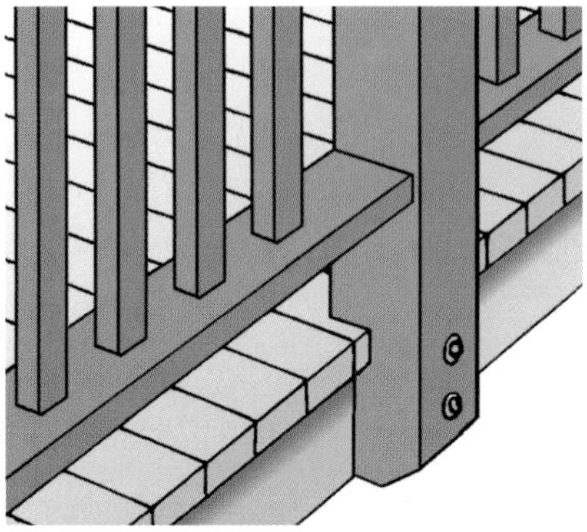

SINGLE CORNER

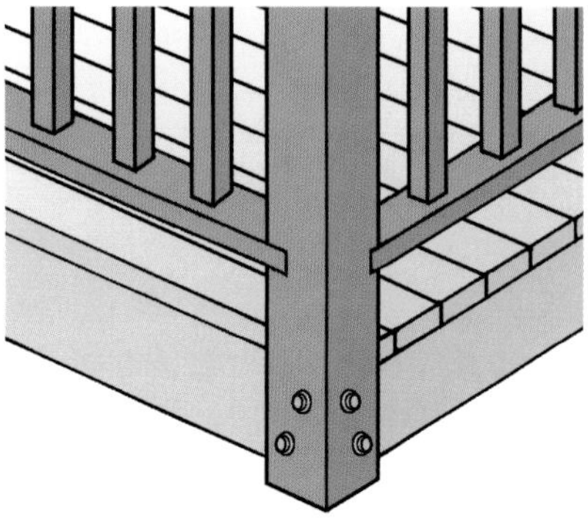

VERTICAL RAIL

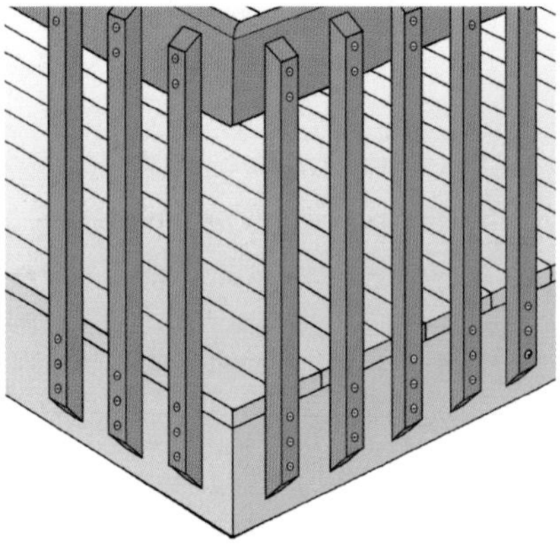

CAP WITH NO RAILS

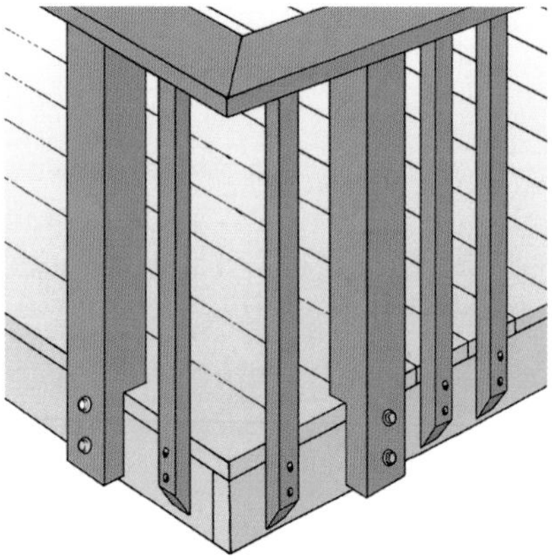

HORIZONTAL RAIL*

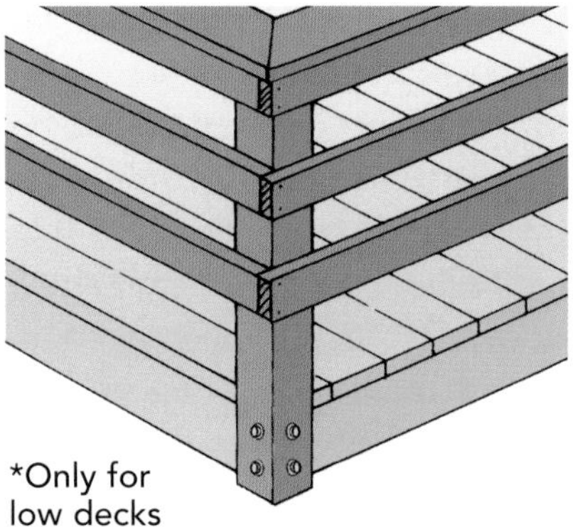

MILLED BALUSTERS

*Only for low decks

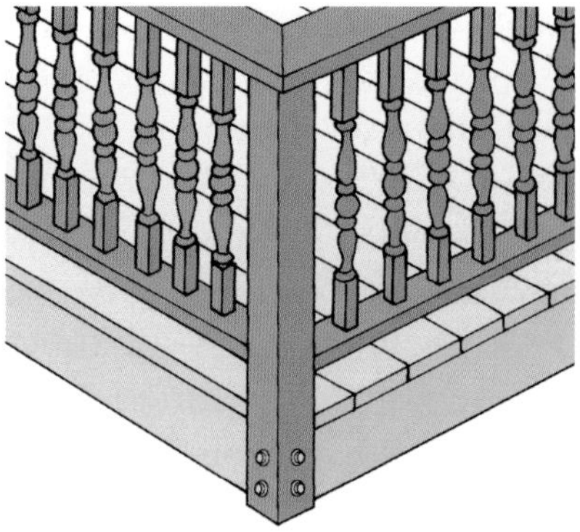

Two Rails with No Cap. In this system, the horizontal lines are as strong as the vertical lines. The lack of a top cap gives a clean look, but affords no shelf space. You may like the look of a wider, more substantial rail on top, such as a 2x6, and a narrower rail, such as a 2x4, near the deck. Attach the top and bottom rails and then the balusters, or build the baluster-and-rail sections ladder-style.

Horizontal Rails. Horizontal lines dominate in this system. (It may not be allowed locally on decks more than 2 or 3 feet high.) You can butt the ends of the rails where they meet over a post or miter them to create an overlap for a more-finished look. The top rail can be made of 1x6, if you want a large overhang on a 2x6 cap. Unless your posts are no more than 48 inches apart, the other rails should be made of two-by lumber. Remember to place rails below the top rail spaced closely enough to conform to codes.

Two Rails with Balusters. This has the look of ladder-style sections between posts, but the rails are continuous, running on the face of the posts (or slightly inset), instead of being butted between posts. This is one of the best approaches because it provides strong horizontal lines and sections of vertical lines with balusters. This helps to give scale and detail to a deck so that it does not look so much like a huge platform stuck onto the side of the house.

First attach posts, which can be 4x4s or 2x4s (spaced and sized according to code); then run the rails and a top cap, if you like, in which case the balusters can butt up against the bottom of the cap.

Sandwiched Panels. This design has several variations, such as using lattice panels, plastic glazing panels, safety glass, or solid panels of siding material. The idea is to build frames for the filler material and attach them to the posts. Another option is to install nailers on the sides of the posts; insert the filler material; and secure it with another set of nailers. A drawback to this design is that water can collect and sit on the bottom rail. So use very rot-resistant materials.

Install the posts, and attach bottom rail and top cap. Install one side of 1x1 nailer pieces, the filler panel, and the rest of the nailers.

Screen with Lattice Top. This uses a combination of designs and provides a lot of visual interest while increasing privacy and cutting down on wind. The potential weak spot is the slats that can become loose over time. At the bottom they can soak up water that sits on the 2x4 bottom rail. So give the cuts a few coats of preservative, and attach the slats firmly with screws.

Cutting the top of the posts to a point will make them less susceptible to water damage. But a simple angle cut will also help. The lattice section on top is constructed in much the same way as the sandwiched panels. Install the posts; build the bottom sections ladder-style; and install them between the posts. Add the topmost rail and one side of 1x1 nailer pieces, then the lattice, and the rest of the 1x1.

Top Rail of 4x6 on Balusters. This is an impressive, unusual railing that does not take a lot of extra work and is no more expensive than many other designs. It is vital, however, that you have extremely straight, dry, and split-free 4x6 pieces for the top rail because there is absolutely no way to straighten them as you build.

The decking has to be cut flush to the joists. The bottom of the balusters are sandwiched between the joists, and the fascia is added after the balusters, creating a 1½-inch gap between the decking and the fascia. This is a good design for avoiding water damage.

Attach the balusters to the deck with two or three screws or nails. Then measure and cut the 4x6 pieces to fit. (With a helper, you can set them on top of the balusters for measuring.) Next, cut the groove in the 4x6 for the balusters. To do this, draw lines for a 1½-inch groove. Be sure you do not cut all the way through to the ends where the groove will be seen in the end grain. Set your circular saw blade to a depth of about 2 inches. First, cut to the lines, then make several passes between the lines, and clean out the groove with a sharp wood chisel. Set the 4x6 pieces in place, and attach balusters with angle-driven screws or nails. Add the fascia board over the balusters.

Crisscross. Making this gridlike pattern will take patience, both to lay it out and to install it. If you want the sections to be squares rather than rectangles, figure how far apart the horizontal pieces will be, and space the vertical balusters in the same way. You can notch the decking for each 2x2 baluster. It's generally easier to install the balusters before the decking. Of course, it would be even easier to cut the decking flush to the joists or fascia. Use screws rather than nails because all those 2x2s will flex if you pound on them.

Figure your grid carefully, laying out the position of all the balusters. You may have to fudge a bit to make the balusters come out evenly spaced. But if you end up with squares that are ¼ inch or so out of square, no one will notice. Install the balusters, the 2x4 top rail, and 2x6 cap. Finish with the 2x2 horizontal rails.

Milled Balusters. Factory-turned balusters, made of treated lumber, vinyl, or composite materials are widely available. These require no cutting (except to length in some cases), which saves you a lot of work. Be sure to inspect each wood baluster carefully for cracks and gouges. Follow manufacturer's installation instructions.

There are many ways you can incorporate these balusters into a railing system. For example, you can build sections of railing ladder style, fastening the balusters to the top and bottom rails with 3-inch screws driven through the rails into the balusters.

INSTALLING RAILINGS AND BALUSTERS

Construction methods vary with different railing designs, but usually you install the posts first, the top and bottom rails next, then the top cap (if you're adding one), and finally the balusters. An alternative approach is to build rail sections ladder-style and install them between the posts. But for most do-it-yourselfers, the piece-by-piece method works best.

PUTTING UP THE POSTS

Once you decide on the railing system, you'll know how to continue—for example, by notching the deck edge for posts. Here is a basic sequence, which you may have to adjust somewhat, depending on the railing system you select. (See "How to Make Posts," below.)

Cut and Notch Posts. Determine the length of your posts, taking into account other railing members and the amount of end joist space the post will cover when it is installed.

For instance, if you have 2x8 joists and want a railing that measures 40 inches high, subtract 1½ inches for the thickness of the top cap, and add 8¾ inches for the thickness of the decking plus the width of the joist, for a post length of 47¼ inches. You also may want to subtract ¾ inch or so to leave a reveal between the bottom

HOW TO MAKE POSTS

TOOLS & MATERIALS
- 2x4s
- Measuring tape
- Combination square
- Circular saw
- Clamps
- Mallet and chisel
- Drill and bits
- 4½-in. lag screws
- Rachet wrench
- Level

You can square cut the ends of the posts, but angled cuts have a more finished appearance.

1 Use a circular saw to make a 45-deg. angled cut at the top end of the posts.

4 Make another set of cuts for the bottom rail. (See step 2.) Clean the recess with a chisel.

5 Notch the deck overhang so that the post lies flat against the joist.

of the joist and the bottom of the post. On decks, this kind of offset generally gives a more finished and professional appearance.

Notch the posts for the railing. If you decide to notch the bottom of the posts rather than the deck overhang, make sure that you don't cut too deeply. **1–4** A cut that approaches half the thickness can expose the post to cracking under pressure. Be particularly careful on corner posts. By the time you make two notches (one for the railing on each side of the corner), the structure of the post may be undermined.

Mark and Notch Decking. On the fascia or joists, mark the positions of all your posts, making them evenly spaced whenever possible.

Make square layout lines so that the posts will fit snugly when you plumb them. You can use a saber saw to make the cutouts or cut the sides for depth with a handsaw, and use a chisel to slice through the back of the notch. **5**

Drill Pilot or Screw Holes. Mark your posts for carriage bolts or lag screws that join the posts to the deck frame. **6** To avoid splits, the fasteners should not go into the deck boards or be driven within 1½ inches of the top and the bottom of the joist, if possible. It's better to have bolts only 4 or 5 inches apart than to set them near the edges of the joists underneath. **7**

Once you have the spacing set, clamp the post in place to be sure the fasteners will connect

2 *Make a series of closely spaced cuts on the opposite side of the posts to create a recess for the top rail.*

3 *Make an angled cut at the bottom outside corner of the post. This will create an attractive detail.*

6 *Drill pilot holes for lag screws where the post will join the deck joist. Countersink to recess bolt heads.*

7 *Attach the post with lag screws and washers. Check for level and adjust as necessary.*

HOW TO INSTALL RAILS

TOOLS & MATERIALS

- 2x4s
- 2x6s
- Measuring tape
- Circular saw
- Drill and bits
- 2½-in. screws
- Router
- Construction adhesive
- Sander

If you can't create a code-approved post spacing layout that is even, leave the odd space next to the house.

1 On long runs that require more than one piece of lumber, create a scarf joint that falls on a post.

4 Continue attaching the bottom rail to the posts. Brace the top of the posts for stability.

5 This top rail projects past posts on opposite sides of a corner. Cut 45-deg. angles in the rails.

solidly to the frame. Then duplicate the layout on the rest of the posts. For through-bolts, drill a hole that allows the bolt to slide completely through the hole. Its threads don't bite into the wood the way they do with a lag screw. For lags, you need a pilot hole that's no wider than the central shaft minus the threads.

To make the holes line up, of course, you need to clamp each post in place (and check for plumb) before drilling through the post into the joist. If you are worried about getting the posts exactly plumb, first drill the top hole and temporarily insert the bolt or screw. Then hold the level to the post and drill the second hole.

Attach the Posts. Secure the posts with car-

riage bolts or lag screws with washers. Some people prefer the appearance of bolt or screw heads that are recessed into countersunk holes. This generally makes a neater, more-finished appearance—and no one will get snagged.

SETTING THE RAILS

Mark and Cut the Rails. When installing rails, it's usually best to hold each piece in place, mark it for cutting, and install it completely before adding another section. Ideally, of course, all of the rails will be single lengths, and you won't have joints except at the corners. (See "How to Install Rails," above.)

But where you must piece the rails, you may

2 To make a scarf joint, cut 45-deg. angles in opposing ends of the rails that meet at the post.

3 Tap the rails into the post notches, and drill pilot holes for the screws. Install two screws per joint.

6 Apply adhesive to the mitered ends; clamp in place; and drive screws to secure the joint.

7 For an added detail, round over and smooth the top of the rail using a router or sander.

want to take the time to make a scarf joint instead of a butt joint, particularly if you have to make the joint over a 2x4 instead of a 4x4 post.

The idea is to cut complementary 45-degree angles where the rails meet, which allows one to slide on top of the other. Clamp the scarf joint in place; predrill; and drive a pair of screws to secure this connection. **1–4** Because this joint requires fewer fasteners than a butt joint, it can reduce splitting. And if the wood shrinks, you won't see an obvious gap the way you would between a butted joint.

As you work your way along the deck, double-check your posts for plumb. You can lock up the posts with a top brace or simply check and

clamp each post to the top rail as you get ready to drive fasteners. There probably won't be much play near the bottom of the posts where you attach the bottom rail.

If you do not have a corner post so that the rails must meet each other between posts, temporarily attach a rail that is too long. Hold the next rail piece up to it, and mark them both at once. You can make a butt joint here, but a miter looks better. **5–7**

Install Stair Railings. The easiest way to mark for cuts on the stair railing is to tack the top and bottom rails in place and scribe the cuts. Check your posts for plumb; then tack the stair rail pieces so that they are parallel with the stringer.

HOW TO INSTALL BALUSTERS

TOOLS & MATERIALS

- 2x4s
- Table saw
- Circular saw
- Sliding T-bevel
- Clamps and horses
- Drill-driver and bits
- 2-in. screws
- Belt sander

If you cut angled tops and bottoms on the main support posts, follow up with the same type treatment on the balusters

1 Mark a sound 2x4 for cutting, and rip the balusters using a table saw.

2 Using the T-bevel, copy the angle on the support posts and transfer it to the balusters.

3 Clamp a group of balusters together, and remove imperfections using a belt sander.

4 Drill pilot holes for the screws in the balusters to avoid splitting the wood.

5 Work your way around the perimeter of the deck, fastening the balusters with screws.

Mark the upper ends for cuts in two directions, flush to the top and to the inside of the deck railing. Use a level to mark the lower ends for a cut that is plumb with the end of the stairway. Mark the lower post to be cut off flush with the top edge of the top rail.

Cut the lower post and rail with a circular saw, and attach the rail to the post with decking screws or galvanized nails, drilling pilot holes for all fasteners.

INSTALLING THE TOP CAP

Measure and Cut. Hold and mark the pieces in place whenever possible. The corners require precise, splinter-free cuts, so use a power miter saw or a guide for your circular saw. It's wise to leave boards long until you get a perfect miter at the corner. Then you can cut the caps to length.

Bevel-Cut the Splices. Avoid butt-end splices if you can, because if the wood shrinks they will look bad and invite moisture into end grain. When splices are necessary, place them on top of posts, and scarf-joint the boards with 45-degree cuts.

Install the Stair Railing Cap. You can use a bevel gauge (or sliding T-bevel) to mark the angle of the upper plumb cut on the stair railing. It's best to mark the cuts with the cap in place. Set your circular saw or power miter saw to cut both ends of the stair railing cap at this angle. Save wasting wood by cutting it a bit long at first, so you can test fit the top end and adjust the angle a bit if you need to. Some end grain will be exposed on both ends, so treat them with some preservative. Get the joint as tight as possible, and smooth the angle transition by sanding.

SETTING BALUSTERS

Estimate Materials and Spacing. You should be able to get a good lumber estimate based on how many balusters you will use per linear foot of deck. If you will be installing a lot of

SMART TIP

USING SPACERS

No matter how careful you are at measuring, there is the chance of making an error. When you measure the same dimension dozens of times, as you do installing balusters, the chances increase. Beat the odds by confirming the margin between two balusters and cutting a block of wood to use as a spacer. Rather than measuring, just hold the block in place. (1) Also use a spacer block beneath balusters to make sure that each one is the same distance up from the bottom edge of the rail. (2)

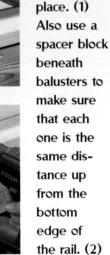

Drainage Details

RAIL CAPS

Angled Cap Sheds Water

Flat Cap Collects Water

POST TOPS

Angled Cut Sheds Water

Square Cut Collects Water

BALUSTER BASES

Face-Mounted Sheds Water

End-Mounted Collects Water

DIY OPTIONS: BUILDING BALUSTRADES

An alternative method for building railings is to construct balustrades, which are complete sections of railings with balusters. You can assemble them flat on the deck as though you were making a ladder. Once these sections are built, you install them between the posts. This system does not have the margin of error provided when you install railings and balusters piece by piece.

Install balusters.

Attach the sections to posts.

balusters in a long, uninterrupted run, pay attention to the spacing between each one, and try to let the odd-size spacing fall next to the house wall.

It is easier to plan spacing in units of balusters between posts. You can figure out the spacing mathematically, but it pays to clamp or tack a set of balusters in place to check your work.

Cut the Balusters. If you have a power miter saw, you can build a jig with a stop block so that you can mass-produce balusters. If you will be cutting with a circular saw, cut one baluster to the correct length; make the angle cuts on the ends if including that detail; and use it as a template for the other balusters. You'll probably cut the stair railing balusters at a different angle than the rest of the balusters, so don't cut them yet. (See "How to Install Balusters," page 246.)

Drill Pilot Holes. You can get away without predrilling on intermediate connections but not near the ends of boards. There you need pilot holes to ensure against splits and to make the joints stronger. And by laying the balusters side by side and drilling straight lines of holes (with a string line to guide you, if need be), you will add a touch of professionalism to your deck. Of course, you need to use a framing square to square-up your balusters before drilling.

Install the Balusters. Figure out the baluster spacing, and cut a spacer block as a guide so that you won't have to measure each installa-

tion. (See the "Smart Tip," page 247.) Use the spacer next to one of the posts and move on down the line of balusters. But double-check for plumb periodically. On long runs, you can make very small adjustments at each baluster (on the scale of $\frac{1}{16}$ inch) to adjust the spacing as needed.

Install Stair Railing Balusters. If you will have stair railing balusters that butt up against a rail cap, find the angle for the top cut by holding a baluster in a plumb position against the top rail and the top cap. Hold a 2x2 spacer on the baluster, and mark the angle. Then check an angle-cut piece in place.

If you are not using a top cap, you can simply attach balusters to the sides of the top and bottom rails. But you will have to increase the offset where the rails run at an angle, or duplicate the angle on the top and bottom cuts of the balusters so that they appear to step down the stairs.

BENCHES

There are many styles of benches and different ways of attaching them to the deck surface and frame. But on almost any deck, it's a good idea to use the same materials on the benches that you use on the decks. This helps the structures blend in with one another.

Bench supports can have a massive look with front and back legs made of 4x4 or larger timbers. But you also can build benches with dimensional lumber, such as 2x10s, cut into a shape that allows one slab to serve as both the seat and back support. These slabs of wood need a supporting front leg, of course, and a brace that securely fixes them to the edge of the deck. But a lot of strength comes from long 2x4 slats that form the seat and back. They can span several of the reinforced uprights and tie them together into a solid assembly.

If you use extended posts that rise through the deck as bench supports, you need to plan ahead and figure out how the benches will attach to the posts. But you can design and build many types of attractive and sturdy benches after the deck surface is completed.

BUILD FOR COMFORT

If you are building a bench with a back, the job will be easy if the seat is level and the back is plumb. This might look good, too, but it won't be comfortable. On a deck where people expect to relax and lounge, you need to slope the back. You also may want to cut an angle into the seat

with a roll-over front edge that makes the bench more like a comfortable chair.

For a bench that takes the place of a railing, be sure to set the top cap so that it does not extend past the back rails. That could lead to a nasty poke in the neck every time you sit down.

BACKLESS BENCH

This low, unobtrusive bench is an attractive way to provide built-in seating. Of course, without a back it won't substitute for a railing.

Build Supports. Before laying the decking, construct T-shape supports of 4x4 uprights and 2x8 crosspieces. (See below.) Make the connections with countersunk 4½-inch lag screws. Add 2x4 blocking to support the decking where needed. Locate supports every 4 feet.

Install the Seat. After the decking is completed, attach the seat pieces to the crosspieces. Install three 2x6 seat slats to the top of the crosspieces with 3-inch deck screws. Make them flush with the sides of the crosspieces and the ends of the end crosspieces as well. There should be a ⅛-inch gap between each slat.

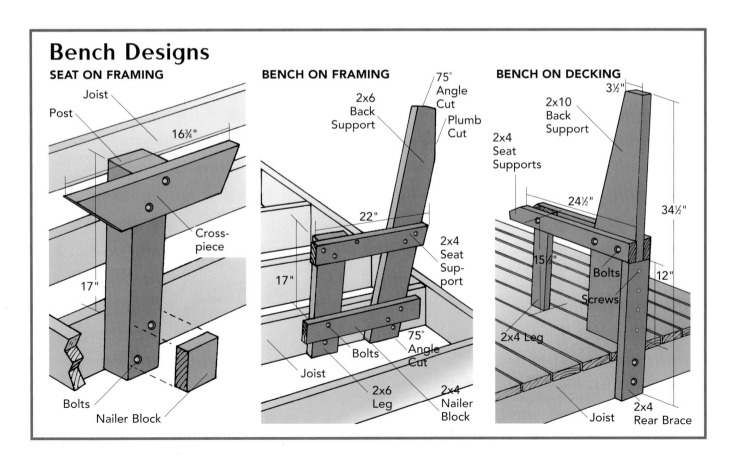

Bench Designs

SEAT ON FRAMING
Joist
Post
16¾"
Cross-piece
17"
Bolts
Nailer Block

BENCH ON FRAMING
2x6 Back Support
75° Angle Cut
Plumb Cut
22"
2x4 Seat Support
17"
75° Angle Cut
Bolts
Joist
2x6 Leg
2x4 Nailer Block

BENCH ON DECKING
3½"
2x10 Back Support
2x4 Seat Supports
24½"
34½"
15½"
Bolts
12"
Screws
2x4 Leg
Joist
2x4 Rear Brace

BENCH ON FRAMING

With this approach, you build the bench supports after the framing is complete but before you attach the decking.

Cut Back Supports. Cut a 2x6 to 36 inches plus the width of your joist, with parallel 75-degree cuts on each end. Then cut off the back of the top.

Construct Supporting Frames. Tack each rear support to a joist, keeping the bottom end flush with the bottom of the joist. Attach the front 2x6 supports and the 2x4 seat supports in the same way. Check that the frames are parallel with each other and that the crosspieces are level. Then drill pilot holes, and fasten each joint with two ½ x 3½-inch carriage bolts with washers.

Provide support for the decking wherever it will butt into one of the vertical pieces you have just installed. To do this, run 2x4 blocking across each pair of front and rear supports, with the top of the 2x4 flush with the top of the joists. You will have to notch some decking boards.

Add Slats and Back Rails. After you've laid the decking, you can finish the bench. Attach 2x2s, 2x4s, or 2x6s across the back supports and seat supports with 3-inch deck screws or 16d galvanized nails. It's wise to lay out blocks to work out spacing (for drainage) and the amount of front overlap you want. Set the top cap so that it will not protrude over the back slats.

INSTALLING DECK-TOP BENCHES

TOOLS & MATERIALS
- 2x4s
- 2x6s
- 2x10s
- Measuring tape and pencil
- Straightedge, horses, and clamps
- Circular saw and handsaw
- 3½- and 5-in. carriage bolts
- 2½-in. screws
- Drill-driver and bits
- Router and belt sander

Plan your spacing so that each support assembly falls over one of the deck joists.

1 Cut the notch for the rear brace and the long angle on the 2x10 back support.

4 With the support system clamped in position, bolt the support brace to the joist.

5 Screw the brace to the seat back. Drill for and install the bolts in the sandwiched seat assembly.

BENCH ON DECKING

You can add this design to a completed deck because the bench frame is a self-contained unit. The main attachment is a 2x4 rear brace bolted to the outermost joist. It extends past the decking and is screwed to the seat frame. (See "Installing Deck-Top Benches," below.) Sand the seat supports before you assemble them.

Cut the Back and Seat Supports. Cut the 2x10 back support with a sloping back and a notch where the 2x4 rear brace will rest. You will need two 2x4 seat supports for every back support. The angle cut at the front of the seat supports allows the last seat slat to roll-over a bit, which makes the bench more comfortable.

Assemble the Supports. Each support unit requires a front leg square-cut to 15½ inches and a rear brace. To figure the brace length, which determines seat height, add 12 inches to the thickness of your decking and the depth of the joists. Attach each front 2x4 leg, sandwiched between the two seat supports, with a 5-inch carriage bolt. Use 3-inch deck screws and 3½-inch carriage bolts to attach each rear brace.

It's easiest to assemble the seat support units on the deck.

Install Seat Slats. Attach evenly spaced 2x4 seat and back slats with 3-inch deck screws. Use a 2x6 cap with the front edge flush with the surface of the back slats.

2 Cut the front seat support. Clamp the support system in position. Mark the bolt locations.

3 Using a handsaw, cut a notch into the deck overhang. The support must be flush to the joist.

6 Screw the 2x4 slats to the support assembly. Leave a small gap for drainage.

7 Screw the 2x6 cap to the top edge of the back support. Remove rough spots using a belt sander.

FINISH AND MAINTENANCE

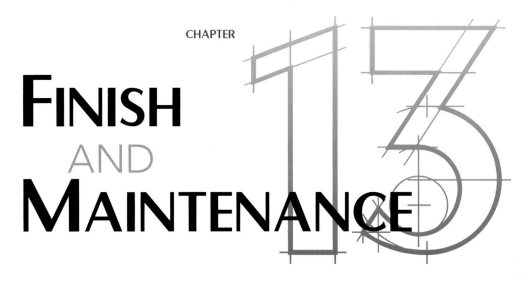

How long your deck lasts and continues to look good depends to a great extent on how well it is designed and built. But even the best-built decks require periodic repairs and maintenance. The idea of maintenance, of course, is to catch imperfections early on, before they develop into serious problems.

SOURCES OF DETERIORATION

How much and how often you need to work on the deck also depends on local weather conditions. In a sunny and relatively dry region, for example, you may need to recoat deck boards every year or two with an exterior-grade clear sealer containing a UV (ultraviolet light) inhibitor. Gradual fading can't be stopped completely, but these sealers can retard the graying effect of the weather. But in a relatively damp region or on a shaded site, moisture, mold, mildew, and rot are more likely to be the ongoing problems.

SUN

The sun's ultraviolet rays break down the binding agent that holds wood cells together. But the rays penetrate only $\frac{1}{100}$ inch, and the damaged cells will actually block further degradation until they are washed away. The sun does contribute to wet-and-dry cycles that can cause wood to crack or distort. But most of the effects cause only cosmetic damage that is easily remedied with a coat of stain or sealer.

MOISTURE

Moisture can cause damage mainly in three ways. First, when wood absorbs moisture and then dries out, it expands and contracts, which can cause cupping, warping, and even splitting. This also puts a strain on your fasteners and can cause nails to pop. Second, moisture provides an environment where fungus and bacteria can cause rot and mildew. Third, in extreme conditions where boards cannot dry out for weeks, the deck can develop wet rot, which produces a dark, charred look.

One simple way to reduce water damage is to sweep your deck frequently, taking care to remove built-up dirt, leaves, and twigs from joints. Dirt and leaves create wet spots that don't dry out easily.

INSECTS

If wood-damaging insects are a problem in your area, expect them to attack your deck unless you use only high-quality treated lumber. Cedar and redwood are decay resistant and to varying degrees insect resistant, depending on how much heartwood they contain.

COATINGS

There are many brands and types of deck finishes. Some allow you to change the color and tone of the wood. These generally lie on the surface. Others seep into the wood.

DIY OPTIONS: FINISHING THE SURFACE

The same deck boards can look dramatically different depending on the type of protection you apply. The most practical are clear sealers and semi-transparent stains. They do not crack or chip like paint and some heavy-bodied stains. These pictures show different coatings on the same kind of Douglas fir. Before you select a finish, test it on scrap deck lumber.

Semitransparent stains allow some grain to show but add tone to the decking. They come in water-based or oil-based solutions.

Solid-body stains cover the wood grain completely. They can also unify deck boards that have different hues and grain patterns.

INGREDIENTS

A deck finish may contain any of the following ingredients in various combinations.

Water Repellents. A good deck finish will repel water but will not form a film that may crack. Most deck finishes contain paraffin, oil, or both, and an agent that spreads the finish.

Resins. A longer-lasting—and more costly—water repellent is resin, often called alkyd resin. Resin will soak into the wood and seal it from moisture without hardening on the surface like polyurethane or varnish. A heavy dose of a finish containing resin will also give your deck a slight sheen that many people find attractive.

Preservatives. Most preservatives contain fungicide, mildewcide, and insecticide in various combinations. All-purpose deck finishes usually contain a small amount of these, enough for a mild dose of protection. If you have serious problems in your area with either fungus, mildew, or insects, you should take other measures.

UV Inhibitors. To maintain the original color of your deck as long as possible (because all wood eventually fades), use a sealer with UV protection. UV absorbers and blockers are pigments that absorb or reflect UV rays to minimize their effects on the wood. But these additives can add color to the wood.

Some expensive finishes contain UV inhibitors designed to disrupt the normal chemical action

SMART TIP

APPLYING SEALERS

Many do-it-yourselfers have some experience with painting. Sealing a deck is easier than painting walls. First, the deck is horizontal, so you don't have to struggle reaching up and down the way you do with walls. Work from a large pan or five-gallon bucket with a roller and extension handle, and you can cover a

large area quickly. Second, you don't have to be neat. The idea is to load up a heavy-napped roller and slop it onto the boards. (1) Brush small areas. (2) Raw wood will soak up one coat and take a second coat the next day.

Paint *provides the most opaque finish, but it lies on the surface rather than penetrating into the wood's fibers.*

Oil-based clear sealers *are the easiest to apply because they are thin and flow readily. You may need more than one coat.*

Latex-based clear sealers *feature easy cleanup, but the finish may not be as durable as a comparable oil-based finish.*

RENEWING A WOOD DECK

TOOLS & MATERIALS
- Rake
- Drill-driver and bits
- Nails or screws
- Plane
- Deck cleaner
- Brush
- Power washer (optional)
- Finish/sealer
- Applicators

Use caution when power-washing under high pressure. The stream may erode the surface of the wood.

1 Drag a garden rake across the deck to locate raised nails or screws. The rake will snag on the fastener.

2 Replace raised nails with screws. Use galvanized or stainless-steel screws ½-in. longer than the nails.

3 Use a plane to reduce raised edges on boards. If necessary, smooth boards using a belt sander.

4 Power-wash the deck to remove dirt and the top layer of decayed wood fibers.

5 When the deck is dry, apply a stain or wood preservative. Sweep up debris, and apply a sealer.

caused by UV light. The advantage here is that no pigment is required, so you get something close to the original look of your wood. But the chemical reactions that occur while UV inhibitors are doing their job may cause them to break down and become less effective. That means you need to reapply them regularly to retard the inevitable weathering process. But to some extent, this is true for all deck finishes. Wood without its bark left out in the weather year-round needs periodic attention.

Most products you can buy will need to be applied every year or two, depending on your climate and how much the deck is used. But some high-end finishes typically last four years, even in regions with harsh weather.

FINISHING PRODUCTS

The products you will find in stores combine the ingredients discussed previously in various combinations.

CLEAR FINISH
Typical clear finishes contain a water repellent and preservative. They have little visual impact (unless they contain resin) and will help your deck last significantly longer than it would if you hadn't applied a finish.

If you are going to use a pigmented finish for the surface of your deck, you may want to use a less-expensive clear sealer for the underside, where you don't have to worry about sun or discoloration. Just be careful that none of the clear sealer gets on to the top, where it can affect the color of the stain.

Some products labeled clear actually contain pigments for UV protection, and so are not really clear. Test a finish in an inconspicuous spot before using it to see whether you like the color.

SEMITRANSPARENT STAIN
Semitransparent stains contain some pigment, but not enough to make an opaque finish like paint. Some of the natural grain will show. If they contain resin or a good deal of oil, they will make your deck look somewhat shiny—when looking at

samples, pay attention to the sheen as well as the color to see whether it's what you want. They will lighten over time and need to be reapplied.

SOLID-BODY STAIN AND PAINT
Solid-body stains and paint often look alike. But stains are generally designed for siding, so will show wear in traffic patterns on decks. For a deep, solid color on your deck surface, it is better to go with a porch-and-deck paint. The drawback is that these pigment-loaded coatings can crack and peel as the deck boards expand and contract with the weather over time. If you don't tend to cracks quickly, water can reach the boards underneath, peel more of the surface coating, and weaken the wood. But as long as the surface is completely covered, you are fine.

APPLYING FINISH COATINGS

Most finishes should not be applied when the temperature is 40 degrees or colder. This is not a big problem because most people don't start building a deck in the middle of winter. However, if you must leave a new deck unfinished for a while because of cold weather and some mildew forms, you can wash the surface with a solution of one part household bleach to two or three parts of water before sealing and finishing.

The main rule of thumb is to be generous when applying a penetrating finish. You want the liquid to saturate the wood fibers. In particular, the end grain of a dried piece (such as the ends of posts or decking pieces) will absorb finish almost as quickly as you can brush it on. Check these spots during application, and reapply until the wood stops absorbing the finish.

As always, you should check the manufacturer's instructions about applying the product and observe all warnings. In most cases, you need to avoid breathing vapors or spray mists, wear rubber gloves and a long-sleeved shirt to minimize the chance of skin irritation, and wear eye protection to guard against splashes and drips.

Here is a look at the basic sequence of applying the finish.

Test the Wood. To avoid sealing in dirt, apply the finish soon after you finish the deck. The

Jacking

To replace a support post, you need to unload the weight it bears. To do this safely, use a house jack set on top of a concrete block or other secure footing centered directly below the main girder that bears on the post. (You may need more than one jack.) Slowly pump the jack until the girder starts to lift. Add extra temporary supports for safety. Then replace the post; gradually lower the jack; and fasten the new post with hardware according to code.

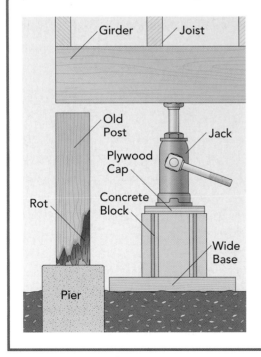

REPAIRING DAMAGED

TOOLS & MATERIALS
- Measuring tape
- Chalk-line box
- Circular saw
- Sealer
- Brush
- 2x2
- Hammer
- 10d nails

When repairing end grain, cut away the damaged sections and recoat the fresh grain or cover it with trim.

3 Don't use a rip fence, because the outer edge is uneven. Cut freehand using a circular saw.

exceptions: treated wood and unseasoned lumber that is still wet. Check manufacturer's data sheets for finishing recommendations.

Prepare the Wood. Sand down any rough spots on your deck, and sweep up any sawdust or other debris. Your deck should be completely clean.

To further increase the finish penetration and produce a cleaner-looking surface, you can sand the entire surface. You can handle a heavy-duty sanding job with a floor-finishing belt sander, but only if the boards are level and all the nails are countersunk or set flush. A raised nailhead will tear through the belt. In most cases, it will suffice to touch up a few areas using a handheld belt sander or random-orbit sander.

Do not sand treated wood. Instead, use a power washer. Allow the deck to dry thoroughly before applying finish.

Apply the Finish. You can cover horizontal deck boards with a roller or spray equipment. Follow the sprayer with a brush to spread out the finish. Wherever possible, also apply finish to the underside of decking and to joists, bridging, girders, and posts. For posts, railings, and stair stringers, brush application is best. Remember that visible end grain will absorb much more than flat surfaces.

If you have grass, flowers, or bushes nearby, take the time to screen them from splashes and drips with plastic sheeting.

DECK EDGES

1 To repair damaged edges, start by measuring the overhang over the joists.

2 Snap a chalk line to guide your cut. Make sure the cut line is not on the inside of the joist.

4 Seal the cut edges with wood preservative. You will need to apply at least two coats.

5 Set a 2x2 over the edges, driving at least one nail per board. Sand the top seam.

DECK
PLANS

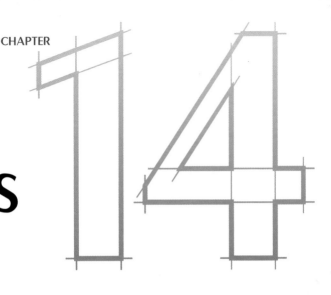

The plans for the three decks presented in this chapter were designed to meet typical building codes, but your local building department may have different requirements so check with the building inspector. If the plans aren't right for your situation, borrow some of the details for your project.

LOW PLATFORM DECK

Two levels, a generous step, decking that runs in three different directions, and the non-symmetrical shape combine to make this a distinctive deck.

You'll need to lay out and install 16 footings for this deck. You might want to try to pour all the footings level with one another so that you can set the girders on top of the concrete. But it is difficult to get 16 footings level with one another. It makes more sense to use short posts that are attached to the footings and then cut flush with the top of the girders. (See "Framing Plan," opposite.)

Because the deck is so low to the ground, you won't have room to put the joists on top of the girders. Instead, attach the joists to the sides of the girders using joist hangers. Make the girders by laminating two 2x6s together using glue and screws, and bolt them to the sides of the 4x4

posts that rest on the concrete footings.

The dimensions given on the drawings accompanying this project are for a deck built in a particular location. It's unlikely that you will locate posts exactly as shown, so use these dimensions as an example only. Measure and cut to fit as you build, adjusting the dimensions as necessary for your project.

INSTALL THE LEDGER
AND FOOTINGS

Bolt the ledger to the house about 2 inches below the surface of the house floor at the threshold to a doorway. Lay out the footings as shown in the framing plan opposite. Dig the holes; install tube forms; and pour the concrete. Insert J-bolts while the concrete is still wet. You'll need to allow the concrete to set before adding girders.

Framing Plan

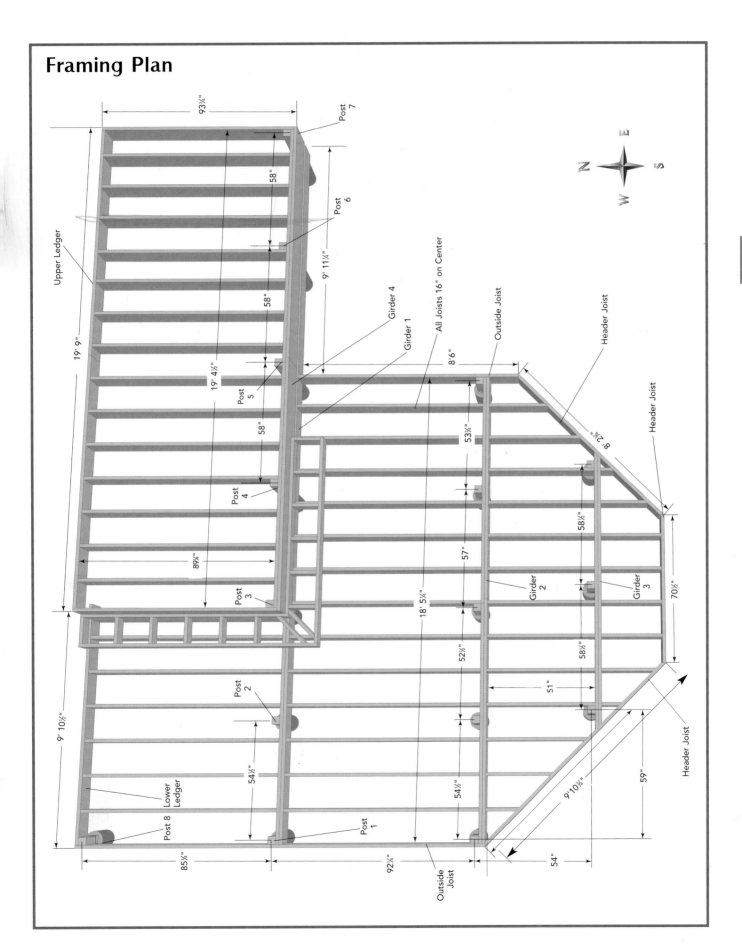

Shopping List

Lumber
- 2 pcs.   2x4   8'
- 2 pcs.   2x4   10'
- 1 pc.   2x4   12'
- 52 pcs.   2x6   8'
- 25 pcs.   2x6   10'
- 7 pcs.   2x6   12'
- 19 pcs.   2x6   14'
- 8 pcs.   2x6   16'
- 7 pcs.   2x6   18'
- 23 pcs.   2x6   20'
- 2 pcs.   4x4   8'

Hardware (Galvanized)
- 16 post anchors with J-bolts, nuts, and washers
- 102 joist hangers for 2x6s
- 8 angled joist hangers for 2x6s
- 5 angle brackets
- 20 lag screws and washers for the ledger
- 32 carriage bolts, ½"x7", with washers and nuts
- 5 lbs. of joist hanger nails or 1¼" decking screws
- 2 lbs. of 2" decking screws
- 30 lbs. of 3" decking screws

Masonry
- 16 concrete tube forms
- Gravel and concrete for 16 footings

Parts List

	Quantity	Lumber Size		Part
Framing	2	2x6	10'	Upper Ledger
	2	4x4	8'	Posts (16 pieces at 2')
	10	2x6	10'	Girders 1 and 2
	2	2x6	12'	Girder 3
	1	2x6	10'	Lower Ledger
	1	2x6	16'	Outside Joist (west)
	1	2x6	10'	Outside Joist (east)
	2	2x6	10'	Header Joists (west and east)
	1	2x6	6'	Header Joist (south)
	48	2x6	8'	Joists
	2	2x10	10'	Girder 4 (ripped to 8½")
	2	2x4	8'	2 Step Headers and 1 Step Joist
	2	2x4	10'	2 Step Headers and 2 Step Joists
	1	2x4	12'	11 Step Joists
Decking	23	2x6	20'	
	7	2x6	18'	
	7	2x6	16'	
	19	2x6	14'	
	5	2x6	12'	
	8	2x6	10'	
	4	2x6	8'	

INSTALL THE POSTS

First, install post anchors. For each post location, place a piece of 4x4 in the anchor; plumb it; and then use a water level to mark the ledger height. If the 4x4 is for an upper-level post location, remove it and cut it to ledger height before fastening it to the post anchor. Cut all the remaining posts to 10 inches below the ledger height before fastening them to their anchors.

INSTALL THE LOWER-LEVEL GIRDERS

There are three girders on the lower level, each made of doubled 2x6s. To locate the girder labeled "girder 1" on the framing plan, measure down 10 inches from the top of posts 3 through 7, and strike a line on their southern faces. Cut three pieces of 2x6 to make the first layer of girder 1, which will span from post 1 to post 7. Of these pieces, cut one to span from the west side of post 1 to the middle of post 3, cut a second to span from the middle of post 3 to the middle of post 5, and a third to span from the middle of post 5 to the east side of post 7. Use 3-inch decking screws to attach these pieces flush with the tops of posts 1 and 2 and aligned with the marks you made on posts 3 through 7. Then add the second layer of girder 1, offsetting butt joints and using two bolts at each girder-to-post location.

As shown in the framing plan, girders 2 and 3 are attached flush with the top of the lower-level posts. Cut, assemble, and attach girder 2 as you did girder 1. Do the same for girder 3, but let it run wild about a foot past each outside post.

INSTALL THE LOWER LEDGER AND OUTSIDE JOISTS

The lower ledger will be attached to the house. Always be sure that you tie ledgers into the house framing. Don't rely on nails or screws into siding or sheathing. To attach the lower ledger, take a 10-foot 2x6 and use a single 3-inch screw to attach it flush to the top and outside of post 8 as shown in the framing plan. Level the lower ledger; then tack it to the house, letting it run wild under the upper ledger. Then bolt the lower ledger to the house, and add three more screws to the connection with post 8. Cut the western outside joist to length, and attach it to girders and posts with 3-inch screws. Cut the eastern outside joist to length. Attach it to girder 1 with a joist hanger, and screw it to the post and the end of girder 2.

CUT GIRDER 3, AND INSTALL HEADER JOISTS

The outer edge of the deck projects out at an angle from the main deck. This means you need to cut the projecting angle on both the western and eastern ends of girder 3. Extend the cut line down both faces of the girder. Cut off both ends of girder 3 with a circular saw set to 45 degrees, cutting from top to bottom on both girder faces.

Cut the western header joist to 9 feet 10¾ inches long and the eastern header joist to 8 feet 2¾ inches with miter cuts on both ends. After making the cuts, attach the eastern and western header joists to girder 3 and the outside joists with 3-inch screws (six at each girder connection). Cut the end header joist to fit between the other header joists.

INSTALL THE LOWER-LEVEL JOISTS

Lay out the lower-level joists 16 inches on center, and install them using joist hangers. Measure the length of the angle-cut joists by marking them in place. Use a framing square to be sure they are at right angles to the girder.

INSTALL THE DECKING

Install the lower-level decking with 3-inch deck screws, running the boards diagonally, as shown in the "Decking Plan," below.

The upper-level girder, labeled girder 4 on the framing plan, is made from 2x10s that are ripped to a width of 8½ inches to meet the top of the lower-level decking. Before making these rip cuts, take a measurement from the top of post 2 and post 3 to the decking, in case your deck varies.

Girder 4 will be attached flush with the tops of

14 DECK PLANS

SMART TIP

LEVELS AND VIEWS

Changing levels by a step or two not only creates separate activity areas, it also offers the opportunity of better views from the elevated level. Because a railing system is rarely required on this type of deck design, there is nothing to interfere with the views.

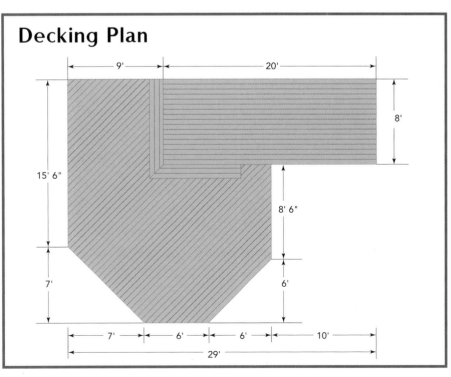

Decking Plan

posts 3 through 7. Cut a piece of ripped lumber to span from the west side of post 3 to the center of post 5, and another to span from the center of post 5 to the east side of post 7. Together, these pieces will be the same length as the upper ledger (19 feet 7½ inches in the deck shown). Temporarily tack these girder pieces to the ledger, and mark the upper ledger and the girder pieces at the same time for joists 16 inches on center.

Use 3-inch screws to attach these two girder pieces flush with the tops of posts 3 through 7. Attach the upper-level outside joists to the ends of the upper ledger and girder pieces. Then install the upper-level interior joists, using joist hangers. Cut two pieces of ripped lumber to complete girder 4, staggering the butt joint a few inches from the joint in the first part of the girder. Attach these pieces to the first part of the girder, driving a 3-inch screw every 12 inches. At every post, drill two ½-inch-diameter holes through the doubled girder and through the post. Install two carriage bolts with washers and nuts. Install upper-level decking perpendicular to the joists.

BUILD THE STAIRS

Assemble a stair frame on top of the decking, as shown in "Stair Framing," below. Cut the 12 short square-ended joists and the inside and outside headers to the dimensions shown. Assemble the frame with the joists 16 inches on center. Set the frame, and attach it to girder 4 with 3-inch screws. Miter one end of each of the mitered joists, and mark them in place for the cuts on the other end. Install 3-inch screws through the face of the outside headers into the mitered joists. Angle-screw the other end of the mitered joists into the inside headers. Angle-screw all the joists to the decking.

Stair Framing

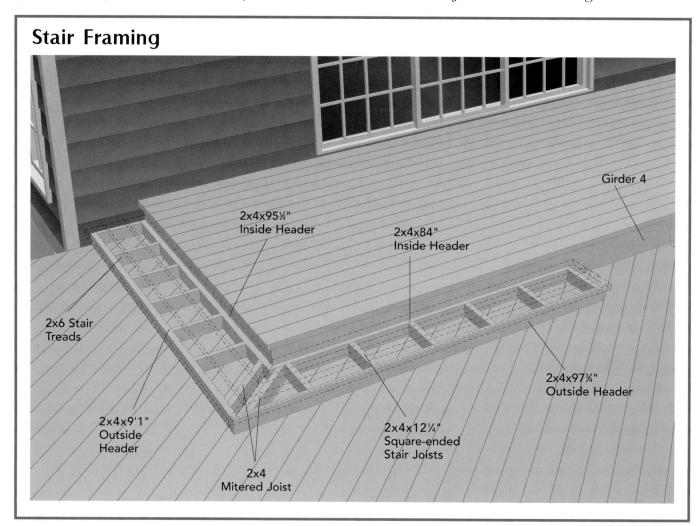

2x4x95¼" Inside Header

2x4x84" Inside Header

Girder 4

2x6 Stair Treads

2x4x9'1" Outside Header

2x4x12¼" Square-ended Stair Joists

2x4x97¾" Outside Header

2x4 Mitered Joist

RAISED RAILING DECK

The railing on this deck has some simple touches that are easy to add. These include nipped corners on the ends of railing caps and bevel cuts on both ends of the balusters and on one end of the posts. The entire deck is made of treated lumber, which will last for many years with minimal maintenance.

Because the site is relatively flat, this deck was designed without posts. A built-up girder made of two 2x12s rests directly on top of the concrete footings. This means you must pour the footings level with one another.

A final note before you build: the dimensions for this project are for a particular deck built at a particular location. It is unlikely that your house has bays exactly like this one. So, use the dimensions given as an example only. Measure and cut to fit as you build, adjusting dimensions to fit your location.

INSTALL LEDGER BOARDS

Mark for a ledger that is 1¾ inches below the surface of the interior floor at the threshold. Take care to make all the ledger pieces level with one another. Install the ledger, using a method appropriate to your house, as described in "Attaching the Ledger," page 159.

As shown in "Framing Plan" on page 269 there is no need to miter the ends of the ledger board pieces.

DIG AND POUR FOOTINGS

Lay out the footings as shown in the framing plan, and install tube forms. Check to see that the four footings for the girder will all be level with one another. The two footings for the stairs should be just above grade. Place J-bolts in the center of each of the girder footings; use a string line to make sure they line up.

Shopping List

Treated Lumber

- 1 pc.   1x10   6'
- 4 pcs.   1x10   14'
- 30 pcs.   5/4x6   14'
- 26 pcs.   5/4x6   16'
- 103 pcs.   2x2   3'
- 2 pcs.   2x2   8'
- 2 pcs.   2x4   8'
- 2 pcs.   2x4   12'
- 1 pcs.   2x4   14'
- 1 pc.   2x4   16'
- 7 pcs.   2x6   10'
- 3 pcs.   2x6   12'
- 2 pcs.   2x6   14'
- 4 pcs.   2x6   16'
- 10 pcs.   2x6   12'
- 14 pcs.   2x8   14'
- 4 pcs.   2x8   16'
- 1 pc.   2x12   8'
- 2 pcs.   2x12   12'
- 2 pcs.   2x12   16'

Hardware (Galvanized)

- 4 J-bolts
- 35 ½"x3" lag screws and washers for installing ledger board pieces
- 32 joist hangers for 2x8
- 4 double joist hangers for 4x8
- 4 angled joist hangers for 2x8
- 4 angle brackets
- 5 lbs. of 1¼" deck screws for joist hangers
- 3 lbs. of 2" deck screws
- 25 lbs. of 2½" deck screws
- 3 lbs. of 3" deck screws
- 3 nail-on tie plates or straps 6"x12"
- 34 ½"x3" carriage bolts with washers

Masonry

- Concrete for 6 footings
- 6 concrete tube forms

Parts List

	Quantity	Lumber Size		Part
Framing	2	2x12	16'	Girders
	2	2x12	12'	Girders
	14	2x8	14'	Joists
	10	2x8	12'	Joists
	4	2x8	16'	Ledger, Header, and Stair Backing
	1	1x10	6'	Stair Backing
Decking	26	5/4x6	16'	
	30	5/4x6	14'	
Fascia	4	1x10	14'	
Railing	7	2x6	10'	15 Posts, 52½" Long
	1	2x4	16'	Bottom Rail
	1	2x4	14'	Bottom Rail
	2	2x4	12'	Bottom Rails
	2	2x6	12'	Top Rail
	1	2x6	14'	Top Rail
	1	2x6	16'	Top Rail
	1	2x6	14'	Rail Cap
	3	2x6	16'	Rail Caps
	103	2x2	3'	Balusters
	22	2x3	5½"	Optional Railing Blocks
Stairs	1	2x12	8'	Stringers
	1	2x6	12'	Treads
	2	2x4	8'	Posts and Top Rails
	1	2x6	8'	Stair Rail Cap
	2	2x2	8'	Balusters

Overall View

Cap Rail

1x10 Fascia

Railing Blocks (Optional)

2x6x52½" Post

Top Rail

Corner Post of Two 2x6s

2x2 Balusters

Bottom Rail

Doubled 2x12 Girder

Stringer

5/4x6 Decking

Stair Post

Stair Footing

2x6 Stair Tread

2x2 Stair Balusters

Framing Plan

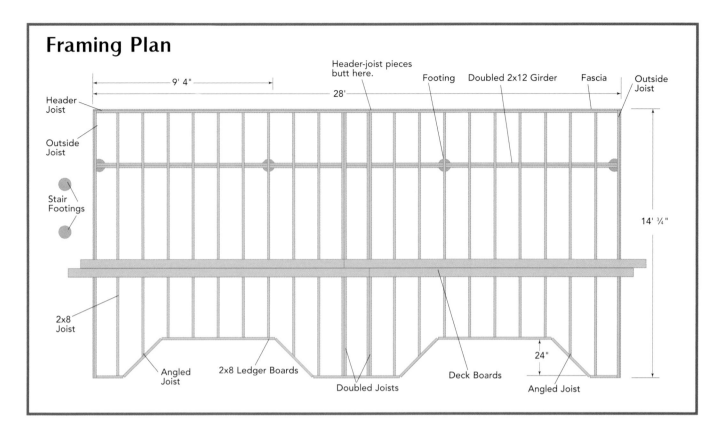

INSTALL THE GIRDER

Build the girder by laminating the 2x12s together with 3-inch screws, two every 6 inches. Stagger the splices. Cut the girder to the length of the ledger, plus 3 inches.

Once the concrete is firmly set, have one or two people help you place the girder on top of the J-bolts so that the bolts are in the center of the girder. Tap lightly with a hammer on top of the girder so that the bolts make an impression on the girder. Remove the girder, and drill holes for each of the bolts. Place the girder on the footings, with the bolts slid into the holes.

ATTACH THE OUTSIDE JOISTS

Attach the outside joists to the outside edges of the ledger, resting them on the girder. These joists are 3 inches longer than the other full-length joists.

LAY OUT THE JOISTS

Cut the two pieces of 2x8 that will form your header joist so that they will butt on a doubled joist. Temporarily attach the marked header joist to the ledger, and mark the header and ledger together for the joists. Use a framing square and level to mark on the sections of ledger that are set back at the bay windows.

INSTALL THE JOISTS

Attach joist hangers to both ledger and header. First, install the longest joists only, slipping them into the joist hangers on the ledger and resting them on the girder. These joists will be made from 14-foot 2x8s. Attach the header to these joists. Next, cut the four angle-cut joists to fit, using 14-foot 2x8s. Now measure for the remaining joists; cut them from 12-foot 2x8s; and install them.

ATTACH THE FASCIA

Cut the 1x10 fascia to cover the outside joists and header joist. Don't worry about getting the corners tight because they will be covered up by the railing posts. Attach it with 2-inch screws.

BACK THE STAIR STRINGERS

Cut a 2x8 to 31½ inches. Rip a piece of one-by to 6½ inches wide, and cut it to 31½ inches long. Use nail-on plates where allowed by code to attach the 2x8 under the rim joist. Attach the one-by pack-out piece under the fascia.

SMART TIP

SETTING JOIST HANGERS

It is best to set the hangers on the ledger with one side free before installing the ledger to the house. This method allows you to make simple adjustments later.

LAY THE DECKING

Begin with the first full piece of decking that touches the house. But be sure to leave a small gap between the board and the siding for drainage. Place one end of each decking board over a doubled joist, staggering the butt joints by alternating the 14-foot decking boards with the 16-footers as shown in the framing plan.

BUILD THE STAIRS

The stair shown has a unit rise of 7 inches and a unit run of 11 inches. However, because terrain varies and no two sites are exactly the same, these dimensions probably will be useful only as an example. Add the treads, cut so that they come flush to the outside of the stringers. Attach the stringers to the backing board (installed as needed) driving 2½-inch decking screws at an angle through the stringers into the backing.

ADD THE RAILING

Cut the 14 2x6 posts to 52½ inches, with 45-degree cuts at both ends. Each of the two corner posts is made of two 2x6s. For these, make a 45-degree mitered rip-cut along one edge of four of the 2x6s. Cut all the railing balusters to 36 inches, with a 45-degree angle at both ends.

Position the bottom of each post flush with the bottom of the fascia. Predrill, and fasten two ½ x 4½-inch carriage bolts with washers.

Attach the 2x6 top rail and the 2x4 bottom rail to the inside of the posts, using 2½-inch screws. Cut the rail cap pieces, nipping some of the corners with 45-degree cuts. Install the rail cap so that it overhangs the inside of the top rail by ¾ inch, and attach the balusters, using a 4-inch-wide piece of scrap lumber as a spacer.

This deck includes decorative railing blocks, which are optional. These are 22 pieces of 1½-inch-thick scrap stock ripped to 3 inches wide and cut to 5½ inches long. Attach one to each side of each post with 3-inch decking screws driven through the inside of the top rails.

BUILD THE STAIR RAIL

To construct the stair rail, first attach the two 2x4 stair posts to the stringers as shown in Stair Details," below. Do not cut the posts to height yet. Next, attach the 2x4 top rails that run parallel with the stair slope. Install the four 2x2 stair balusters, spacing them equidistant from the deck posts, stair posts, and each other. Cut the tops of the stair posts and balusters flush to the top of the top rail; then install the rail cap.

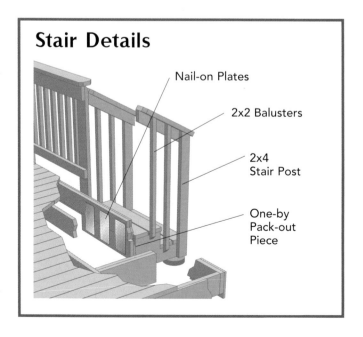

Stair Details

Nail-on Plates

2x2 Balusters

2x4 Stair Post

One-by Pack-out Piece

CANOPY-COVERED DECK

Here's a truly elegant freestanding deck. The deck itself is nothing spectacular—just a simple rectangle. What makes it special are the railings, benches, and the overhead structure. Generous and comfortable benches with attached tables provide plenty of room for reading, lounging, and conversing. The distinctive railings will show off your craftsmanship. And the overhead structure filters midday light gracefully.

You may be able to buy the large timbers for the overhead in cedar. If not, treated wood is a good choice. It may take a lot of shopping

around before you find pieces this large that look good. Another option is to build up a beam.

The railings and benches are not as complicated as they look, but they do require accurate, clean cuts. If you have good basic carpentry skills and some patience, you will be able to do it. If you have a power miter saw or radial-arm saw, a table saw, and a router, the work will be much easier. To build the top rails with those distinctive overhangs, you will need to make a lap joint. (You will see how to do this later.) The railing posts do not actually come up through the railing caps; the tops are separate post caps, which match the

Shopping List

Lumber

- 4 pcs.   1x3 12'
- 2 pcs.   1x4 14'
- 2 pcs.   1x8 10'
- 2 pcs.   1x8 14'
- 1 pc.   2x2   6'
- 2 pcs.   2x3   8'
- 4 pcs.   2x4   8'
- 4 pcs.   2x4 10'
- 1 pc.   2x4 12'
- 5 pcs.   2x4 18'
- 4 pcs.   2x6   8'
- 17 pcs.   2x6 10'
- 1 pc.   2x6 12'
- 21 pcs.   2x6 14'
- 3 pcs.   4x4   8'
- 3 pcs.   4x4 10'
- 2 pcs.   4x6 14'
- 3 pcs.   4x6 16'
- 4 pcs.   6x6 12'
- 2 pcs.   6x6 18'

Bamboo Poles and Reed Fencing

- 9 poles at 16'
- 4 poles at 18'
- 3 Reed Fencing at 6'x15'

Hardware (Galvanized)

- 6 elevated post bases
- 18 joist hangers for 2x6
- 4 angle brackets
- 2 lbs. of joist hanger nails or 1¼" deck screws
- 1 lb. of 2¼" deck screws
- 5 lbs. of 2" deck screws
- 15 lbs. of 3" deck screws
- 26 pieces ¼"x3½" lag screws
- 3 pieces ¼"x3" lag screws
- 1 lb. of U-shaped stainless-steel wire ties
- Copper wire

Masonry

- Concrete and gravel for four large postholes and 6 footings
- 6 concrete tube forms

tops of the bench posts to complete the illusion.

Begin by building the main part of the deck, following "Framing Plan," opposite. Then proceed to the benches and canopy.

CUT AND NOTCH THE BENCH POSTS AND RAILING POSTS

Cut the posts as shown in "Cutting Posts," opposite. There are four bench posts; two rail posts dadoed on the left; two rail posts dadoed on the right; three rail posts dadoed on both sides; and three dadoed and notched corner rail posts.

Parts List

	Quantity	Lumber Size		Part
Deck Framing	2	4x6	14'	Girders
	11	2x6	10'	Joists
Fascia	2	1x8	14'	
	2	1x8	10'	
Decking	21	2x6	14'	
Railings	3	4x4	10'	9 Posts
	4	2x4	10'	Rails
	1	2x4	12'	Rails
	1	4x4	8'	1 Post and Post Caps
Benches and Tables	2	4x4	8'	4 Posts
	1	2x4	8'	4 Back Supports
	1	2x6	8'	4 Seat supports
	1	2x2	6'	4 Legs
	2	2x4	8'	Back Bands
	6	2x6	10'	12 Seat and Back Slats
	1	2x4	8'	Front Apron, Angled and Outside Apron
	1	2x6	8'	Shaped Aprons
	2	2x3	8'	Cleats
	2	2x6	8'	Tabletop Slats
	1	2x6	12'	2 Seat Bands
Nosing and Bottom Fascia Piece	2	1x4	14'	Nosing
	4	1x3	12'	Bottom Fascia Piece
Overhead Structure	4	6x6	12'	Posts
	2	6x6	18'	Beams
	3	4x6	16'	Crossbeams
	5	2x4	18'	Rafters
	9	16' Bamboo Poles		Top Pieces
	4	18' Bamboo Poles		Cross Ties
	3	6'x15' Reed Fencing		Lattice

Framing Plan

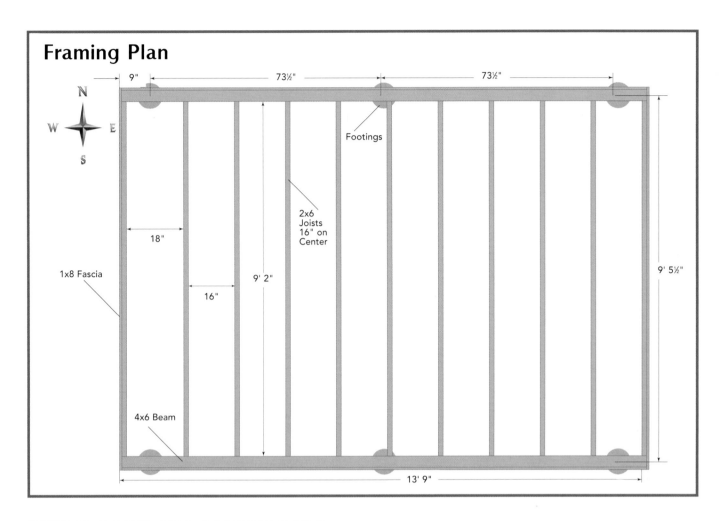

INSTALL POSTS AND BOTTOM RAILS

Install the corner posts then the middle posts, positioning them as shown in "Decking/Seating Plan" on page 274. Attach each post to the deck with two countersunk 3½-inch lag screws. On the deck shown, the screws are covered with wood plugs made from pieces of dowel. Cut the bottom rail pieces to fit, making a rabbet cut at the end of each piece. Cut ¾-inch dadoes on the corner edges of each front post as shown in "Posts and Rails," page 275. Install the bottom rail rabbets into the post dadoes. Secure each joint by driving two 3-inch deck screws at an angle from the bottom of the rails.

CUT AND INSTALL THE TOP RAILS

Cut the top rails to the lengths shown in "Decking/Seating Plan," page 274. Then chamfer all four sides of the rail ends. Lay out cut lines ½ inch from each end of the rails, on all four sides of the rails. Then tilt the blade on a power miter saw to 45 degrees, and cut four chamfers on each rail end.

At the three corners, make ¾-inch-deep dadoes in both top rails to create half-lap joints, as shown in "Posts and Rails," page 275. Secure the rails to the posts with ¼ x 3-inch countersunk lag screws. Use one screw at each connection, driving it through both rails at the half-lap joints.

Cutting Posts

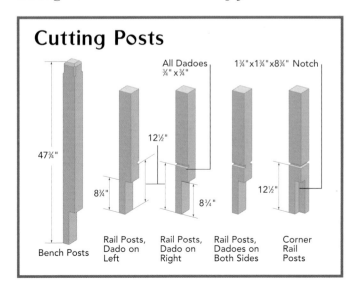

Deck/Seating Plan

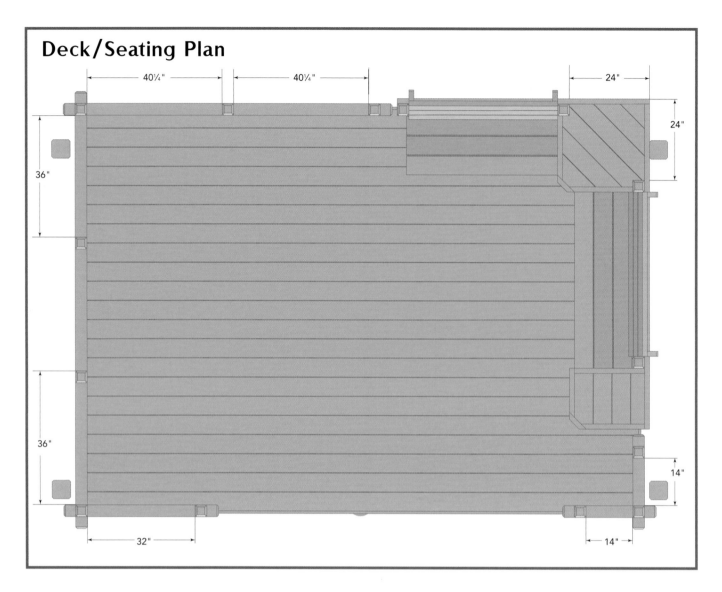

MAKE POST CAPS, AND COMPLETE THE BENCH POSTS

The post caps and the bench posts are all chamfered at their tops and all four sides. Because the post caps are only 4 inches long, for safety you need to make the decorative chamfer cuts before cutting the pieces to length.

Start with a piece of 4x4 about 8 inches long. Square one end, and lay out stop lines on opposing faces, 3 inches from the end as shown in "Making Post Caps," opposite. Set a chamfering bit in your router for a chamfer of about ½ inch. Clamp the 4x4 in place. Make a 3-inch-long chamfer on each edge of the 4x4.

Now tilt the blade on your power miter saw to 45 degrees. Chamfer all four sides of the ends of the 4x4, just as you did the ends of the rails. Cut the 4x4 off at 4 inches, and repeat the process

six more times. Now rout and cut the same chamfer details on the ends of the bench posts.

On the deck shown, a biscuit joiner was used to attach the post caps. The simplest way to attach the caps is with 4d galvanized casing nails driven into predrilled angled holes on both sides of each cap. The procedure for chamfering the bench posts is the same as for the post caps except that you won't cut off the chamfered part.

CUT THE BACK SUPPORTS

Cut four pieces of 2x4 to 18¾ inches long for the back supports. On one piece, lay out the angled cut as shown in "Back Support Layout," opposite. Along one edge, make marks at 1¼ inches and 7⅝ inches from the bottom. From the 7⅝-inch mark, measure over 1½ inches as shown in A, and strike a line down about 1 inch.

Back Support Layout

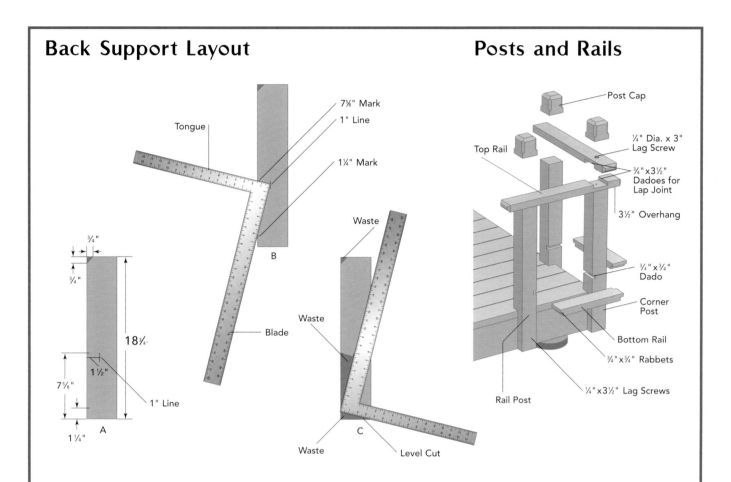

7⅝" Mark
1" Line
1¼" Mark
Tongue
Blade
B
Waste
Waste
Waste
C
Level Cut

¾"
¾"
18¾"
1½"
7⅝"
1" Line
1¼"
A

Posts and Rails

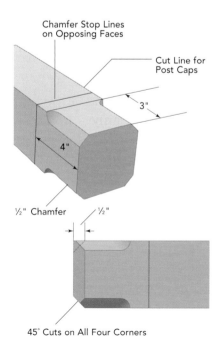

Post Cap
¼" Dia. x 3" Lag Screw
Top Rail
¾" x 3½" Dadoes for Lap Joint
3½" Overhang
¾" x ¾" Dado
Corner Post
Bottom Rail
¾" x ¾" Rabbets
Rail Post
¼" x 3½" Lag Screws

Seat Side View

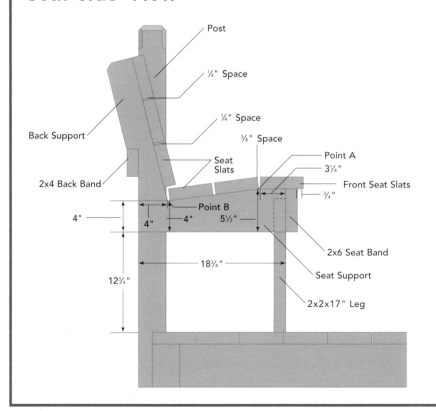

Post
¼" Space
¼" Space
⅜" Space
Back Support
Seat Slats
Point A
3¼"
Front Seat Slats
¾"
2x4 Back Band
Point B
4"
4"
4"
5½"
2x6 Seat Band
Seat Support
18¾"
12¾"
2x2x17" Leg

Making Post Caps

Chamfer Stop Lines on Opposing Faces
Cut Line for Post Caps
3"
4"
½" Chamfer
½"
45° Cuts on All Four Corners

Overall View

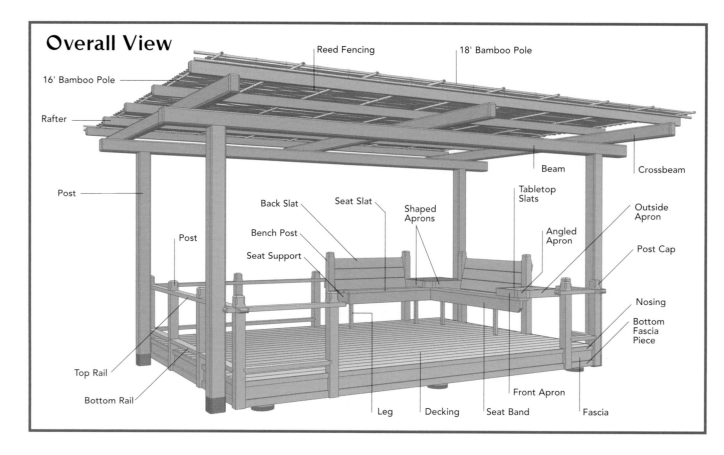

Reed Fencing · 18' Bamboo Pole · 16' Bamboo Pole · Rafter · Post · Beam · Crossbeam · Back Slat · Seat Slat · Shaped Aprons · Tabletop Slats · Outside Apron · Bench Post · Angled Apron · Post Cap · Post · Seat Support · Nosing · Bottom Fascia Piece · Top Rail · Bottom Rail · Leg · Decking · Seat Band · Front Apron · Fascia

To lay out the notch, place your framing square on the board as shown in "Back Support Layout," part B, page 275.

To lay out the level cut, align the square to the notch and the bottom corner of the square as shown in "Back Support Layout" C, page 275 Cut one back support, and use it as a template to lay out the remaining four.

CUT THE SEAT SUPPORTS

Now cut four pieces of 2x6 to 18¾ inches long for the seat supports. Lay out a seat support as illustrated in "Seat Side View," page 275. Make a mark along the top of the board 3¼ inches from the right side to locate Point A, as shown. Then draw a 4-inch-long horizontal line located 4 inches from the bottom of the left corner to locate Point B. Draw a line from Point A to Point B to create the slightly angled seat shape. Cut the board, and use it as a template to make the remaining seat supports.

ASSEMBLE THE BENCH FRAMES

Cut the legs to 17 inches long. Measure up 12¾ inches from the deck along the seat posts to mark where the seat supports will go, as shown in "Seat Side View," page 275. Align the bottom of the seat supports to the line, check that they are level at the bottom; and secure each support with three 3-inch deck screws.

Position the 2x2 legs as shown, and secure each to the front inside edge of a seat support with two 3-inch screws. Cut the seat bands to the dimensions shown in "Bench and Table Construction," opposite, and screw them to the front of the seat supports with three 3-inch screws at each connection.

Position the back supports with their plumb notch cuts flush to the outside of the posts and the level cuts sitting on the seat supports. Secure with 3-inch screws.

Cut 2x4 back bands to the lengths shown above in "Bench and Table Construction." Tuck them against the top of the back support notches, and secure them to the posts with two 3-inch screws at each connection.

INSTALL SEAT AND BACK SLATS

For each bench back, cut three 2x6s to fit between the posts. Attach them to the supports with three 3-inch deck screws at each connection. It's wise to predrill your holes to prevent splitting, particularly near the ends of boards.

The front seat slats on each bench are longer than the other slats because they continue under the tables. Cut these slats to the same length as the seat bands. Use 3-inch screws to fasten the longer slat to the right seat band flush at both ends with a ¾-inch overhang at front. Attach the shorter slat to the left seat band, butting it against the other slat with a ¾-inch overhang at front. (This will give you a ¾-inch overhang on the left end.) Cut two slats to 45¾ inches long, and attach them to the left bench flush with the left end of the front slat. Cut two slats to 55 inches long. Attach them to the right seat supports with equal overhang on both ends. For comfort, rout a ½-inch roundover along the outside edges of the front seat slats.

CUT THE SHAPED TABLE APRONS

The corner table is supported by both benches and the back band. The end table is supported by the extended front bench slat and the back band. The distances between your posts and the dimensions of your bench may vary a bit, so the best way to construct the tables is to scribe and cut the pieces to fit. Also, rout a ½-inch roundover on the top outside edge of the table aprons before you install them. Otherwise the router base will hit the post before the chamfer is complete.

First, rip a 6-foot 2x6 to 5 inches wide. Cut two pieces to 19 inches long with 45-degree angles on one end of each. These will make the shaped aprons for the corner bench. Cut a third piece to

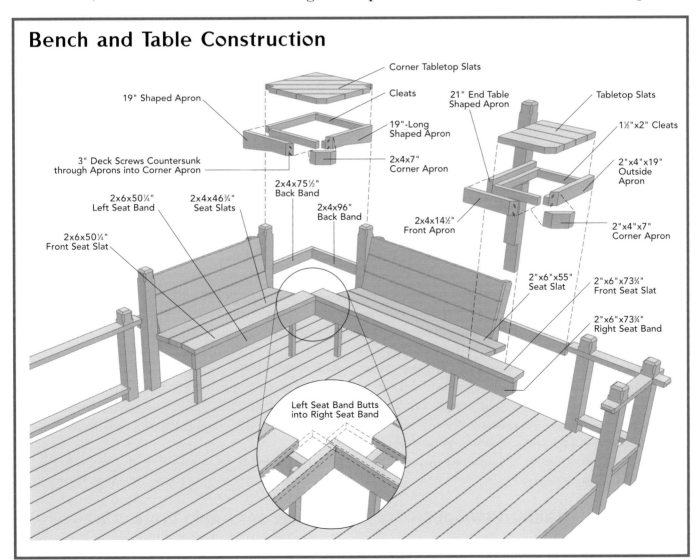

Bench and Table Construction

Corner Tabletop Slats

19" Shaped Apron

Cleats

21" End Table Shaped Apron

Tabletop Slats

19"-Long Shaped Apron

1½"x2" Cleats

3" Deck Screws Countersunk through Aprons into Corner Apron

2x4x7" Corner Apron

2"x4"x19" Outside Apron

2x4x75½" Back Band

2x6x50¼" Left Seat Band

2x4x46¾" Seat Slats

2x4x96" Back Band

2"x4"x7" Corner Apron

2x4x14½" Front Apron

2x6x50¼" Front Seat Slat

2"x6"x55" Seat Slat

2"x6"x73¾" Front Seat Slat

2"x6"x73¾" Right Seat Band

Left Seat Band Butts into Right Seat Band

Scribing Table Apron

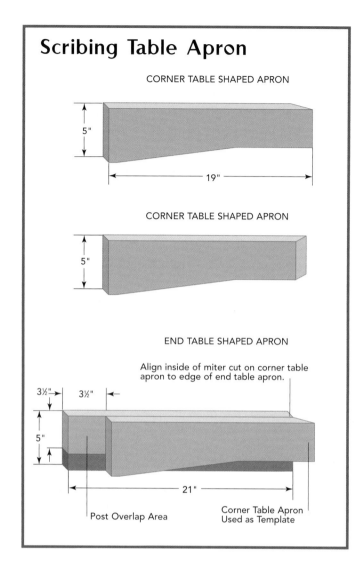

CORNER TABLE SHAPED APRON

5"

19"

CORNER TABLE SHAPED APRON

5"

END TABLE SHAPED APRON

Align inside of miter cut on corner table
apron to edge of end table apron.

3½"   3½"

5"

21"

Post Overlap Area

Corner Table Apron
Used as Template

21 inches long (square on both ends) to make the end table shaped apron.

To obtain the shape of the bottom cut on the three shaped aprons, butt one of the 19-inch pieces against the post at the left side of the left bench. Align the bottom of the piece to the bottom of the front seat slat, as illustrated in "Scribing Table Aprons," above. Run your pencil along the top of the seat slats. Cut the piece, and use it as a template to make the other corner table shaped apron. Lastly, use one of the corner table shaped aprons as a template for the end table shaped as shown. The 3½-inch-square area on the end table shaped apron will be screwed to a post.

INSTALL THE SHAPED TABLE APRONS

Butt the longer shaped apron against the back band, and screw it to the side of the post with 3-inch deck screws. Make sure the apron is square to the bench; then fasten it to the bench with two 3-inch screws through the bottom of each seat slat. Drive two screws through the back band into the apron ends.

Butt both shorter shaped aprons against their posts, and fasten them to the bottom of the seat slats with two screws each. Hold a piece of 2x4 against both 45-degree faces to make sure that they are in the same plane. If not, shorten one before fastening with more screws. Put a length of 2x4 in the corner apron position, and mark the position of the 45-degree cuts on both ends.

COMPLETE THE TABLES

Cut the end table front apron and one corner apron to the dimensions shown in "Bench and Table Construction," page 277. Fasten them together with two 3-inch screws as shown. Screw this assembly to the front of the end table shaped apron. Make sure the aprons are square; then measure for the length of the outside end table apron in case it varies from the 19 inches shown. Cut the outside apron to fit with a 45 degree angle on one end.

Rip 2x3s to 2 inches wide to make cleats to support the tabletop slats. Cut the cleats to fit around the inside perimeter of the table as shown in "Bench and Table Construction," page 277. Use 2¼-inch deck screws to attach the cleats 1½ inches below the tops of the aprons.

Cut 2x6 tabletop slats to fit between the aprons as shown. Note that the corner table slats are positioned 45-degrees to the bench slats, while the end table slats are parallel to the bench slats.

ADD NOSING

Rip 1¾-inch-wide pieces for the nosing. Attach the nosing and the 1x3 fascia trim around the perimeter of the decking using 2¼-inch screws.

INSTALL 6X6 POSTS

The posts that support the overhead structure are butted against the nosing and bottom fascia trim. They are located 10½ inches from each corner as measured from the outside of the nosing. Dig 42-inch-deep postholes that are 10 inches in diameter. (Hole depth requirements may vary regionally; check with your building department.) Pour some gravel in the bottom.

Rout a ½-inch chamfer on all four sides of each post, stopping about 2 feet from what will be the top end of each post. Leave the bit in the router. Set the posts; pour the concrete.

The bottoms of the posts in our deck are clad in copper, an Asian method for avoiding rot.

CUT THE POSTS, AND SHAPE THEIR TOPS

Cut the posts to 8 feet high. In the deck shown, the top of the roof posts are shaped to match the chamfered beams. The procedure is shown in "Shaping Roof Post Tops," below. First, lay out two lines along the top of the posts, ½-inch from parallel sides as shown. Set your circular saw to a 45-degree angle. Then set the cutting depth to ½ inch. Make two angled cuts as shown.

Reset the blade to 90 degrees, and reset the cutting depth to ½ inch. Make kerfs as shown. Use a chisel to knock out the waste. Use the router to cut chamfers to the tops of the posts.

COMPLETE THE CANOPY

Cut the 4x6 crossbeams to 15 feet. Rout a ½-inch chamfer on all edges of the crossbeams

and the 6x6 beams, including the ends.

Raise the 6x6 beams in place; check that they overhang the posts equally on both sides; and then fasten to the posts with angle-driven 3-inch screws. Set the three 4x6 crossbeams on top of the 6x6 beams, and attach in the same way.

If the beams you are using are just too heavy to lift to the top of the posts in one step, build lift stages. Do this by securely tacking and clamping 2x4s across the posts so that the ends project about 6 inches. Install several sets at different heights. Then you and a helper can lift the beams in manageable stages from one set to the next.

Lay out 2x4 rafters, as shown in "Overhead Structure," below, and fasten them to the crossbeams with angle-driven 2-inch screws. Lay out the bamboo poles, and fasten them by driving 3-inch screws through the poles into the rafters.

Finish by laying rolls of reed fencing on top of the bamboo poles or 2x2s. Fasten these with U-shaped stainless-steel wire ties driven every 6 inches into the bamboo poles or 2x2s.

At the north and south ends of the roof, the 16-foot-long bamboo pieces are sandwiched between two 18-foot bamboo cross ties. With a helper, hold the pieces in place, and tie them together with copper wire at each joint.

Shaping Roof Post Tops

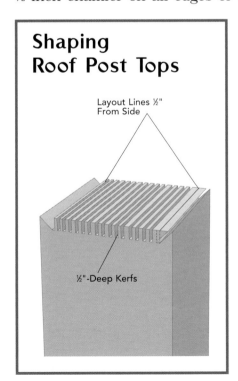

Layout Lines ½" From Side

½"-Deep Kerfs

Overhead Structure

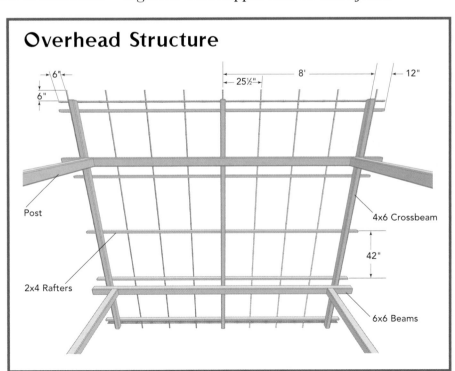

6"
6"
25½"
8'
12"

Post

2x4 Rafters

4x6 Crossbeam

42"

6x6 Beams

RESOURCE GUIDE

The following list of manufacturers and associations is meant to be a general guide to additional industry and product-related sources. It is not intended as a listing of products and manufacturers represented by the photographs in this book.

Arch Wood Products manufactures preservatives used in the treatement of exterior wood products. Brand names include Wolmanized and Natural Select lumber.
1955 Lake Park Dr.
Smyrna, GA 30080
Phone: 770-801-6600
www.wolmanized.com

California Redwood Association offers technical information about the use of redwood in decks and other structures, including grade distinctions, structural applications, and finishing characteristics.
405 Enfrente Dr.
Novato, CA 98411
Phone: 888-225-7339
www.calredwood.org

Grabber Construction Products is a construction supply company that specializes in screws and fasteners. Its Web site offers a full catalog plus technical information about its products.
205 Mason Circle
Concord, CA 94520
Phone: 800-477-8876
www.grabberman.com

Deckmaster is the creator of the Hidden Deck Bracket System, a patented deck board fastening system. The company's Web site offers additional information about the system, as well as testimonials and reviews.
P.O. Box 4060
Concord, CA 94524
Phone: 800-869-1375
www.deckmaster.com

KK Mfg. Co, Inc., manufactures the Lumber Loc, a hidden deck fastener designed to work with all types of woods, as well as plastic lumber. Order and installation information is available at the company's Web site.

4915 W. 120th Pl.
Overland Park, KS 66209
Phone: 913-908-9445
www.lumberloc.com

Dixie-Pacific says that its porch posts and railing systems are designed for installation by the tradesman and DIY homeowner alike. Get more information at the company's Web site.
1700 West Grand Ave.
Gadsden, Alabama 35901
Phone: 800-468-5993
http://consumer.schlage.com/brands/dixiehome.htm

Durable Deck by Anchor Systems, Inc., is a vinyl top deck designed to cover a current wood or concrete surface. The company's Web site offers installation instructions and FAQs about the deck product.
1101 N.W. 31st Ave.
Pompano Beach, FL 33069
Phone: 954-969-0122
www.durabledeck.com

Royal Crown Limited is a leading manufacturer of vinyl fence, deck, and railing products. Find out more about the product lines at the company's Web site.
P.O. Box 360
Milford, IN 46542-0360
Phone: 800-488-5245
www.royalcrownltd.com

TimberTech manufactures wood composite decks and railing systems. The company's Web site offers an interactive Deck Designer that allows customers to tailor a deck to their own unique specifications.
894 Prairie Rd.
Wilmington, OH 45177
Phone: 800-307-7780
www.timbertech.com

Trex Company, Inc., specializes in composite decking materials made from recycled plastic and waste wood. Check out its photo gallery of deck design ideas and find an installer at the company's Web site.
160 Exeter Dr.
Winchester, VA 22603
Phone: 800-289-8739
www.trex.com

Regenex Corporation produces home improvement supplies made entirely from recycled PVC. The company specializes in small parts, but it also offers solutions for deck and fence work. Visit Regenex's Web site for its mission statement and catalog.
P.O. Box 608
West Middlesex, PA 16159
Phone: 724-528-5900
www.regenex.com

Correct Building Products manufactures the CorrectDeck line of products. This light composite decking material is available with either a hidden or traditional fastening system. View the company's color selector at the Web site.
15 Morrin St.
Biddeford, ME 04005
877-332-5877
www.correctdeck.com

BW Creative Wood Industries, Ltd., is a leading manufacturer of interior stair components and exterior deck accessories. See its Web site for more information about its products.
23282 River Rd.
Maple Ridge, BC V2W 1B6
Phone: 604-467-5147
www.bwcreativewood.com

Elk Composite Building Products, part of Elk Corporation, is the manufacturer of CrossTimbers composite lumber. For a product gallery and technical information, visit its Web site.
15500 West 108th St.
Lenexa, KS 66219
Phone: 866-322-7452
http://composites.elkcorp.com

Genova Products, Inc., offers a variety of PVC products for the home, including plumbing, fencing, and decking materials. Its Web site offers information about its various products.
7034 East Court St.
Box 309
Davison, MI 48423-0309
Phone: 810-744-4500
www.genovaproducts.com

Vaughan & Bushnell Manufacturing Company offers a comprehensive catalog of ergonomically designed tools for professional contractors and tradesmen. View the company's Web site for a full listing of hammers, hatchets, and axes.
11414 Maple Ave.
Hebron, IL 60034
Phone: 815-648-2446
www.vaughanmfg.com

L.B. Plastics provides PVC solutions for many home improvement tasks, including deck and railing projects. The company's Web site offers a full catalog of products.
482 East Plaza Dr.
P.O. Box 907
Mooresville, NC 28115
Phone: 800-752-7739
www.lbplastics.com

Southern Pine Council is a trade association that offers information on deck building with treated lumber. Its Web site provides information on product selection, installation techniques, and locating treated wood products.
P.O. Box 641700
Kenner, LA 70064
Phone: 504-443-4464
www. southernpine.com

Timber Holdings Ltd. imports exotic hardwoods under the Iron Wood brand. The company offers a free catalog and deck building brochure.
2400 West Cornell
Milwaukee, WI 53209
Phone: 414-445-8989
www.ironwoods.com

GLOSSARY

Actual Dimension. The exact measurement of a piece of lumber after it has been milled, generally ½ inch less each way than the advertised size. For example, a typical 2x4's actual dimension is 1½x3½ inches.

Architectural Scale Ruler. A three-sided ruler that enables you to convert large dimensions to a small scale in a drawing, including ⅛-, ¼-, and ½-inch scale.

Balusters. The vertical pieces, generally made of 2x2s, that fill in spaces between rail posts and provide a fence-like structure.

Beam. The term for any large framing member of four-by or doubled two-by material. On a deck, the main horizontal beam used to support joists is generally called a girder.

Breadboard Edge. A long strip of wood, typically 1x2 or larger, fastened along the edge of a deck to cover the end grain of decking boards.

Bridging. Usually short, solid blocks of lumber made of joist material that are cut to fit snugly between the joists to prevent twisting.

Building Codes. National and local rules regulating building practices. Generally, codes encompass structural, electrical, plumbing, and mechanical remodeling and new construction. Code compliance is checked by on-site inspections.

Building Permit. An authorization to build or renovate according to plans approved by the local building department. Generally, any job that includes a footing or foundation or that involves any structural work or alterations requires a permit.

Cantilever. The outer part of a deck floor frame that extends beyond the main girder, floating without additional support.

Carriage. A cut stringer with a sawtooth shape on its top edge that runs at midspan on wide stairs.

Countersink. A shallow hole drilled to house the head of a lag screw or bolt. The hole diameter is generally the size of the washer used with the fastener.

Curing. The slow, ongoing chemical action that hardens concrete.

Dado. A channel cut across the grain of a piece of wood to house the end of another component in a joint.

Dipping. A treatment in which wood is immersed in a bath of preservative for several minutes, then allowed to air-dry.

Fascia. A facing board (generally one-by material) that covers the exposed ends or sides of deck framing.

Footing. A masonry base, usually concrete, that supports a post, girder, or steps.

Frost Line. The maximum depth at which soil freezes as specified by local building departments, which require footings below the line to prevent heaving.

Grade. Ground level. At-grade means at or on the natural ground level.

Header Joist. The outermost joist, also called a belt, set at right angles to and across the ends of the on-center joists that support the decking.

Joist. Horizontal structural member, usually two-by lumber, commonly set 16 inches on center to support deck boards.

Joist Hanger. A U-shaped metal connector that joins a joist, generally at right angles, to another board such as a ledger. Similar hardware is available for other structural joints.

Kickback. The lurching, backward action of a power saw when the blade binds in a cut.

Lattice. A cross-pattern structure generally used for skirting that is made of wood, metal, or plastic.

Ledger. A horizontal board attached to the side of a house (bolted into the framing) that supports one end of the deck joists.

Nominal Dimension. The identifying size of stock lumber, such as 2x4 and 2x6, even though the boards are a half inch smaller each way.

Penny. The colloquial measure of nail length, generally abbreviated with the letter d, as in 10d (ten penny). (2d, 1 in.; 3d, 1¼ in.; 4d, 1½ in.; 5d, 1¾ in.; 6d, 2 in.; 7d, 2¼ in.; 8d, 2½ in.; 9d, 2¾ in.; 10d, 3 in.; 12d, 3¼ in.; 16d, 3½ in.; 20d, 4 in.; 30d, 4½ in.; 50d, 5½ in.; 60d, 6 in.)

Pier. A masonry support, similar to a footing, generally made of concrete poured into a form that extends from below the frost line to a few inches aboveground.

Plan Drawing. A drawing that shows an overhead view of the deck and specifies the locations and sizes of components.

Plumb. Vertically straight in relation to a horizontally level surface.

Plunge Cut. A cut with a circular saw that starts in from the edge of a board.

Post. A vertical component, usually a 4x4, that can support girders, joists, and railings.

Post Anchor. A metal fastener that secures a post to a concrete pier and inhibits decay by holding the post a bit above the concrete.

Posthole Digger. A clamshell-shaped tool used to dig holes for posts.

Power Auger. A tool (generally rented) powered by a gasoline engine that excavates post holes with a large auger screw.

On Center. A point of reference for measuring framing that is installed in a modular layout. The spacing, typically 16 inches, is figured from the center of one framing member to the center of the next; abbreviated o.c.

Rabbet. A ledge-shaped recess cut along one edge of a board.

Rail. A horizontal component placed between or on a row of posts.

Rip Cut. A cut made with the grain on a piece of wood.

Riser. A vertical board (set on edge) that closes off the open space between treads.

Site Plan. A drawing that shows your project at a scale small enough to include the house, yard, and nearby property lines. To obtain a permit, a site plan is typically required, along with drawings that show construction details.

Skirting. Material that covers or screens the space between the edge of the deck and the ground, generally made of narrow slats, such as 1x2s, or lattice.

Span. The distance on a horizontal component, such as a joist, between supports. Span limits for all types and sizes of lumber are controlled by building codes.

Stringer. A wide, angled board that supports stair treads and risers. Cut or housed stringers run on the outside edges of stairs.

Synthetic Decking. Any engineered decking material made from plastics and/or recycled wood products.

Toenailing. Joining two boards together by nailing at an angle through the edge of one board into the face of another.

Top Cap. A horizontal piece of lumber laid flat across the tops of posts or top rails.

Tread. A horizontal stair board (generally several spaced boards in deck construction), laid flat on stringers.

Treated Lumber. Wood that has had preservative forced into it under pressure to make it decay resistant. In the past, arsenic was used to treat wood. Today, alkaline copper compounds are the primary treatment chemicals.

INDEX

PHOTO CREDITS

All project photography by John Parsekian/CH, unless otherwise noted
page 1: Jessie Walker page 2: John Parsekian/CH page 6: Brian Vanden Brink page 7: *top* Garden Picture Library/ Marie O'Hara; *bottom* Mark Lohman page 8: Mark Lohman page 9: courtesy of Trex Decks page 10: *top* courtesy of California Redwood Association; *bottom* John Parsekian/CH page 11: courtesy of Trex Decks pages 12-13: Brian Vanden Brink page 14: Brian Vanden Brink, architect: Rob Whitten page 15: *top left* courtesy California Redwood Association/Kim Brun; *top right* courtesy of California Redwood Association/Geoffrey Gross; *bottom right* Jessie Walker; *bottom left* Bill Rothschild pages 16-17: *top right* Brian Vanden Brink; *bottom right* Brian Vanden Brink, design: Weatherend Estate Furniture; *bottom center* Jessie Walker; *bottom left* Brian Vanden Brink; *top left* Bill Rothschild; *top center* Randall Perry page 19: Michael Thompson pages 20-21: *top left* Brian Vanden Brink; *top right* Brian Vanden Brink, architect: Dominic Mercadante; *bottom right* Jessie Walker; *bottom left* Michael Thompson page 22: Brian Vanden Brink, design: Weatherend Estate Furniture page 23: *top* Tria Giovan; *bottom* Carolyn Bates

page 24: Carolyn Bates page 25: Tria Giovan page 26: Brian Vanden Brink, architect: Pete Bethanis page 29: Brian Vanden Brink, architect: Stephen Blatt page 30: courtesy of California Redwood Association page 31: John Parsekian/CH page 32: *top* Mark Lohman; *bottom* Michael Thompson page 33: *top* Brad Simmons; *bottom* John Glover page 34: Randall Perry page 35: *top* Garden Picture Library/Ron Sutherland; *bottom* Jessie Walker page 36: Jessie Walker page 37: *top* Brad Simmons; *bottom* courtesy of California Redwood Association/Ernest Braun page 38: Tria Giovan page 39: *top*: Garden Picture Library/Ron Sutherland; *bottom* Brad Simmons pages 40-41: courtesy of California Redwood Association/Eli Sutton/HBM page 43: *top* Brian Vanden Brink; *bottom right* Randall Perry; *bottom left* Jessie Walker page 45: Carolyn Bates page 46: Charles Mann page 48: courtesy of California Redwood Association/Geoffrey Gross page 49: *top* Brian Vanden Brink; *center* Randall Perry page 51: *top* Brian Vanden Brink; *bottom* courtesy of California Redwood Association/Geoffrey Gross/Denver Decks page 52: *all* Tria Giovan page 53: *top left* courtesy of Arch Wood Protection; *top right* courtesy of

TimberTech; *bottom left* courtesy of California Redwood Association pages 54-55 *all* Mark Lohman page 56: Mark Samu page 57: Positive Images/Ann Reilly page 59: Randall Perry pages 62-63: Brad Simmons page 64: Carolyn Bates page 65: Brad Simmons page 66: *top* Bill Rothschild; *bottom* courtesy of California Redwood Association/Kim Brun page 67: Mark Samu page 68: courtesy of California Redwood Association/Kim Brun page 69: Brian Vanden Brink page 70: Tria Giovan page 71: courtesy of TimberTech pages 74-75: Brian Vanden Brink, architect: Dominic Mercadante page 76: *top* Randall Perry; *bottom* Jessie Walker page 77: *top* Brad Simmons; *bottom* Derek Fell page 78: Brian Vanden Brink page 79: *top right* courtesy of Trex Decks; *right center* Brian Vanden Brink; *bottom right* Randall Perry; *bottom left* Garden Picture Library; *top left* Jessie Walker pages 80-81: Bill Rothschild pages 92-93: Tria Giovan page 94: Brian Vanden Brink page 97: Jessie Walker page 98: Carolyn Bates page 103: courtesy of TimberTech pages 108-109: Randall Perry page 110: Carolyn Bates page 111: *top left* John Glover; *top right* Bill Rothschild; *bottom right* Tria Giovan; *bottom left* Garden Picture

Library/Maria O'Hara **pages 112-113:** *top left* Tria Giovan; *top right* Jessie Walker; *bottom right* Mark Samu; *bottom center* Brad Simmons; *bottom left* Tria Giovan pages 114-115: Brian Vanden Brink page 117: Jessie Walker page 120: Garden Picture Library/Maria O'Hara page 123: Brad Simmons page 124:Mark Lohman pages 132-133: Brian Vanden Brink page 134: Derek Fell page 140: *bottom left* Jessie Walker page 141: *bottom right* Carolyn Bates pages 148-149: Jessie Walker pages 150-151: *bottom center* Brad Simmons page 155: *bottom right* Randall Perry pages 173-174: Garden Picture Library/Henk Dijkman page 176: *bottom* Jessie Walker page 179: *top left* Brad Simmons page 192: *top* Brian Vanden Brink page 193: Samu Studios/Andy Letkovsky page 196: Jessie Walker pages 198-199: Brian Vanden Brink, architect: Rob Whitten page 203: Carolyn Bates page 209: courtesy of TimberTech pages 216-217: Mark Samu pages 234-235: David Duncan Livingston page 236: Carolyn Bates page 245: Bill Rothschild pages 252-253: courtesy of California Redwood Association/Ernest Braun page 262: Maurice Victoria page 267: Maurice Victoria page 271: Edward Gohlich

Have a home improvement, decorating, or gardening project? Look for these and other fine Creative Homeowner books wherever books are sold.

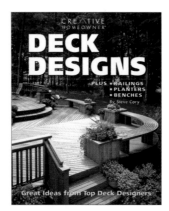

Plans from top deck designer-builders. 300+ color photos, illustrations. 192 pp.; 8½"×10⅞"
BOOK #: 277369

Design your own deck. 250+ color photos. 128 pp.; 8½"×10⅞"
BOOK #: 277155

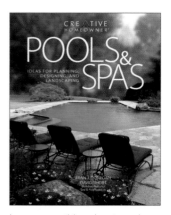

Learn everything about pools, from planning to installation. 300 color photos. 224 pp., 8½"×10⅞"
BOOK #: 277853

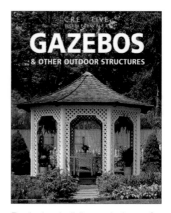

Designing, building techniques for yard structures. 450+ color photos, illustrations. 160 pp.; 8½"×10⅞"
BOOK #: 277138

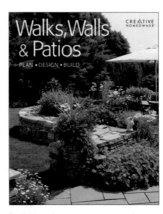

Build landscape structures from concrete, brick, stone. 370+ color illustrations. 192 pp.; 8½"×10⅞"
BOOK #: 277994

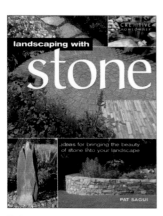

Enhance your landscape by using stone in its design. 375+ photos, illustrations. 224 pp.; 8½"×10⅞"
BOOK #: 274172

Design ideas, planning advice, and projects. 460+ color photos, illustrations. 160 pp; 8½"×10⅞"
BOOK #: 274804

How to build 20 furniture projects. 470+ color photos, illustrations. 208 pp.; 8½"×10⅞"
BOOK #: 277462

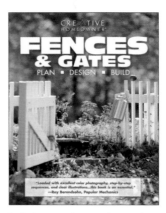

Includes step-by-step instructions for building fences. 400 color photos. 144 pp.; 8½"×10⅞"
BOOK #: 277985

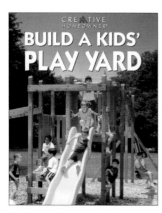

Build, step by step, the play structures kids love. 200+ color photos, drawings. 144 pp., 8½"×10⅞"
BOOK #: 277662

Complete guide to designing and planting with emphasis on solving problems. 870+ photos and illustrations. 384 pp. 9"×10" paper
BOOK #: 274610

Lavishly illustrated with portraits of over 100 flowering plants; planting and care tips; 500+ color photos. 208 pp.; 9"×10"
BOOK #: 274032